BLESSED
MARY CELESTE
CROSTAROSA

BLESSED MARY CELESTE CROSTAROSA

Mystic and Foundress of the Redemptoristines

BY THE

VERY REV. FR. FAVRE, C.SS.R.

Translated by a Redemptoristine of the Convent of
Chudleigh

MEDIATRIX PRESS
MMXXII

ISBN: 978-1-957066-30-1

Nihil Obstat
Joannes Simcox, D.C.L., M.A.
Censor deputatus

Imprimatur
✠Joseph Butt,
Vic. Gen.

Westmonasterii,
die 31a *Julii,* 1935

Mediatrix Press
607 E 6th Ave.
Post Falls, ID 83854
www.mediatrixpress.com

CONTENTS

FOREWORD

HERE was sore need in the skeptical, godless, licentious eighteenth century for a mighty champion of God's cause, a persuasive messenger of Divine Truth; for an Apostle who would unite in himself at once the wisdom, the personal saintliness, and the exquisitely human tenderness that marked the public ministry of Our Blessed Lord Himself. Such an Apostle, such a champion, such a messenger was raised up by God in that critical necessitous time in the person of a young Neapolitan lawyer, Alphonsus de Liguori, who put aside position, rank and fortune, to follow Jesus Crucified. But the divine charity, which filled the heart of Alphonsus, did not stay there; it forced its way out to reach his fellow-men and set the world on fire. Alphonsus—felt he could not truly love Jesus without loving the souls for whom Jesus died, and so he founded his Congregation of Missionary Priests of the Most Holy Redeemer.

The work of Alphonsus—his sacred learning, his eloquent magnetic preaching of God's Word, his life of regulated mental prayer, has continued in the Redemptorist Congregation ever since. In our times Redemptorists pray and go about preaching their Missions throughout the Christian world. To how many thousands of the poor and the abandoned have Redemptorist Missions opened up a new horizon of hope, and brought abiding solace of God's salvation? In these modern days of fretful rush, amid the buffeting of human policies and passions, how many date the beginning of peace, of true happiness, to these same Missions? How many walk the remaining journey in cloistered quiet places, living dedicated lives apart, who heard the first low whisper of Jesus, who felt the first stirrings of heroic love well up in their hearts, during Redemptorist Missions?

FOREWORD

Only God alone who knows the secrets of human lives and human hearts, and can see all the yesterdays and all the to-morrows, is able to measure the glory of this wonderful Apostolate founded by St. Alphonsus de Liguori.

From the day when Alphonsus turned his back upon the law courts of his country, God took, and God kept unchallenged and without rival, the first place in his heart. The one passion, which henceforth dominated his life, was to prove his love for God, by doing in all things God's Most Holy Will. "O Will of God" he cries out, "how dear you are to me. I wish to live and die united to You. What pleases You, pleases me. What You desire, I wish to desire. My God, make me live only to will what You will, to love what You love."

God did not fail His servant. He made known to him His Divine Will, and the chief instrument God used to reveal to Alphonsus that his life's principal work was to be the foundation of the great Missionary Apostolate was Maria Celeste Crostarosa. Maria Celeste! Charming name of a beautiful and saintly soul, the story of whose life is now presented to English readers in this admirable translation.

The drama of Maria Celeste's life, and the reading of this biography will show that it was a drama, enacted amid the most charming and peaceful landscape on earth. Those with leisure and a sufficiency of means to enable them to travel know the beauty of the coast of Southern Italy from Naples to Salerno. Between these two towns stands the pretty little village called Amalfi. Behind Amalfi the ground rises precipitously, and the road wends its way upward. Brilliant gold orange trees, interspersed with patches of vineyard and dull green olive trees border the right-hand side of the road as one climbs, but on the left hand one has the uninterrupted view of the sparkling lapis lazuli coloured sea. The village of Scala stands upon the crown of this hill overlooking Amalfi, and the Gulf of Salerno. Standing in the village street one commands a most beautiful view over landscape and sea. The reader of this biography will be told a great deal about Scala, and the two small townships Nocera and Castellamare. It may be well to have a mental picture as the background of one's thoughts. Imagine therefore an equilateral triangle, whose sides are ten miles long, and the apex of which points to the west on the Gulf of Naples. That apex is Castellamare. Then Nocera and Scala will occupy the other angles of the triangle; Nocera to the east and Scala to the south; while Foggia lies about 100 miles to the east, near the Adriatic.

It is at Scala that the story of Maria Celeste opens. She had been a Carmelite, but on the advice of Father Falcoia, she entered the Community, living under his direction at Scala, when the Carmel, to which she had belonged, was dissolved and its Community disbanded. It was at Scala that the Rule of the Congregation of the Most Holy Redeemer was revealed to her. It was she who, through the same Mgr. Falcoia, now Bishop of Castellamare, made known to Alphonsus God's Will in his regard. If the world and mankind have benefitted greatly by the Apostolate of Alphonsus and his sons, has not this saintly Nun a share in the merit? Is she not even now enjoying the reward of God? It was finally from Scala that Bishop Falcoia had her expelled because she could not in conscience bind herself by vow to follow his direction of her soul, and his direction alone. This action of the saintly Bishop only goes to prove that God sometimes permits such errors of judgments, in order to purify by tribulation souls devoted to His glory, and make them do greater work for Him.

The closeness of the friendship between Maria Celeste, St. Alphonsus, St. Gerard and the other early companions of St. Alphonsus will appear as the story of her life unfolds itself to the reader.

Maria Celeste was a contemplative and a mystic, and her life, abounding as it does in the miraculous, has one great antecedent recommendation to all well versed in spiritual things. Judged by human standards her life was a failure. The shadow of His Cross, who was the greatest failure of all in the eyes of His contemporaries, hangs over the life of this holy Nun.

Catholics know that they are not called upon to believe in the incidents which claim to be miraculous in the lives of God's servants as a matter of religious faith, as they are, for instance, in the miracles narrated in the Scriptures. It is lawful for Catholics to deal with them on rational lines, and by the ordinary judgment of human reasoning accept them or reject them, or suspend their judgment upon them, according to the weight of the evidence with which such miraculous incidents come before them. Before a Catholic accepts a miracle, unmistakable evidence is required.

Speaking generally, in these days in which we live, the world, particularly the intellectual, the educated world, is not a religious world. God, in the sense of a personal God, with His code of laws and punishments, hardly comes into its philosophy. It occupies itself exclusively with this present life and does not trouble itself about any life beyond the grave. It deals with the material universe, with what we can see and handle and analyze, and with that alone.

The very mention of the word supernatural arouses its opposition. For some years there has been a number of intellectual men thinkers, writers of distinction, who in dealing with questions of Christian belief, have antecedently implanted in their minds one principle, fixed, fundamental, irrevocable. Miracles are impossible and therefore all miraculous incidents, whether in the Scriptures, or in the lives of the Saints, are either apocryphal, fictitious or false, or else they must be capable of some kind of plausible interpretation, which will strip them of their supernatural character.

They are inconsistent, because they claim to believe in God as the Supreme Being, who made the Universe and who fixed the laws by which it is uniformly and normally governed and yet go on to deny to God the power to suspend or deviate for any reason or purpose whatsoever from the laws- He Himself has made.

God was under no necessity to create the world in one way rather than another. If He is omnipotent, He could have constructed a different world, and could have subjected it to laws different from those which He has actually imposed upon this world.

Is it not irrational to deny to an Omnipotent God the power to deal with His own Creation, and for His own wise purposes, perhaps unknown to us as He pleases? Cannot God in His own time and way suspend or modify the action of laws, which are not necessary in themselves, and of which His own free will has been the origin and the source? A God who cannot work a miracle is not Omnipotent and is therefore not a God at all.

If such men believe in God, they do not believe in the Christian God. They do not believe in *our* God.

The miracles narrated in this biography depend entirely upon the evidence brought forward in each particular case.

On September 14th, 1755, the Venerable Maria Celeste died at Foggia, while her Nuns were reading aloud to her the Passion of Our Blessed Lord. As they read aloud the words "Consummatum est," she gently breathed out her soul to the God whom she had loved so well. Saint Gerard was on that day in September, 1755, lying seriously ill in the Redemptorist house at Caposele, which is about 100 miles away from Foggia. Yet he turned to Brother Stephen, who was attending upon him and said, " Mother Maria Celeste is to-day about to receive the reward of her great love for Jesus and Mary. I have just seen her soul take its flight for Heaven." Brother Stephen, astonished at the words of Saint Gerard, noted the time and it was afterwards found that at that very moment, the holy Prioress of Foggia had breathed her last.

May the reading of her life inspire the imitation of her virtues, and especially of her abandonment to the Holy Will of God. May her Children, the Redemptorist Nuns, living the same

FOREWORD

devoted, prayerful lives, on a hillside of our own glorious Devon, be encouraged by her example to advance their own personal holiness, and to pray earnestly that God may one day glorify His Servant, their foundress, Maria Celeste before the world.

PETER J. DEERY, C.SS.R.,

Sup. Prov. Ang.

June, 1935.

PART I

NAPLES AND MARIGLIANO

CHAPTER I

CHILDHOOD

HAT magic there is in the words "city of Naples"—that spoilt child of Nature and of grace. Set as a jewel amongst some of the most enchanting scenes of the world, the town seems to have been from its earliest days smiled on by God Himself. How many saints and holy persons have lived and died within the walls of that sun-kissed city, cradled on the shores of the deep blue Mediterranean!

From St. Januarius and the early martyrs down to St. Alphonsus de Liguori, and even to our own times, the long list of God's chosen ones in that favored spot has known no break. It was in that privileged city that the subject of this biography was born.

When in September, 1696, the aged St. Francis Jerome took into his arms the newly-born son of Don Joseph de Liguori and prophesied for him a long life in the service of God and His Church ... did he foresee the mighty influence that was to be exercised on that life by a little girl who was born within a stone's throw of the Liguori Palace? It would be interesting to know. But so it was. God, Who destined that little child to be the guiding star of the great doctor of the Church, and to be His instrument in making known to His servant the work he was destined to do for the Church, gave her birth on October 31st, 1696, just one month after Alphonsus, who was born on September 27th of the same year.

St. Alphonsus was raised up by God to combat one of the two great evils of the eighteenth century—Jansenism. In the Ven. Maria Celeste we have the living refutation of the second evil, the errors and blasphemies of the philosophers. They denied Providence, Grace, the whole supernatural world. Maria Celeste demonstrated vividly in her life and person the reality of the mysteries of our holy Faith and the supernatural life, in all its radiant beauty.

The parents of this favored child came of an old and illustrious family. Already, in 1150, we find the names of the Lords of Rosa chronicled in the archives of Aquila as men renowned in war and in the government of their native town. Anthony Rosa was the friend and confidant of Charles I of Anjou. John Anthony commanded under Charles V and received as his prize the right to quarter the Imperial Eagle in his coat of arms. Francis Rosa fell fighting gallantly at the Battle of Lepanto. While the young John Baptist, Chevalier of the Order of SS. Maurice and Lazarus, was raised to the dignity of a Roman citizen. Many others kept up the family tradition for valor, while not a few made the name of Rosa still more illustrious by their sanctity. Blessed James Rosa from a brilliant soldier became a humble Celestine in the monastery of Collemaggio, at Aquila, and after his death was famous for his many miracles.

Blessed Gabrielle Rosa, whose praises are sung by Walding and other historians, was one of the first companions of Antonia of Florence, who founded the Poor Clare Convent at Aquila.

Father Evangelist Rosa, a Dominican, was one of the most renowned writers, theologians and preachers of his Order. Maria Celeste's great-grandfather was a royal magistrate at Naples, distinguished for the masterly tact with which he put an end to the bloody strife between the towns of Cittaducale and Amatrice. His only daughter, Creseida, married Signor Crosta, and their son assumed the name of Crosta-Rosa, thus adding his mother's family name to that of his father, and he became a barrister like his father. He married Paula Baptistine, of the noble family of Caldari, and God blessed their union with three sons and three daughters. Maria Celeste was their fifth child. The little girl was so frail that, fearing for her life, she was baptized immediately after her birth. However, to the great joy of all, she revived, and the next day was carried with great ceremony to the parish church of St. Joseph the Great. Here the ceremonies of the baptismal rite were performed, and the child received the names of Julia Marcella Santa.

The child grew stronger each day and was the delight of her family. Three brothers, Michael, James and Francis, and a sister, Ursula, had welcomed the little Julia, and a few years later they were joined by a new baby, Jane. They were a merry party, and Julia outshone the others by her gaiety and wilfulness. Their pious mother began early to train her little daughter in the love of God, and the Divine Master did not delay in granting special favors to this innocent soul. Speaking of herself in the third person, Maria Celeste says in her autobiography: "It is the way of our most loving God to shower His Divine mercies on His creatures, and to show forth His greatness and power in the most miserable. That is why, gazing down upon this soul, He gave her choice graces from her very childhood. She was a little child of only five or six years when Our Lord deigned to communicate Himself to her passively, by making her realize and know His Divinity: and that with so much sweetness that she had no longer any desire but to love and seek Him; all the more so because God had given her an intelligence and understanding far beyond her years. She continually sighed with love towards God, and her longing to serve Him well was so intense that she knew not how to satisfy it."

From this time Julia listened with greater avidity to all that her parents taught her about the Christian Faith, and she delighted in the lives of the Saints, which were read aloud; especially was she interested in those who loved God most, and made great efforts to learn to read them for herself. She adds in her Memoirs: "At the same time, the Lord spoke interiorly to her heart, and in a few brief words urged her to advance in His love. The child was too young, however, to understand the extraordinary graces with which she was favoured, and lived in this manner until she was nine years old."

At this age Julia was as attractive as a little Neapolitan can be. Her large dark eyes shone with ardour and vivacity, her whole bearing was marked by an extraordinary dignity and grace. Like all Southerners she was far more mature than the children of the North, and thus was easily influenced by some of the servants of the house, in whose company she delighted to be. In spite of her natural attraction for piety, and of the graces she had already received from God, she was not dead to the charms of the world. She had her weaknesses like other less favoured mortals. The Neapolitans are a song-loving, dance-loving, gaiety-loving people; their surroundings and the very air they breathe is intoxicating, and soon Julia learned to love the gay songs and the frivolous conversation of other girls.

There is no hint of real sin in all this, but the child's spiritual fervor naturally cooled, and Our Lord, Who destined her indeed to be a "vessel of election," never ceased to reproach her with her coldness. According to Julia's own account, she was endowed with an extraordinarily ardent and sensitive nature and might easily have been led very far astray, but God watched over His chosen one. Let us quote her own words:

". . . Who can ever explain the mercies of the Lord, and His infinite goodness towards the souls He has redeemed. If we, His creatures, were capable of understanding the least part of it, we should be carried away by a very passion of love for this Divine Savior Who runs after souls to draw them into the way of eternal salvation." And she adds, always speaking in the third person: "It was thus He acted towards this soul of whom we are speaking, notwithstanding the efforts that she made to separate herself from Him in every way and by every means." She tells us that though the little girl felt great fears and remorse she discontinued neither the conversations nor harmful amusements. "Our Lord in His goodness pursued her, giving

4

her scruples and doubts as to whether she had sinned or not." The poor child began to ask herself if God were not disgusted with her conduct, for, although she had confessed her faults, the priest had never told her if they were sins or not. ". . . The God of all goodness continued all this time to flood her soul with His mercies and graces, communicating to her great interior lights."

Sometimes He would say to her: "Leave creatures, and love Me alone." And again: "Come to Me—give yourself wholly to My love, and I will give you true contentment." Touched at last by so much goodness, Julia resolved to make a general confession, and on the Feast of St. Joseph she went with her mother to the Dominican Church of St. Thomas Aquinas, in Naples. The child, who was now eleven years old, explained carefully all her doubts. The priest was not slow to see that he was dealing with a very favored soul, and unhesitatingly explained how dangerous such frivolities would be for her. Julia then asked the Father to teach her how to make mental prayer, being ignorant that she had practice it for some time under the guidance of Our Lord Himself.

Understanding that she could read, the Dominican advised his little penitent to make use of the Meditations of St. Peter of Alcantara, and the "Manna of the Soul," by Father Segneri, which she found amongst the books of a pious aunt who lived with them. Filled with remorse at the thought of having offended God, Julia resolved to begin a new life and to Practice meditation as the priest had taught her. She read the meditations on the Passion of Our Lord and made her act of Faith, but immediately, she says, "a mysterious force drew her into the innermost recesses of her soul, and she was inflamed by a most ardent love and recollection. The book was useless, and the time passed without her perceiving it." The poor child began again, with the same result, and sometimes whole hours passed in this way, and she could not understand the reason of it. Often, too, during the day she was drawn into this state of profound recollection, so that she was incapable of taking part in the conversations around her.

The Divine Master was gradually attracting this pure soul to Himself. One day, when meditating on the thrust of the lance, which Our Lord had received on the Cross, she became so wrapt in ecstasy at the thought of the ineffable love of Our Divine Savior, Who invited her to come and make her abode in His Heart, and at the same time she was so wounded with love that she never again used a book for meditation. Her soul remained thus illuminated and in profound recollection for two months. This is Sister Mary Celeste's own account of her state at that time. Her prayer became more and more profound.

"The more the Divine Master loaded her with His caresses, the more her sorrow increased at the remembrance of her ingratitude." Her desolation was extreme, for she had no one in whom she could confide.

Julia was now preparing for her First Communion. Unfortunately, no details have been preserved to us either of her preparation for that great event, or of the First Communion itself. But she tells us of several favors accorded to her at this period, which were not only to console her in her loneliness, but to change her whole outlook on life. She says:

". . . One Sunday morning she went to Communion, and after she had received the Sacred Host, Our Lord showed her His open side, saying: 'Enter into this Wound, and I will purify you from all your sins.'" Then, not noticing how she was giving away the secret she wished to guard, she goes on: "Then I began to shed abundant tears, but of such sweetness that I entered into a profound recollection, during which Our Lord said to me: 'I wish , to be your Guide, I will lead you, look for none other than Me alone; I will be your Master, love no creature, but only Me.'"

Julia's delight and astonishment were unbounded, especially as this was the first time that Our Lord had favored her with an interior vision. She went home firmly determined to give herself wholly to God and to begin a really saintly life, resolutions enkindled by the Divine Presence which she felt within her heart, and which she had never hitherto experienced.

She says: "This Presence was none other than that of Our Lord Jesus Christ, and it was so real that the soul could not help expressing her vehement love by words of fire, and she was obliged to hide herself in solitary places away from the indiscreet looks of others, in order to allow free course to the tears she could not restrain, for God so enlightened her mind that she recognized her immense obligations towards Him, and remembered her past ingratitude to His infinite goodness. He so overwhelmed her with His mercies and graces that she would gladly have been consumed with love for Him: for she had always in her heart the consciousness of His Divine Presence."

A little later Our Lord for the first time gave her some notion of what her essential vocation was to be, but it was only by degrees that He made known to her His whole design. "You must imitate My life," He said to her, "and perform all your actions in union with those I accomplished on earth."

Julia understood that she must now live a more mortified life and, having heard that Our Lord went about barefoot, she left off her stockings, not daring to go without her shoes for fear of being seen. It was winter-time when she did this. She also made for herself a discipline of small chains and began to deprive herself of dainty dishes at table, but so cleverly as not to be noticed by others. The child was far from strong, and even then suffered greatly from indigestion and could take but little food. Nevertheless, she began her lifelong practice of making an hour's prayer in the middle of the night. She was now spending six hours in prayer every day, and soon she tells us that, owing to the great consolations she experienced, both food and sleep became impossible.

Julia was fourteen when Our Lord told her that He wished

her to keep secret all that He did in her soul. He also told her that He wished her to reproduce His hidden life on earth, which He had loved so much. He made her understand the grandeur of this hidden life, and she loved it and sought for it close to her Beloved.

Hitherto Julia had been the life and gaiety of the house, and her brothers did not at all approve of the change that had come over their lively sister. They thought it was a case of scruples and tried to laugh her out of it; but Julia, having once been privileged to converse with Our Lord, found it almost impossible to spend her time in useless amusements, and suffered much in consequence from all their teasing.

The Divine Master now began to teach her more and more of the lessons He wished her to learn. One day He called her and said: " Look at the sun and see how it gives light and heat, how it makes the plants grow, so that they may produce flowers and fruits, and also how it makes the whole world rejoice by its brilliancy. It shines on everyone, except on those who, shutting their windows, refuse to admit it and by their own fault remain deprived of its light, turning aside from its splendor. This sun which you admire in the visible world has been created to symbolize the Divine Sun which My divine Presence produces in hearts created by Me, and which gives light to the interior world of souls. In this spiritual sun you must behold My divine Perfections, and you will see how with the fire of My Spirit of Love I make the plants of virtue grow in souls and make them produce flowers and fruits for eternal life. I give light to the soul, and by enkindling it with My divine Fire of Love, I burn up all the weeds produced by disorderly passions and consume all imperfections. Those who keep the eyes of their soul open, and do not close them by sin, let in My divine Light. In looking on the material sun, you must remember what I have taught you, and let it be the subject of your continual meditation."

This instruction was a revelation to Julia. She was deeply

impressed and sought at once to put it into practice. She tells us that from early morning, when gazing at the dazzling light of the sun, she felt herself at once drawn into the invisible and divine splendor which resulted from the presence of her Well-Beloved. In this sublime contemplation she received continually fresh lights and an ardor that consumed her unceasingly. Incapable of thinking of anything else, she used to withdraw to the most secluded room in the house so that, entirely absorbed in this divine Light, she might enjoy it for hours together, oblivious of the flight of time.

Let us listen to the Venerable Mother herself describing the action of the Holy Ghost in her soul at this period. " While seeming to do nothing, this soul enjoyed ineffable sweetness and such an ardent love of God that she was overwhelmed by it. Sometimes, when thinking of God dwelling above the clouds, she would receive sublime knowledge of Heaven and its magnificence. Thus, the Lord gave to her innermost soul a wonderful appreciation of Himself, and of His Divine Uncreated Immensity and Eternal Being." "At another time," she adds, " He gave her to understand how Our Lord Jesus Christ is the Divine Sun of Justice, shining in the eternal glory of Heaven, and how in like manner He is the Sun of die just soul on earth." For more than a year Julia remained in this exalted way of prayer, and each day she received fresh lights and such admirable knowledge of the attributes of God that it would be impossible, she tells us, to relate them in human words.

9

CHAPTER II
GIRLHOOD

ULIA had just attained her fifteenth year. Now in the parish of Saint Joseph it was the custom to celebrate every year the seven Wednesdays in honor of the glorious Patriarch, before his Feast on March 19th. People flocked to the church in such crowds at this time that the parish priest was obliged to call in several neighboring priests to help with the confessions. Amongst them this year was a priest from the Cathedral, a very learned man, who appeared to be well versed in the spiritual life, but who was so young that he was usually only permitted to hear the confessions of men. On this special occasion his faculties were extended for hearing women's confessions also. Ursula and Jane Crostarosa, fired by the example of their sister, had begun to lead very pious lives, and together with her they went to confession to this young priest. After her confession the Father asked Julia if she devoted herself to the spiritual life, and who was her director? She told him she had none and simply went to confession to the parish priest. She told him about her way of prayer and the extraordinary graces she received. Hearing all this, the confessor was much surprised and interested, and, adds Julia with delightful simplicity, "Being quite young and inexperienced in such things, he told her that God wished to lead her to a high degree of sanctity."

In a second interview he examined her at length, and, becoming more interested in his penitent, he spoke to her of the love of God and told her it was not right for her to remain without a director. He then offered himself to be her spiritual guide. Julia asked for nothing better, and the proposal was accepted. He thereupon commanded her to write down all that took place in her soul. The child had never learned to write. ... This is not surprising at the time in which she lived even for a young girl in her station of life. In Naples, as in France, much instruction was considered unnecessary for a woman, and the Abbe Fleury quoted the general opinion of the period when he declared: "It would be a paradox to say that women should learn anything else than their catechism, and how to sew and embroider."

Nevertheless, since her confessor ordered it, Julia set herself to do as she was bid, and, trusting in Our Lord, without the help of a master was soon able to write. She then wrote down the experiences of her interior life and entrusted these pages to her confessor. The manuscripts of the Venerable Servant of God are written in a clear, bold hand as admirable as is the beauty and simplicity of her style. The same favor of writing without any teaching was granted also to St. Catherine of Sienna and to Ven. Anne of St. Bartholomew.

It was at this time, Julia tells us that she came to have a certain attachment for this young priest, and he for her; spiritual, it is true, and perfectly innocent, but nevertheless a hindrance to her intimate union with God, and at once the Divine communications became less frequent, and Our Lord even reproached her in this regard. She was very unhappy but did not know how to withdraw herself from the situation. She has left us some very wise counsels on this subject, having learned wisdom by her own experience. "It is very necessary," she says, "for all who wish to lead a spiritual life to be most careful in their choice of a director. They should pray much and have recourse to God in humility and confidence. They should beg for light and grace in so important a matter, for their advancement and progress in the spiritual life depend on this choice. Let them be careful to inquire about the qualifications of the priest. Above all, he should be holy, learned and experienced. It would be far preferable for souls to depend wholly on God than to fall into the hands of an inexperienced confessor. Their choice should in no way depend on natural inclination. God will choose for them if they wait patiently, trusting in Him; for He is faithful to the soul that loves Him, and He will lead her Himself in the way of perfection until she finds the guide who is to help her in the spiritual life." These words are but the echo of St. Teresa's own sentiments on this subject.

For two years Julia continued to be directed by this young priest; then one day he informed her that, as he had finished his four years of residence at the Cathedral, he would now be able to come and hear her confessions, and thus she could tell him of the state of her soul in words instead of in writing. Julia was pleased, because she had been obliged to take from her prayer the time she had spent in writing to him.

The three sisters had continued to allow themselves to be directed by this young priest in spite of the disapproval of their mother, who wished them to go to the parish priest as she did herself. The young girls, however, complained that the latter was too old and did not understand their way of prayer. Nevertheless they came to realize that to oppose their mother's wishes must be wrong, and Ursula, the eldest, now set about seeking a more suitable director for herself and her sisters. In her autobiography Julia writes: ". . . The Lord permitted these contradictions because it was not His Will that the young priest should be their spiritual guide."

After much prayer they at last found a most virtuous and learned priest who was well known in the town as a holy director. This was Don Bartholomew Cacace, who belonged to the Apostolic Missions of Naples. After thinking the matter over and praying about it he consented to come and hear the Sisters' confessions every week in their parish church. The Venerable Sister tells us that she was seventeen at this time, and that, "the obstacle being removed, it pleased the Lord to inundate her soul with a torrent of graces." The great advantage to Julia in this new direction was that her soul was now at peace. After a careful examination of her dispositions and the graces accorded to her, Don Bartholomew assured her that her way was from God, and that she must follow it in all simplicity. He ordered her to go to Communion daily and, feeling sure of God's designs on this chosen soul, allowed her to make the vow of perpetual chastity. Our Lord bestowed many favors on her at this time. In particular she tells us of one occasion when she went to a window to adore the Blessed Sacrament, which was being carried to the sick, and saw instead of the priest Our Lord Himself carrying the ciborium. He appeared in great majesty, and was so beautiful and resplendent that her heart was wounded with love and sweetness. She adds that it was not with the eyes of her body, but with those of her soul, that she saw the Redeemer. From that time forward Our Lord remained more intimately united to her, and this continual presence of the Sacred Humanity of Jesus, though without sensible form, consumed her with love and tenderness for her Beloved.

Another time, after Communion, she was given great lights concerning the Blessed Sacrament. Touched by the manner in which Our Lord was teaching her, she considered her past life, her many infidelities and her ingratitude towards Him, and burst into a torrent of tears. Unable to repress her great sorrow, she began to confess her sins aloud. At her words the people about her were in great admiration, for they knew her well from seeing her in church, and they could not but smile, knowing how young she was and how innocent her life had been. They therefore tried to console her, but in vain. Julia only answered that she had greatly offended God, and that her sins were very grievous, and the poor child continued to sob and cry.

When she returned home, she was unable to take any food, but ran and hid herself in her favorite retreat and passed the day in transports of love and repentance.

Two more years passed during which Our Lord continued

to show Himself to His servant as the Light of Truth. He guided her step by step, sometimes allowing her to hear words by which He taught her the meaning of the sublime truths of the Gospels, sometimes inflaming her with love by such invitations as the following:

"Love Me alone, I alone am Thy Guide, in Whom thou must confide, never in men. ... I have chosen thee as My spouse, I desire thee to be pure and simple. ... Do not attach thyself to any creature—to anything on earth, to anything made by creatures ... I am jealous of thy heart, because I have chosen thee for Myself alone."

But let Julia herself describe the action of Him Who was forming her in silence according to the divine ideal He had conceived for her. Turning to Our Lord she says:

"... From time to time it pleased Thee in Thy divine love to draw my soul to Thee so sweetly, so gently and with so much mercy, that Thou seemedst to forget that I was not yet purified from my bad habits, and that I was still full of imperfections and of my self-love. I ignored it, being always alone and absorbed by Thy most pure and divine Light, which overwhelmed me entirely and enkindled my soul. Thy divine sweetness was so great that it not only filled the superior part of my soul, but also the inferior and sensible part, so that my spirit and my soul no longer experienced any revolt or contradiction."

Then she goes on:

"O my Love, Thou didst not disdain each morning to come into this heart so full of self, full too of imperfections, and still subject to bad habits, this heart not yet purified by Thee. Each time that I received Thy most divine Sacrament Thou didst manifest Thyself to my soul in diverse and most wonderful ways, sometimes Thou didst declare Thyself to be my only Spouse, saying: 'I am thy All.' At other times Thou didst instruct me about the truths of Faith, accompanying Thy words with thousands of caresses, and bringing light to my soul." Julia here speaks with the sincerity and humility of the saints, making allusion to her imperfections and to a necessary purification, for it is true that those to whom God vouchsafes special favors and whom He calls to an intimate union with Himself, must first be cleansed from the slightest stain of sin and thereby rendered pure as crystal. Such a soul is not freed at once from all imperfection. Therefore, God is now about to lead His servant by the way of sorrow, called passive purification.

Julia says plainly: "In spite of so many favors, I disregarded Thy will," and she did. At this time the young confessor to whom Our Lord did not wish her to address herself came, as he had promised, to their parish church. A very natural desire came to the girl to see him once more and to have a long talk with him: she therefore gave herself this satisfaction. This act was for her the starting- point of the terrible trial which she was now to undergo. Hardly had she left the confessional when she realized that she ought to have made the sacrifice of this meeting which was not pleasing to God. Her sensitive soul felt the Divine displeasure, and she says:

"... Thou, O my Love, didst correct me promptly and severely; darkness entered my soul, and I was filled with profound remorse for the fault I had just committed.

"I no longer felt Thy sweet Presence nor the Divine Light which taught me the way of truth and faith, there remained nothing in any of the powers of my soul but darkness and obscurity." Temptations of all kinds assailed her. She describes her state in the following words:

"I experienced such a terrible interior revolt that my soul, plunged in sorrow and as it were crucified, was absorbed in its own misery. It was as if I had lost my reason, or at times had become like a statue, incapable of movement or resistance. I felt as if I were in the hands of enemies, conquered, miserable, lost, without any hope of breaking the chains which bound me. I could no longer think of Thee, O my God, nor invoke Thy sweet Name, O my Love. Thus incapable of any good action, I endured this struggle for many hours and thought I had become like the demons." Hoping to find some relief, Julia went to Don Bartholomew, who assured her that she had not really offended God and must not worry. "You are passing through two cruel trials at the same time—the purification of the senses and that of the spirit," he said. "This painful state cannot last long, the good God will soon relieve you." He seemed surprised to see her in such a state, and, finding that he was able to do her no good, advised her to go to some other priest. This she did, but God, Who wished that she should have no human succor to support her during her period of trial, gave no grace to his words, and Julia was only plunged into deeper distress. Her confessor told her to continue her practice of daily Communion in spite of all her feelings, and she forced herself to go each morning to the church. But her terror was increased, for it seemed to her "as if a dart of fire came from the Tabernacle and struck her violently, and, despite the darkness in which her spirit was plunged, she saw it enter the secret recess of her soul, not to console, but to fill her with anguish."

This agonizing state lasted, she tells us, for three months, during which time no trial was spared her, neither in the undue and unmeant severity of her confessor, nor the relations she was obliged to have with her family, in spite of the grief she was enduring, nor the constant dread of being cast off by God.

It was on Holy Saturday, 1716, that relief came. Julia had gone to church as usual, but did not dare to raise her eyes to the altar. When the first notes of the "Gloria in Excelsis" sounded, her soul, so long buried in darkness and misery, felt as if the stone of the sepulcher had been rolled away. She raised her eyes and saw Our Lord looking at her with infinite sweetness. He made a sign, and in an instant all her sufferings, and even the memory of them, disappeared. She says:

"My mind and my memory, forgetting their prolonged sorrow, the powers of my soul fell as it were into a refreshing sleep, and my will was sweetly inflamed during this repose. I was like a person who, being overtired with hard work, falls into a life-giving sleep; I remained thus during the whole of Mass. At the Communion I approached the Holy Table, and Thou, O my Love, coming to me, said in Thine own divine language, 'May peace be in thy heart!' At these words my soul melted, becoming wholly pacified and absorbed in Thee, not seeking to know where its powers resided. My senses, exterior as well as interior, seemed no longer to exist—I was as one sleeping peacefully. This state lasted all the time I was in church. Returning home in a very different frame of mind from that in which I left it, I seemed to be bereft of everything. I could not even form a single thought, either spiritual or temporal, so that I became incapable of any exterior action. I seemed to be like a tiny child, not knowing how to make a single reflection." Seeing herself in this state to be useless, Julia ran to hide in solitude. As at the time of her first ecstasies, the hours passed imperceptibly, whilst she prayed in the words of St. Paul: "Lord, what wouldst Thou have me to do?" Then, her soul being now purified, she heard the voice of God inviting her to leave her father's house and dwell with Him on Mount Carmel.

CHAPTER III
THE CARMEL OF MARIGLIANO

ULIA had long cherished a religious vocation; in fact, she had never had any other idea than that of belonging entirely to God, but her health had always been an obstacle, and she had been especially delicate during the trials through which she had just passed. The doctors could only order strengthening remedies for her state of anemia; time would do the rest. Julia waited for God to give her some sign as to when He wished her to leave the world and enter the cloister. A chance occurrence was to show her what were His designs.

Not far from Naples, in the little town of Marigliano, a Carmelite Convent had been founded lately according to the reform of the Venerable Seraphine of Capri. Ursula Crostarosa desired to become a Nun there, and her mother agreed to take her with a friend to make the acquaintance of the Prioress. After much persuasion, Julia was allowed to go with them. The visitors were most cordially received, and at the end of their interview the Superior, struck by the ardent look in Julia's eyes, turned to her and asked if she would not also like to remain in Carmel? The latter answered yes with so much joy and vehemence that all were astonished and impressed. Ursula on her part declared that she would be very glad not to return to Naples. A long argument ensued, as Madame Crostarosa had no desire to leave her daughters there without their father's permission. At last she was obliged to give way, but the two girls promised to leave the Convent at once if their father insisted on their returning home. The joy of the two sisters was indescribable when Don Crostarosa expressed himself quite satisfied to allow them to remain at Marigliano.

Julia was only twenty years of age and, rejoicing in her vocation and freedom from worldly ties, thought only of uniting herself to God. But very soon she began to have a forewarning that God had other work for her to do. Although the Carmel of Marigliano was in its first fervor, the Sisters enjoyed great liberty as regards regular observance and visits to the parlor. As they were nevertheless a very simple and upright community, they led perfectly innocent lives under a Superior who, herself pious and almost childlike in her simplicity, saw nothing wrong in what was being done and made no attempt to correct it.

Our Lord evidently loved the Community very much, and, knowing that such practices might become harmful to them, He made use of Julia to put an end to them. He sent her to the Superioress, ordering her to speak in His Name. Hard as the task was, the postulant faithfully performed it, and also said that she herself would never take the veil in that Monastery while these relaxations were allowed. The holy Superioress accepted with her whole heart the instructions sent to her by Our Lord, and at once set to work to ensure regular observance. Julia, overjoyed and greatly edified, was strengthened in her intention of becoming a Nun in that Convent. At the end of six months, on November twenty-first, the Feast of Our Lady's Presentation, she was clothed in the Carmelite habit. On this happy day Our Lady appeared to her and accepted her as a daughter forever. On His side Our Lord enlightened her mind, showing her that He, the Divine Word, was the true Spouse of her soul, Who would never separate Himself from her. She tells that, thus favored by Mother and Son, she was all the more confused at seeing herself so poor and destitute of virtues. "Unworthy as I was," she cried, "I did not know how to repay my Lord for all the graces and mercies without number with which He loaded me, but my Jesus promised that He Himself would teach me the way in which I was to walk."

At the clothing ceremony Ursula received the name Sister Maria Illuminata, and Julia that of Sister Maria Celeste del deserto. The holy Mother seems to give us the clue to this somewhat strange name, "del deserto," when in her book "The Mystical Ladder," describing the third degree or rung of the ascent, which was evidently her state of soul at this time, she says:

". . . The greatest of our weaknesses and miseries consists in only living for things of earth, engulfed by our senses, our passions and the thousand and one ever-changing accidents that occur on our way. These are like clouds that shut out the light of eternal life; we are as it were in an unclean earthen vessel which emits foul and impure odors, thus preventing us from enjoying the pure air of the Divinity. It follows that we are like the blind, not able to distinguish our supreme good, and are therefore deprived of those consolations which would make us happy. But no, we rest on what is exterior; on the senses which are the cause of so many vicissitudes and sorrows, and make this land of exile so bitter for us. Our poor spirit, made by God for God, has become a slave; its nobility is buried beneath vileness and falsehood. Seeing this, our good God has compassion on the misery of His creatures and, by the light of faith, sends some rays of truth into those souls who wish to be united to Him by love."

"Thus passively and through knowledge enlightened by faith. He shows the soul how He is the All in the being of every creature. This ray of truth destroys in man all that is false and unreal and shows him the unreality of the things of this world. God gives the soul by this means the grace of annihilation of self and of all created things, and by this act the soul discovers her true center, divine Truth, and she ascends to her true origin, the supreme Good. ... Such a soul can have no complacency in herself; while esteeming and recognizing the gifts she has received from God, she does not consider herself at all, but only her most amiable All, Whom she adores and loves always. Each time that the Lord grants her this state of prayer He gives her for a few short seconds a foretaste of His Glory. She there drinks with satiety, so that she may fill all the void in her soul, and, quenching her thirst at this fountain, the desire grows within her to humiliate herself and to die to herself and everything else as far as she can. For souls who receive this grace the world becomes a desert. ... Nothing in it consoles them. The conversations and amusements of creatures are most painful to them and cause them a real martyrdom. They look upon themselves as already dead. O my God, let my tongue be silent, because in truth it could never know how to express what the soul feels in this case." We must always remember that in this extraordinary life of the Venerable Sister Maria Celeste, Our Lord was first and last the Director and the Guide of His privileged daughter. In her book of "Soliloquies" she explains this as follows:

"At the beginning, in my childhood. Thou didst communicate Thyself to my soul and Thy divine Presence overwhelmed me with Thy love. Thou didst Thyself teach me to despise the world and to love poverty and humiliation. Thou didst instruct me in the Holy Gospels, showing me their divine meaning and the mysteries they contained. Thou didst excite me to love Thee with a great and constant ardor, yet so sweetly withal, and Thou didst beseech me to be entirely Thine. I saw Thy Divine splendor as though it were always near me, drawing me to Thee in an indescribable manner. Then, when I reached girlhood, I began to feel Thy divine Presence in a more spiritual way; it was an intellectual light, a divine brilliance, which made me see Thine unspeakable Beauty. This was so wonderful that my soul seemed to go out of itself with the joy I experienced. Then it was that I began to feel a great bodily weakness, accompanied by ecstasies and a sort of spiritual joy which was almost continual."

After Sister Mary Celeste's entrance into Carmel, Our Lord continued to instruct her, and to teach her the true way of religious life, as He had promised to do on the day of her clothing. He gave her these seven rules, which we copy from the Autobiography written by Julia under obedience.

"THE FIRST RULE.—My well-beloved daughter, from early morning you shall withdraw yourself into Me, your Creator, flying all conversations and useless words. You must guard with great jealousy the chamber of your heart, in order that I may take my repose therein. Remain as far as possible retired and in solitude, allowing only Me to enter into your heart, and from henceforth your sacred cell shall be in My Divine Heart; there you must make your home, praying continually, and so I shall live in your heart and you in Mine. Listen to the most pure voice of My divine Love, and in My Light you will see your omissions and faults in order to humble yourself in My divine Presence, then you go to receive Me in the Sacrament of the Altar, abase yourself at the sight of so incomparable a gift and annihilate yourself by true humility. When you have received Me in this great Sacrament, lose yourself in the immensity of My love, for within your heart is now a treasure, Infinite, incomparable, and ineffable. It can be understood by Me alone. Then abide in My pure love.

"SECOND RULE.—My well-beloved daughter, listen to the voice of Purity. See how you must conduct yourself in the two most difficult actions, where Nature is most to be found —that is to say, at meals and at recreation. You must leave your senses unoccupied with these two actions, keeping your mind always attentive to Me by love. Avoid leaving your house empty, therefore in the refectory nourish yourself by My Spirit without attending to the corporal food. You must go to recreation in a spirit of gentleness and kindness, seeing all the actions of others in a favorable light. You must bear any hurtful word in a spirit of humility, single-mindedness, and sincerity. You must not stop to judge the actions and motives of others. Do not give way to frivolous gaiety, and do not leave your beloved cell, that is to say, My Divine Heart. Whenever you can, in conversation with others, try to speak of spiritual and pious subjects. Do this always. If others begin to talk of worldly affairs, do not answer and do not listen to them. Never meddle in the affairs of the Monastery, either now or at any other time, unless obedience obliges you to do so.

"THIRD RULE.—Be most careful to retire to your cell at the hours prescribed for silence, which you will observe most faithfully, unless obedience or charity obliged you to do otherwise. During the time of silence and recollection, you will remain withdrawn within yourself, and live in My Heart, paying great attention to all that I shall show you. You will also at this time remember the three most painful hours that I passed on the Cross, overwhelmed by anguish both of Body and of Soul. I gave My Life for love of you and for the salvation of souls which are so dear to Me, so you must remain beneath the Cross and gather up My Blood so as to offer It to My Father for the salvation of sinners.

"FOURTH RULE.—My daughter, unite every beat of your heart to My Spirit, renouncing absolutely all that is not pure love. Do all your actions with uprightness and purity of intention, solely for My glory. As the body breathes the air which surrounds it, so you should breathe in and for Me at each moment of your life and in each act of your heart. My Will should be yours, and the end of all your desires and in all your sorrows and crosses, you must rejoice, and you should do the same in the time of aridity and desolation, as well as amidst consolations. As fire produces h brilliant flame from dry wood and not from green, so My divine Love consumes the soul more ardently by true charity in the time of aridities and sufferings. Have only My Honor and Glory in view and do not count on yourself or lean on the world or on creatures. Be constant in your zeal for My glory, even if you should lose your life thereby, for it is thus I acted for love of you.

"FIFTH RULE.—There are three exercises to which you must apply yourself as long as you live upon the earth. The first is to accustom yourself to live amongst creatures solely for the good of their souls, and to help them to arrive at eternal salvation without mixing yourself up with temporal affairs. The second is to have your mind always anchored in God and united to Jesus, as the Word was united to His Eternal Father and to the Holy Spirit. This was His habitual exercise while He lived on earth. The third is that you must no longer occupy yourself with either your past, present, or future life, but think only of your one Love, the supreme and eternal Good, your first Principle and Last End.

"SIXTH RULE.—You must love your neighbor, and never complain of anything he does to you, remaining always in your own nothingness. As My greatness is infinite, so in a sense are your poverty and misery. Know that you have never received sufficient light to understand them as they are. When you learn of the graces and gifts which I impart to your neighbor, you must rejoice and thank Me for them as if I had given them to you. This will be for you fruitful to humility and an increase of charity, and for Me it will bring accidental glory. Receive with meekness every insult for sins merit for man infinite sufferings and evils, and for this reason you should consider contumely as nothing, and make no account of it. You must never say words that could pain your neighbor, but treat him with respect as the living temple of God, and you must receive with humility every kind of injury as I did for love of you.

"SEVENTH RULE.—You must honor your Superioress, considering her as My representative on earth, and you will see in your Sisters the Holy Apostles and My disciples. In this religious house as in the Cenacle, you must live in their company in a spirit of gentleness and charity. When you go to the choir to sing and proclaim My praises you must unite your spirit to Mine, because while I was on earth I glorified My Heavenly Father, and thus I and not you will be living with your life. In the same way all the spiritual gifts, graces and consolations that, you receive from My Mercy will be received not in you but in Me. Then I will rejoice in you by My pure love. You must act in this way in all the actions of your life, as when you eat or sleep. I am the life of love in your soul. You must love Me by this pure love, hidden from all creatures, and I must live hidden in your heart."

To these Rules, which He ordered her to write down. Our Lord added further instructions. During the Divine Office He taught her the mystical meaning of the Psalms, the beauty of which, she tells us, wounded her soul, so that she was no longer able to continue chanting. At Holy Communion also she experienced the same suspension of her senses. One day, on hearing the Name of God pronounced, she received as it were a wound of love, which recurred as often as the Sacred Name was pronounced, and more especially if it were the name of Jesus. Many times Our Lord said to her "Thou are Mine and I am all thine, do not leave Me alone in thy heart." But Maria Celeste herself owns that sometimes, through human weakness, she failed to remember this Sacred Presence, and that then, to her great confusion, Our Lord would reproach her with her want of vigilance. When she had been only eight months a novice the Superioress seeing her great virtue, named her Portress and gave her other charges. This caused no little disturbance and was especially resented by the Mother Vicar, whose right it was to hold these offices. Maria Celeste herself recognized the inconvenience of her appointment, and only accepted it out of obedience. It was not long before the displeasure of the Sister gave way to petty persecution, and the Novice found herself denounced to the confessor as a visionary.

This priest was not the director of the Servant of God, but he forbade her to receive Holy Communion so frequently, and reprimanded her severely on account of the complaints made by the Mother Vicar. The humble Sister made no answer to the accusations and simply obeyed, but the Superioress advised her to write all that had occurred to Don Bartholomew, and he arranged matters with the confessor. For three months longer the persecution continued; in fact until the death of the Mother Vicar. After this peace reigned in the little community. At the end of her year of novitiate Julia made her Solemn Vows, for which Our Lord Himself had prepared her. On the day of her Profession, He gave her in a special manner Our Lady as her Mother, and St. Catherine of Sienna for her mistress in the spiritual life. The perfume of her virtues was already beginning to attract others, and the Servant of God herself tells us the following anecdote:

"When I was *touriere,* two postulants entered the Convent, the younger daughters of a Neapolitan barrister. They were accompanied by their eldest sister, who was very fashionably dressed, as she was shortly to marry a rich nobleman. She came into the Convent with her sisters, as at this time the relations of postulants were allowed to come into the downstairs cloisters. Soon after she had come in she entered our room and sat down; then looking at me very fixedly, she said: 'Servant of God, I wish to remain in this monastery in your company and to give up the world.' Knowing of her engagement, I told her it could not be, and that the house was already full to overflowing, but she answered: 'I am determined to stay with you, God calls me.' I told her it could not be done so suddenly, and reminded her of her betrothal. I spoke to her for a very long time, but she only wept and said she would never go home, and then went to look for the Superioress, to obtain the desired permission. Her relations began to expostulate, but at last agreed to her staying."

She then asked the Superioress to allow her to be under the

direction of Sister Maria Celeste, through whose means God had called her to the religious life. The narrative continues: "On this same day on which Our Lord called this soul to His service in so extraordinary a manner one of her sisters, on hearing that she could keep nothing of her own, and that everything in the Community was shared in common, made up her mind to return home with her relations." The elder sister, after an heroic life of mortification and humility, during which she was favored by extraordinary graces in prayer, died in the odor of sanctity, and Sister Maria Celeste adds that her body was kept in a special place apart on account of the many miracles that God worked after her death.

In the May of 1717 Sister Maria Celeste was made Mistress of Novices, and in spite of the fact that her life from this time onwards seemed to become more and more extraordinary, she discharged the office with wonderful success, to the great profit of the souls under her care. About this time she gives us a graphic account of a prolonged ecstasy with which Our Lord favored her. She says: "One morning I went to the choir to hear Holy Mass. It was a Feast day. Scarcely had I entered than I experienced such a fire of love for God that, fearing to fall into an ecstasy, I returned to my cell so as not to be noticed by anyone. Immediately I was favored with a wonderful vision, wholly spiritual and not corporal, for I have never experienced corporal visions. I beheld Our Lord Jesus Christ in resplendent majesty and incomparable beauty.

A ray of light from His divine side entered my heart and wounded it, causing me great pain, while at the same time I was filled with ineffable joy and love. In the meantime the hour for receiving Holy Communion had arrived and, according to the custom in that monastery, I should have conducted the Novices to the Holy Table. Not seeing me in choir, they came to our cell to call me. Finding me prostrate, they rushed in great fear to the Superioress, saying that their Mother was dead. Thereupon all the Sisters came running to our cell and began to shake me and call me, and the Superior commanded me by holy obedience to rise and go to Communion. Sighing deeply, I awoke as out of a sweet sleep and, though aching in every limb at being thus forcibly aroused from my ecstasy, I went, supported by two Nuns, to receive Holy Communion."

For long after this Sister Maria Celeste could not move without great pain, and was subject to attacks of fever for over a year. Her health became so bad that she was forced to keep to her bed entirely until a command from her director, joined to her implicit faith and obedience, restored her to perfect health. It was evident, however, that her state was incompatible with the care of the novices, and at the end of a year she was made sacristan. Great was the joy of the young Nun to be able to pass so many quiet hours near the tabernacle, but here again her physical weakness betrayed her. Her constant ecstasies reduced her body to a state of complete prostration, and she was unable to cope with material things. One of the Sisters, finding her in tears at her inability to get through her duties, offered to aid her, and things went better. On one occasion, having mounted a ladder which she had fastened insecurely, she fell down with the ladder on top of her, but on that occasion God preserved her from harm almost miraculously, and He watched over her continually. She tells us of one charming little incident showing the Divine goodness. She was in bed, suffering greatly and unable to take any food, but the idea came into her head that she could eat a certain kind of little tart that was sometimes made in the house on feast days. It was night and no one was about, but next morning she was surprised to see a lay Sister come into her cell with a little tart, quite hot. The Sister told her that the Mother Vicar had said she was to eat it at once. She says: "Great was my astonishment, as I had spoken to no one. I asked the Mother Vicar how she had known, and she said that very early, before getting up, she had heard a voice telling her quite plainly to have a little tart of puff paste made for me, and that I was to eat it as I had need of it."

CHAPTER III: CARMEL OF MARIGLIANO

On another occasion during her illness she tells us that chestnuts were served for supper; all that were sent up to her were full and very good, but all those that went to the refectory were empty. She says: "I was greatly confused at these favors, and I could fill a book with similar occurrences." It was during this year that Our Lord began to lift the veil which hid His designs on this favored soul. One day she was enveloped by a brilliant light, and felt sensible of the Divine Presence within her. Then Our Lord showed her a legion of religious souls whom she had never seen before, and He said to her: "I desire to make you the Mother of many souls whom I shall save by means of you." Sister Maria Celeste was stupefied and, not being, able to understand the mystery, resolved to think no more about it. A few days later a mission opened in that part of the country, preached by the Fathers of the Congregation of Pii Operarii, established at Naples. Some of the Fathers were named for the different convents, and Father Falcoia came to that of Marigliano. Being fully satisfied with her own director, Maria Celeste had no thought of opening her soul to the Missioner, but during the following night, while in prayer. Our Lord told her to go to this Father and tell him the whole state of her soul. "In the morning," she says, "I wrote him a note asking him to come to the grille so that I might speak to him about my interior life, as that was the Will of God. After the morning sermon he sent for me, and I told him all that had happened to me, and what Our Lord had told me concerning him. He answered that God had also enlightened him concerning me, when he was praying the night before. He told me I was to write to him for the future, while still being directed by Don Bartholomew, that Our Lord wished it so, and he assured me that all my spiritual life came from God."

This interview lasted two hours, and was accompanied by sensible graces which strengthened these two great souls. Except on this occasion, however, they never fully understood one another, and the Venerable Mother wrote later on: "If the

Lord placed me in the hands of this Father, it was to make me enjoy the precious fruits of the Cross hitherto unknown to me. ... He was, nevertheless, a great servant of God."

The result of this long interview was to fill Maria Celeste with scruples as to whether she had done wrong or not in opening her heart to a stranger. Falcoia tried to persuade her that it was only a temptation of the devil, and at last succeeded in calming her fears. Then for the first time the servant of God heard the name of Scala.

Father Falcoia spoke to her several times of a monastery he was trying to found there. She little thought of the work God was reserving for her in that monastery.

At the end of her year as sacristan Sister Mary Celeste was renamed Mistress of Novices and Postulants, and she tells us that "with great consolation she set herself to cultivate this little garden of the Lord." Her hunger and thirst to help souls was ardent, and she desired above all things to make them love God with the whole of their being. She tells us also that Our Lord gave her wonderfully efficacious lights on the words: "I am the Way, the Truth and the Life, no one cometh to the Father but by Me." She was allowed to see the admirable work of the divine union in an upright soul. She saw how Jesus is the Way, by His works and virtues as applied to our soul; the Truth, by the light of Faith infused into us; the Life, by the grace which makes us live with the life of our Divine Head. Sister Mary Celeste speaks here in the third person and says: "She saw also how the soul mounts to the Father only by Jesus, for He is the mystical ladder by which man ascends from earth to Heaven. The Word came down from the bosom of the Father by astonishing humiliations, in order to make Himself like unto us, so that, made like to Him and united to Him, we might ascend to Heaven with Him and through Him, for He only can of right ascend to Heaven who has come down from it. The Lord has made the sky so far from the earth, in order to show us that, if man does not leave all earthly visible and sensible things, he can never ascend to Heaven with Him Who descended from there." "I thought," adds the Servant of God, "that I had already arrived in Heaven when the Lord, in an effusion of His Love showed me all these wonders, and I imagined that I was already in possession of that great good." "It was my profound ignorance, notwithstanding all that ought to have enlightened me. Oh, I was indeed far from that sublime state, being still too much attached to the earth, and not being as yet purified by the water and fire of suffering and tribulations. I was full of myself, and thought I was pure because I was clothed in the purity of my Jesus, which perfumed me and surrounded me with light."

How sublime must be the height of perfection to which the human soul is invited, when a soul such as that of the Venerable Mother, fashioned for so long by the Hand of God Himself, found herself at so great a distance from this ideal. She herself gives us a very instructive comparison on this subject when she says: "We are like the Israelites, who only took possession of the Promised Land after much fighting, many struggles and great labor. This is why the Lord arms the soul with the Cross, so that during many years she may Practice virtues, fight and triumph until she reaches the Promised Land, that is to say, the divine and intimate union with the Word of God."

The health of Sister Maria Celeste improved considerably, but it never became good. "I don't remember ever to have enjoyed good health," she owns. "From my childhood I always had a delicate stomach, and was subject to frequent attacks of sickness." Now, however, that she was stronger. Our Lord enjoined on her certain corporal penances, and she adds: "Having obtained permission from my spiritual Father, I began fo put into execution the orders Our Lord gave me, and I was filled with an ardent desire to suffer for Him Who loved me so much."

At this time Sister Maria Celeste was enjoying great peace

of soul, and the Carmel of Marigliano was a home of joy to her. It was the oasis in which Our Lord allowed her to repose before she once more entered the scorching desert where fierce storms awaited her. For the time had come for her to leave this happy retreat.

The Convent was, unfortunately, to a great extent under the domination of a rich and powerful nobleman, who now began to cause the Nuns indescribable worries and annoyances. He not only confiscated a great part of their property, but intimidated the clergy so much that the Nuns were deprived of their confessors; moreover, he threatened worse vengeance for the future. Powerless to help the Sisters, the Bishop resolved to close the Convent, and he ordered that the dowries of the Nuns should be given back, and that each one should find a home in another convent. Thus the Carmel of Marigliano was dissolved, to the great grief of those whom it had sheltered for so many years. When the day of separation came the Superioress, herself a most holy soul, took her dear daughter Maria Celeste in her arms and, embracing her, said: "Pray for me; you will do many things for the greater glory of God." This was the second time Our Lord had manifested His designs in regard to Sister Maria Celeste, but the holy Sister dismissed the matter from her mind, thinking herself incapable of doing anything.

The Carmelites had communicated to their relations the decision taken by the Bishop, and Maria Celeste wrote also to Father Falcoia, with whom she kept up correspondence for a year and a half, as he had requested her to do. She made him acquainted with the circumstances, and asked him what she and her sisters ought to do. Her eldest sister was now a professed Nun, and the youngest a postulant. Father Falcoia immediately replied that God wished them to go to the monastery of Scala, of which he was the spiritual Father.

From this time onwards Sister Maria Celeste placed herself entirely under his direction, having lost Don Bartholomew, who had guided her for so long. Thus the Divine Master cut all the cords which bound her to the past so as to lead her into the harbor he had prepared for her, and where He awaited her with His Cross. Whilst Father Falcoia was endeavoring to procure the entrance of the three sisters at Scala the latter went home to their parents, who did all in their power to console and help them. They took them for a change of air to the town of Portice. During the month spent there Don Crostarosa entered into negotiations with certain ecclesiastical authorities with a view to founding a monastery at Tramonti, near Naples. There he wished to establish his daughters as foundresses, and thus to have them settled near their old home. Many reasons were brought forward in favor of this proposition, and Sister Maria Celeste hardly knew how to refuse when one morning, after Holy Communion, Our Lord said to her: "It is My Will that you should go to the monastery at Scala; there you will exercise yourself in humility, and you will be amongst the Sisters as the least of all."

This was decisive. All doubts and hesitations vanished from her soul. She spoke at once to her father, respectfully expressing her determination to go to the convent at Scala. After much discussion Don Crostarosa gave way so as not to displease his daughter, whose judgment he trusted. In all these events it is to Julia that her sisters look for advice and guidance. Ursula, in particular, was not attracted to the monastery of Scala, but when Julia told her that it was God's Will for them to enter there she at once put aside her objections and felt at peace on the matter. It was thus that the Sisters made their final preparations and set off for this monastery to which the Voice of God so clearly called them.

PART II

SCALA

CHAPTER I
THE CRADLE OF THE ORDER

 HE traveler landing at the town of Amalfi from the Gulf of Salerno is immediately struck with the beauty of the surrounding country. Amalfi nestles among verdant hills covered with cedars and orange trees. The blue sea lies below, reflecting a sapphire sky; on either side rise high and wooded mountains. To the east, and forming a background, rises the pointed cliff on which stands Scala, opposite to its twin town, Ravello. Scala and Ravello seen from afar resemble eagles' nests, so near to the sky, but a closer view, showing their serene and smiling aspect, would remind us rather of the home of doves.

Scala and Ravello were formerly important towns and bishoprics, but at the present day they form part of the archdiocese of Amalfi, and it was at Scala that God had chosen to place the cradle of a religious order whose special aim would be to imitate the hidden life of the Savior of men. His providence was already preparing the way.

In 1719 Father Maurice Filangieri and Father Thomas Falcoia, the first Superior-General, the second a well- known member of the Congregation of "Pii Operarii," were preaching a mission in Scala. Anxious to secure for the inhabitants all possible help and grace, they resolved with the approbation of the Bishop of Scala to found a monastery of Visitandines in that beautiful and solitary spot, where the majesty of the mountains and the vast expanse of sea seemed favorable to contemplation. The following year Father Filangieri was able to acquire a house and chapel which had originally been destined for an association of pious widows and young girls who did not wish to take religious vows. This work died out after a few years, and Father Filangieri was thus able to buy the house, which he determined to transform and raise to the dignity of an enclosed monastery under the Rule of St. Augustine and the Constitutions of St. Francis de Sales.

The next difficulty was to find suitable vocations, and the two missionaries sought earnestly for souls pleasing to God. Their choice fell on Mathilda and Theresa de Vito, young girls of good family and distinguished by their virtue, who afterwards became Sister Mary Raphael and Sister Mary Angela; these were joined by Angelique and Grazia Bellini, daughters of a celebrated lawyer of Naples. They took the names of Mary Seraphine and Mary Michael respectively. Also at Naples they found Catherine Schisano, who was already over fifty years of age. Several years of her youth had been spent in the Carmelite Convent of Massalubrense. On account of her age and practical experience of religious life Catherine Schisano was appointed Superior of the future Community under the name of Mary Joseph of the Cross.

Soon these first Sisters were joined by Helen and Frances Montes, daughters of a Spanish nobleman formerly Governor of the town of Majori. They took the names of Mary Archangel and Mary Emmanuel. Then Justine and Anne de Natale entered, and became Mary Catherine and Mary Cherubina. Finally Ursula and Angela Galdo, in religion Mary Gabriel and Mary Theresa. These were the first fervent souls with which the foundation began. The inauguration of the Monastery took place on the Tuesday after Pentecost, May 21st, 1720. The ceremony was most impressive, and was attended by all the clergy and the Cathedral Canons. The Bishop presided at the solemn clothing of the postulants, and Father Falcoia preached, taking as his text "*Accipe jucunditatem glories vestra*," from the Introit of the day. At the conclusion of the ceremony the Sisters were led in procession to the Convent Chapel, the Bishop carried the Blessed Sacrament, and placed the Sacred Host in the Tabernacle. The enclosure door then closed behind the new

Sisters, who began their monastic life with joy and thanksgiving.

The Monastery was very poor, containing only six rooms. The choir was low and narrow, so low that it was difficult for the Sisters to avoid knocking their heads against the ceiling. Yet these difficulties did not quench their ardor, and, thanks to their dowries and to the generous charity of Father Filangieri, they were able to enlarge the house and to begin the construction of an enclosure wall. Father Filangieri had confided the spiritual direction of the Nuns to Father Falcoia. Under his guidance the Sisters made rapid progress in the way of perfection, and eighteen months after their clothing, on December 22nd, 1721, made the three religious vows according to the Rule of St. Francis de Sales. The holy reputation of the Convent soon attracted good vocations, and their numbers grew rapidly. Yet one thing was wanting to them. They had begged in vain for a Nun from the Visitation of Naples to come and form them to religious life. Their request was not granted, and they could only obtain a copy of the Rules and Constitutions. Thus they felt that they were not truly Visitandines, having neither papal enclosure nor solemn vows, and it grieved them to think that they were only half religious. This state of things was providential, for it left them canonical liberty to establish a new Order. But the Sisters were ignorant of God's designs for them. The Divine Master did not wish the Convent of Scala to become a Visitation Convent. He wished to found there the first Monastery of the new Order with which He was to enrich His Church. Already at Naples He was preparing the apostle who was to accomplish this work. Father Filangieri and Father Falcoia had tried to found a Visitation Convent, but God intended St. Alphonsus to found there the first Monastery of the Order of Redemptoristines.

CHAPTER II
PREPARATION OF THE WORK

T the beginning of the year 1724 Maria Celeste and her sisters entered the Convent of Scala. Their friends and relations accompanied them on the journey, and Father Falcoia made all arrangements for the travelers. Nevertheless the journey was not without accident. No doubt the enemy of all good wished to place obstacles in the way of the Divine plans. First the coachman became drunk, and the horses, finding themselves uncontrolled, rushed off, nearly dragging the carriages over a precipice. One of the carriages overturned, throwing Jane and her brother Francis to the ground. The wheels actually passed over their legs, but, "thanks to the protection of the holy Virgin," says Maria Celeste, they received no injury, and all arrived safely at the monastery. There the postulants received a warm welcome from the Nuns. Far from asking for a dispensation in consideration of the eight years spent in the Carmel of Marigliano, Julia and Ursula begged to recommence their novitiate. The three sisters received the habit of the Visitation on February 9th, 1724. Jane took the name of Mary Evangelista of Jesus, Ursula kept the name of Mary Illuminata of the Holy Cenacle, and Julia that of Mary Celeste of the Holy Desert. The Convent of Scala was small and inconvenient. The room which served as the Novitiate was also used as a dormitory, in which were seven beds. Mary Illuminata suffered much from this state of things, but Mary Celeste noticed nothing and thought herself in Paradise after the trial of having been outside the cloister walls. Such fervor reigned in the

Noviceship that several of the Professed Sisters obtained permission to follow the Novitiate exercises, so that altogether there were twelve novices vying with each other in the race along the path of perfection and in the practice of all religious virtues. Silence was so well kept that nothing could be heard but the singing of the birds. All were fervent in the Practice of mortification and penance, and many were the nights spent in prayer.

The Novice Mistress, Mother Mary Angela, was only twenty-two years old. In fact, all the professed Sisters with the exception of the Mother Superior were still young. In spite of her youth, Mother Mary Angela was a truly spiritual Nun, endowed with eminent virtues and rare prudence. She could not, however, know what great designs God intended to accomplish through one of her novices; in short. Our Lord in His mercy destined to form a new Order in the Church which should have no other aim than to reproduce as perfectly as possible the example and virtues of His own life, and to continue His work of redemption. This Order was to comprise, first, Nuns imitating His hidden life and sacrificing themselves in the silence of the cloister for the salvation of souls; secondly, apostles who would, after His example, preach the Gospel to the poor.

And it is in the little town of Scala that Jesus wished to place the cradle of this Order. For this reason He, in His Divine providence, had brought Mary Celeste there. From the very first days the Divine Master prepared her for her great mission. "During the Novitiate," she says in her autobiography, "Our Lord loaded me with His graces and mercies. The most precious moment of all for me was that of Holy Communion, which I received daily by order of my spiritual Father. Amongst many supernatural gifts that I received, the greatest was the transformation of my being into that of Jesus. By a divine light He impressed on my soul the admirable virtues of His most holy life when He was the Man-God upon earth. These communications absorbed me the whole day, and caused me such great joy that my soul was entranced." "About this time, by order of my spiritual Father and of the Novice Mistress, I wrote a book in the form of soliloquies, and also by obedience I wrote 'A Mystical Ladder of the Degrees of Prayer.'

"One morning after Holy Communion I heard in the very center of my soul these words of the Credo: '*Consubstantialem Patri, per quem omnia facta sunt.*' I was, as it were, embalmed and penetrated with the perfume of it, and my heart overflowed with joy in God. In this Essence were all the virtues of the Word of God made Man, by the power of which He communicates life to all men. I understood that these Divine Virtues were to be the rule of all my actions. Another time Our Lord said to me: 'Prepare thyself, for this Lent I will give thee a grace.' And consequently I was overtaken by an extraordinary and continual state of recollection, and that during the whole of Lent. I was so absorbed that the Nuns around me seemed to me but as shadows. I worked at exterior occupations with the help of a Sister, My spirit seemed to be elsewhere, and my recollection was so profound that the powers of my soul, far from all created things, found themselves absorbed in the Word of God my Beloved. But the greatest grace of all was received one day after Holy Communion, when it was shown to me how from the Divine Word gushed forth an immense fountain, which flowed into my heart. Our Lord Jesus Christ, in His infinite love, gave me His Divine Heart, which He enclosed in my breast in place of my own. The sweetness I experienced was such that I began to shed abundant tears in an ecstasy of love. Jesus made me inviolable promises, assuring me that He would unite me to Himself eternally in Faith, Hope and Charity, and it seemed to me that the Holy Spirit operated the union of my will with the Will of my Divine Spouse, Jesus the Man God. From this moment I appeared to enter into a new life of love, a life in God. He covered me with His Divine Beauty, all my deformities, so that I was unconscious of my poverty and misery." Thus Our Lord prepared the heart of His Servant for the work He had in store for her.

CHAPTER III

SISTER MARY CELESTE'S MISSION

 E have now reached a stage in the history of Mary Celeste which is inseparable from that of the foundation of the Redemptoristines and Redemptorists. In order to understand this important period of her life it is necessary to cast a glance at the part assigned to her by God in these events. What, therefore, is the part played by Sister Mary Celeste in the foundation of the Order of the Most Holy Redeemer? Her providential mission is a double one: on the one hand public, on the other hidden.

The Servant of God is first of all the confidante and messenger made use of by Jesus to establish in His Church this new Order. To her is revealed the Divine Will concerning the foundation, to her Jesus dictates the Rule which, with the Church's approbation, will be definitely adopted in its substance by St. Alphonsus for his sons and daughters. What Our Lord told her in secret she will repeat faithfully, however great the cost, by order of the Divine Master Himself. Thanks to her heroic courage the foundation of the first monastery of the Most Holy Redeemer will be laid, from which will spring all the others.

On leaving Scala she will don again the habit of her Order as soon as she is able; as for the Rule, she never for a moment ceased to observe it.

In the Convent at Foggia which she is afterwards to found under the name of the Most Holy Savior (this name was later changed to that of the Most Holy Redeemer, in order not to confound it with the Order of Canonesses of the Most Holy

Savior) she will continue until her death to Practice and to teach the Rule she had received from Jesus. As regards the Congregation of Missionaries founded by St. Alphonsus, it is through Mary Celeste that the saint first knew the Will of God concerning the work itself, and concerning God's designs for him personally.

We cannot sufficiently insist on the fact that the Rule left by St. Alphonsus to his sons is that which was revealed to Mary Celeste, with the additions, explanations, and adaptations which St. Alphonsus considered necessary for its working, and in no way incompatible with the supernatural origin of this same Rule. Let us add that Sister Mary Celeste's revelations regarding the double Order have proved themselves to be true by their complete realization in the course of years.

So much for the Sister's public mission. Her hidden life was still more beautiful, and from a human point of view harder to fulfil.

The thought in the mind of Our Lord in creating the new Order, as He told His Servant, was to form generous souls who would imitate Him, whose constant preoccupation would be to reproduce His Virtues, that is, to imitate His human life and to suffer in union with Him. For Jesus redeemed us on the Cross, and on the Cross the sufferings of His most Sacred Heart were the greatest. Like St. Alphonsus, Mary Celeste was therefore to conform herself to this ideal. It would not suffice for her to be holy, and thus to imitate the virtues of her Lord; she was also to be misunderstood, shamed, reviled, persecuted. Thus she would reproduce in all things the example of Jesus Christ. The Divine Redeemer knew beforehand the bitterness of His chalice. To Mary Celeste the divine Spouse showed the Calvary she would have to climb, showed her the persecutions and humiliations which awaited her, and above all the abandonment she would have to endure in imitation of His abandonment of the Cross. She on her part offered as a sacrifice to God her life and her honor. Jesus kept His word to her, while always protecting her He yet allowed her to be crucified and annihilated. She accepted this crucifixion, she endured her annihilation—if such should be the Will of God, even to the end of time—seeking only to love her Spouse and to resemble Him. For did not Christ say: "Except the grain of wheat fall to the ground and die, it cannot bear fruit." Her life was spent in hidden sacrifice for God alone, and how much fruit was it to bear? Who can say what part her sacrifice played in the foundation of the double Institute, which, without subtracting anything from St. Alphonsus, can indeed recognize her as its Mother, since without her it would not have existed? After two centuries it is indeed time that the veil which hides this heroic life be lifted. Yet for those who do not understand the hidden ways of God's Providence the life of Sister Mary Celeste will ever remain a mystery.

CHAPTER IV
THE REVELATION OF THE WORK

HE first revelation concerning the new Order to be founded by Our Lord was received by Sister Mary Celeste on Wednesday, April 25 th, 1725. Five years later St. Alphonsus asked her to write an account of this revelation; she obeyed, and it is this account, carefully kept by the Saint, which we now endeavor to translate as literally as possible:

"PRAISED BE JESUS CHRIST!"

"Reverend and Dear Father in Christ,

"In obedience to your request, I am writing a short account of what happened to me regarding the foundation of the new Order. The facts, as far as I can sincerely recall them, are these: A few years ago, on Rogation Day, after I had received Holy Communion, I was filled with an ardent love of Jesus. At the same time I felt drawn towards Him with my whole soul, and in the midst of an infinitely pure light He showed Himself to me in Divine beauty and splendor such as no human language could ever describe, uniting me to Himself through His Hands, His Feet, and His Side (the five wounds of Our Lord) with inexpressible joy and love. After this short vision I was again able to see myself, and in the midst of a bright light I saw that His finger was writing in my heart with His Blood. During this time, He made me understand the full value of His life and told me that He wished to found a new Order which would remind the world of all that He had done for man. At the same time, I received clearly and distinctly a full and entire knowledge of all that was to be contained in the Rule, and He ordered me to write everything down in His Name as He had revealed it to me.

"Another morning, after Holy Communion, He again showed Himself to me, full of majesty, covered with a garment similar to the habit to be worn by this Order. I could never forget this vision.

"The first day this happened to me, I became unconscious through joy and wonder. I recovered consciousness after a few hours, nevertheless I was so much impressed by what had happened that I had not the courage to speak of it for several days. I kept my anxiety to myself, not knowing what to think nor whether to tell all to my spiritual Father or not. I remained thus troubled and uncertain as to whether the communications came from God. Doubtless it seemed to me that God was truly the Author of it; yet, on the other hand, it appeared to me impossible that God could treat me thus, where there were in the world so many really holy souls to whom Our Lord could have communicated Himself. They would more readily have been believed on account of the goodness of their life; whilst in me there was not that virtue which would make me a worthy instrument for procuring the glory of God. Because of my way of living everyone would refuse to believe me, and above all my spiritual Father. Moreover, I was only a novice in this monastery, occupying the lowest place in the Community. I spent many days without revealing my secret to anyone. But one morning, after Holy Communion, my Spouse reproached me for my silence. He said to me: 'Why will you not speak?' You are afraid of being despised, know that your silence proceeds more from self-love than from love of Me.'

"At the same time He united my spirit to His own. He showed me in a flash all that I should have to endure, such as blame, desolation and persecution, and that I should be delivered over to the same abandonment as He had endured on the Cross. He showed me in particular the people through whom I should suffer; but He assured me that He would always protect me. At the sight of this vision, of so many tribulations, all of which my soul saw distinctly, my body became cold and inert, but my mind—strengthened and resigned—was ready to obey and to reveal my secret. I offered to God the sacrifice of my honor, my life, also of all esteem, and I resolved to speak openly to my spiritual Father and to my Superiors. In the meantime I could not sleep at night, because the communications of my Divine Spouse were uninterrupted. It was as though fifty Doctors of the Church had spoken to me at once. My soul listened, transported with admiration. What I have reported of these communications, either in the Rules or in the writings which are in the hands of my director, is still only the quarter of what I heard. I received great promises from my Spouse. I do not relate them here, for that would necessitate speaking of other favors granted to me.[1]

"He ordered me to write the Rule after Holy Communion, during which time He would dictate it to me. When that time was past I was unable to write a syllable, apart from that moment I could not continue writing."

Fortunately, we are able to complete this short account from Sister Mary Celeste's Autobiography. During the ecstasy with which the holy Sister was favored on Rogation Day she says: "My soul was absorbed in a divine spiritual purity which I had never yet experienced, it seemed to have left this present

---

[1] In a passage of her 'Dialogues," Mary Celeste reveals to us one of these promises, she speaks thus to Our Lord: "In Thine infallible Truth, Thou hast made me see all the contradictions, sufferings, persecution, doubts and anguish which I shall have to endure for the glory of Thy Name. As reward. Thou dost deign to promise me the glory of the Martyrs, and a place for eternity in the midst of them. Oh, how is it possible that a God of such majesty could choose so miserable a creature as the object of His love? Is it possible Lord, that Thou canst have made so bad a choice? Do not trust me, of myself I can only fail Thee, unless Thou dost protect me and bind me by chains of love."

life and already to rejoice in the eternal Beatitude. Our Lord told me that not only did He imprint His divine Seal on me, but also on many souls who, through me, should be saved and have eternal life in Him. Then He made me understand that in the new Order which He wished to found, all the Rules and Laws observed therein would be in imitation of Him. I saw written, as it were in an open book, the infinite perfections of the Divine Lamb, and all this remained imprinted in my soul and in my heart. I was carried out of myself and was so absorbed in God as to be unconscious of all that happened around me. The Rogation Procession was organized according to the custom of the Monastery, but I heard nothing of all this. Seeing that I did not move, the Sisters left me in peace, thinking, not without reason, that I was in a supernatural state, for they knew that I often suffered from the suspension of my faculties and from ecstasies. I remained thus until the hour of noon. As soon as this intimate communication with God was over, my soul was overwhelmed with fears and doubts. My spiritual Father was in Rome, and I feared to speak to my Superiors of the state of my soul, thinking that I might have been deceived by the devil. I therefore decided to take no notice of what had happened to me, lest it were but a device of Satan to trouble my peace. I felt also that I was only a novice in this Monastery, and the least worthy of all the Sisters to do anything for the glory of God. I remained thus for several days without mentioning my secret to anyone. Withdrawn into the deepest recesses of my soul, my recollection was so great that I seemed to be no longer of this world. But on returning to myself I was again troubled by all the devil suggested to me. At recreation I had lost all my usual gaiety, and was sad and silent. Seeing this, my eldest sister, who was a religious of great purity of life, questioned me as to the cause of my sorrow. She urged me so strongly that in the end I told her all. I told her how impossible it seemed to me that Our Lord should want to make use of me for so great a work, I who was the last in the monastery, and I thought that the idea must be a temptation of the enemy to take away my peace. On hearing this, my sister encouraged me, and advised me to tell the whole affair to the Mistress of Novices. She added that I ought not to try to forget about it, but to allow myself to be guided by holy obedience in the matter and to put all my trust in God. I saw that she was right and resolved to confide in my Superiors without delay. At the same time I was con soled interiorly. Our Lord showed me all I should have to endure in making known this secret, but He assured me also that the communications were from Him, that it was His Will and that He would protect me always.

"Accordingly the following day I sought out my Novice Mistress and told her all. I feared that she would be alarmed at the thought of such a work, but on the contrary she shed tears of joy and said: 'May the Lord be praised. Who has heard and answered our prayers and desires; for so many years we have been beseeching Him to perfect our monastery. Now the time has come when He is about to give us a solid basis for religious life.' She then gave me a long account of all the Sisters had suffered since the foundation, as they had never been really affiliated to the Visitation Order. Finally, she told me to write down all that had happened, so that it could be shown to the spiritual Father when he came back from Rome. Two days after this conversation with the Mistress of Novices I was about to go to Holy Communion, being still full of fear and trouble regarding what had happened to me; I humbled myself profoundly before God, beseeching His help and support. Raising my eyes to the Blessed Sacrament, all my fears vanished, and in the Sacred Host I saw Our Lord wearing the habit of the Order, of a dark colour and the shape of that the Religious were to wear. This vision lasted but a moment and was altogether spiritual.

"Though not seen by bodily eyes, it was of such wonderful brilliancy that no comparison could make it understood. The mantle appeared to me as a clear blue sky, and the tunic resembled crimson, so resplendent was it, it clearly showed me the colour and make indicated in the Rule. At the same time Our Lord assured me that the work was from Him and that it pleased Him that I should imitate His life. All this occurred while the priest was distributing Holy Communion to the Sisters. When I had received Our Lord, I was carried out of myself, as on the first day of these Divine communications, and this happened each day, lasting all the time while I was writing the Rules. In the morning, when I was thus transformed into His likeness, He made Himself visible, writing in my heart with His most precious Blood. He blessed me and ordered me to write the Rules of the Order in His Name, but always after Holy Communion. This I did for about an hour from what He had imprinted in my heart and in my memory. Then He explained to me the signification of the garments, also the actions and the spirit in which the Rules were written. He told me that in this Order there was to be neither Founder nor Foundress, but that He was the foundation stone. That the evangelical counsels were to be the cement, that my heart was to be the ground of this edifice, and that His Father was the Divine Worker. He ordered me to fast for forty days, that is to say, all the time I was writing the Rules. Also I was to pray, to observe silence, and to purify myself more and more, divesting myself completely of self, so as to mix up nothing of my own will in all this, but to remove all the obstacles, in order that His Divine Majesty alone might operate in me. He said I must be as a tiny child at the breast of its mother, who can do nothing of itself, but just follows the impulsion she gives it. Finally, He ordered me to write ail to my spiritual Father, this being His Divine Will."

Having thus revealed His designs to His faithful servant, Our Lord is now about to prove the authenticity of the mission He has confided to her.

CHAPTER V
SIGNS PROVING THE DIVINE ORIGIN OF THE WORK

OD in His Wisdom deigned to surround the revelations of the new Order with signs proving its Divine origin. Such a work, it is true, could not rest on the authority of Mary Celeste alone, though it is she who will have to bear the full weight of contradiction which all holy enterprises entail. Witnesses and signs are not wanting, however, to prove definitely that Mary Celeste was but the faithful messenger of God's designs. These testimonies and proofs have been brought forward by Sister Mary Raphael, who in the world was Mathilda de Vito.

Her name has already been mentioned among the first foundresses of the Convent of Scala. This Nun was most holy and fervent. Thirty-two years of dreadful illness, which made her days and nights one continual martyrdom, could draw no complaint from her lips other than the generous cry: "I give glory to God." Owing to her prudence and virtue she was elected Superior three times, in 1741, 1744, and 1757, and was chosen by St. Alphonsus as the first Superior of the Redemptoristine Monastery founded by him in the town of St. Agatha of the Goths in 1766. She has left us an account of the revelation made to Sister Mary Celeste, and of all the accompanying circumstances. This account was written under obedience, and she declared herself ready to confirm it on oath.

Sister Mary Raphael also tells us that, while she still ignored the revelation made to Mary Celeste, she herself about this time felt an extraordinary desire for the spiritual good of her sisters, and one day after Holy Communion the Divine Master told her to have confidence, for He would make these souls like unto

Himself. "Since that day," she adds, "I seemed to see them all transformed into Jesus Christ, whilst Our Lord granted me a great love towards my neighbor."

The Mistress of Novices, Mother Mary Angela, of whom we have already spoken, was a sister of Theresa de Vito. Sister Mary Raphael does not hesitate to speak of her as an exemplary religious whose soul was adorned with great virtues, and who for long years served God with fidelity and love. It was true, for St. Alphonsus held this Sister in great esteem. Sister Mary Angela informed her sister that when, as Mistress of Novices, she received the confidence of Mary Celeste regarding the revelations, she experienced great joy of soul, while an interior force seemed to oblige her to believe in the divinity of the revelation.

Sister Mary Raphael provides us also with the testimony of two other Sisters—Sister Mary Seraphine and Sister Mary Michael. The first of these two Sisters, while still in the world, had been told by a holy woman that she would one day join a new Order shortly to-be founded, and which would do much good for God. When the young girl entered what she thought to be the Visitation Order she forgot all about this prediction until the day when the change of Rule and habit was actually affected. Her sister, Sister Mary Michael, had not been very happy in the Convent. "For," says Sister Mary Raphael, "not having been formed by a Nun of our Order, we were ignorant in many ways, and faults crept into our observance of Community life." One day, as Sister Mary Michael was grieving over thus, she heard a voice within her soul telling her to rejoice, for the Monastery would be transformed by the adoption of the new Rules.

Finally a lay Sister, Sister Baptistine, several months before the revelation of the new Order, learnt from Our Lord that He intended to make use of Sister Mary Celeste to accomplish great things in this Community. Later on, seeing Mary Celeste writing every morning, she asked what she was doing. As the latter refused to reply, Sister Baptistine exclaimed: "I will tell you what you have to do; it is to transform our Rules!" The next morning this lay Sister, after Holy Communion, suddenly saw Mary Celeste dressed in a red habit and blue mantle, with the picture of our Savior on her breast. At the same time Our Lord told her that all the Sisters would one day be dressed thus, and that the new Order would give glory to Him. Sister Mary Raphael, after having told us that several other Sisters—for example, Sister Mary Felix and Sister Mary Antoinette, had also received lights more or less precise regarding the new Order, furnishes us with another and very different proof as to the divine origin of the revelations. These are the persecutions inflicted by demons on the Monastery, as soon as the new Rule became known, in order to prevent the Nuns from accepting it. Dreadful apparitions, terrifying noises and cries, are mentioned. We know also, though Mary Celeste, that certain Sisters were struck by invisible hands, and that threatening voices were heard at the time when the Council of Theologians had met together at Naples to examine the new Rules.

But according to Sister Mary Raphael the most convincing proof that the work came from God was the marvelous renewal of fervor which showed itself in the Community when the Rule became known. "From that hour," she says, "our souls sought after closer union with Jesus Christ and gave themselves up to the Practice of solid virtue. I myself, on the day I first heard it, experienced such joy as I had never felt before, and this is true of all the Sisters who heard the Rule before it was read to the general Community."

Finally, an outstanding miracle placed the seal of God on the work. For some years one of the Nuns, Sister Mary Madeline, had lost her reason. Her uncle, Vicar-General of Scala, wished to withdraw her from the Monastery, where she gave great trouble. However, through the charity of Sister Mary Raphael, she was allowed to remain, for the latter offered to watch over her day and night. It was in answer to her prayer that the miracle was granted.

"Oh, God," prayed the holy Sister, "if this Rule comes from Thee, cure our sick sister." The manuscript of the Rule was then placed on the head of the poor mad Nun, and she was instantly cured.

CHAPTER VI
HOW THE WORK WAS RECEIVED

E have seen how Mary Celeste's revelation was received by the Novice Mistress, Mother Mary Angela, and how the latter told the Sister to write an account of all that had happened. The same advice was given to her by her confessor. She was also told to write down the Rules under the conditions required of her by Our Lord. "During the time of writing," says Sister Mary Celeste in her Autobiography, "I experienced a very special assistance from Our Lord, joined to an extraordinary recollection. Sometimes my soul, in possession of its powers, was able to reflect on what it had to write. At other times it seemed as if someone were dictating to me. I was helped as much as if several Doctors were explaining to me what I had to say, and again at other times I did not even perceive what I was writing.

"But once the hour of thanksgiving was over I could not write one word, and I was obliged to leave off till the next day after Holy Communion. All this time I was faithful to the fast which God had imposed on me, taking only some bread and a little fruit, and also performing corporal penances. In spite of all this, I had never been so well since my childhood, for I was naturally of a sickly and weak constitution. Yet I now seemed perfectly strong and able to do all my work."

The seven Nuns who had received lights from God as to His designs regarding the new Order fasted and prayed in union with Sister Mary Celeste during these forty days. This period was marked by a wonderful occurrence. Every evening celestial music made itself heard. It was audible to the whole

Community, without anyone knowing from whence it came, and it brought great spiritual joy, particularly to those Sisters who were acquainted with the revelations about the new Order. They spent the nights in continual prayer, absorbed in the love of God, nor was their health in any way affected by these prolonged vigils.

In the meantime the spiritual Father had returned from Rome. The Novice Mistress sent to him the full account of the revelations written by Sister Mary Celeste, but not the Rules, which were as yet incomplete. From this time onwards begins the long series of obstacles which seemed to rise like barriers in front of the work of Providence. Father Falcoia wrote to Mary Celeste, condemning her revelations as the product of imagination and pride, and ordering her to throw the Rule into the fire.

The gentle Sister replied by a letter full of humility and obedience, but asked permission on the advice of both her confessor and Novice Mistress to wait before burning the Rules until after Father Falcoia's expected visit to Scala. This reply only annoyed the spiritual Father still more, and to punish Sister Mary Celeste for not having burnt the Rule immediately he forbade her to communicate until the Feast of the Assumption. It so happened, however, that this letter, written on June 30th, only reached Scala on August 17th. This was a visible intervention of Providence, for it was the first time that the Monastery correspondence had gone astray. Mother Mary Angela, receiving no reply from Falcoia, took advantage of the moment to send him a copy of the now completed Rules, when a third letter arrived from Falcoia retracting the order to burn the Rule, as he had suffered much inwardly on this account, and stating that he would examine the matter fully in August, when he intended to visit the Convent. In the meantime he ordered complete silence on the subject.

This letter was received before the preceding letter, as we have explained, and caused great surprise both to Mother Mary

Angela and Sister Mary Celeste, as they could not understand it until the delayed letter arrived explaining matters. At last Father Falcoia came himself. He had examined the Rule and gave his opinion in the following terms: "The thing may come from God, but the fact that according to Mary Celeste's vision the new Order is to be founded at Scala makes me fear that it is but an ambush of the enemy to trouble the peace of this fervent monastery established under the Rule of St. Francis de Sales." Thus he neither condemned nor approved, and for three months he refused to believe in the divine origin of the revelation. This was only natural, for it meant undoing his own work in order to substitute something entirely different.

Yet if it should prove to be God's Will, the upright soul of the old priest would not oppose it. Finally, he decided to submit the Rule written by Mary Celeste to a council of eminent theologians at Naples. This famous council put the powers of darkness to flight. Before the unanimous approval of the theologians Falcoia submitted. The Convent at Scala not being affiliated to any other Order, it would be permissible to introduce a new Rule if the professed Sisters consented to accept it. He therefore returned to the Monastery, bringing with him his Superior-General, Filangieri (who was also in favor of the new Rule), with the intention of proposing the change to the Community subject to the Bishop's approval. It therefore seemed that the Order desired by God was about to be inaugurated without delay. But Divine works are not established so easily. "The mills of God grind slowly" and contradictions are inevitable. The obstacles in this case were to come both from Mary Celeste's own Superior and from Father Filangieri, the Superior of Father Falcoia.

CHAPTER VII
THE FIRST STORM

HE Superior of Scala, Mother Mary Joseph of the Cross, was a simple soul, full of good intentions, but with no aptitude for spiritual direction. For this reason Father Falcoia, from the beginning, had advised the Nuns to speak only to him of what passed in their souls, and in the case of Sister Mary Celeste he had commanded her to keep a strict silence regarding her revelations, until such time as they should be proved to have come from God. Thinking that this time had come, after the favorable decision of the Council of Theologians, Father Falcoia himself proposed the change of Rule to the Nuns of Scala assembled in Chapter. His discourse was so fervent and inspiring that all the Sisters began to praise and thank God, and expressed their willingness to embrace the new Rule of divine origin. Only the Superioress showed signs of disapproval. She was not unnaturally hurt at having been kept in the dark so long concerning what had been revealed to one of her subjects, and could not see that Sister Mary Celeste had only been acting under obedience, which wisely prescribes the greatest prudence in speaking of such matters. Full of her grievance, Mother Mary Joseph sought out Father Filangieri and succeeded in completely changing his mind regarding the revelations which hitherto he had been prepared to accept. She implored him to use his authority as Father Falcoia's Superior to induce the latter to give up all idea of change. Father Filangieri, now completely won over to the Superior's way of thinking, reproached his subordinate. Father Falcoia, with having been

too credulous regarding the whole affair. The spiritual Father submitted his judgment to that of his Superior and ordered the Sisters to think no more about a change of Rule. He also considered it his duty to reprimand Mary Celeste in public, assuring her that her revelations were illusions, and that she ought to have great remorse for having troubled the peace of the Community, and to humble herself before God, asking for light to walk henceforth in truth. The Sister listened without making any reply, then retired to a room near the sacristy, where she wept silently. After a time Our Lord deigned to console her and to disperse the cloud of doubt and unrest which surrounded her, saying: "My spouse, it is I, it is not the devil. All that shall be done to you with regard to this work I shall consider as done to Myself. Trust in Me, and be assured that you shall see this Order established." After these events Filangieri returned to Naples; but he still feared that the new Rule might be established in spite of all. Therefore in order to prevent this he forbade Father Falcoia to return to Scala, and ordered him to cease all communication with the Monastery. The submission of the venerable religious in these circumstances was truly admirable. With entire resignation he wrote the following edifying letter to the Monastery:

"I now see how much God loves you, for He is providentially removing from you the obstacle to your perfection. His Hand will know how to re-establish that good order among you which has been disturbed not by your fault, but by my clumsiness. Rest assured that the Father-General has treated me as I deserve in accusing me of incapacity and illusion. Be at peace, therefore, regarding the prohibition made to me of mixing myself up in the affairs of your Convent. Always live under obedience and pray for me to the Divine Majesty. As far as I am concerned I shall never cease to pray for my dear daughters, whom I bless for the last time from the depths of my heart."

Yet this did not satisfy Filangieri. Full of mistaken zeal, he resorted to still stronger measures. He called together the Vicar of Scala and several theologians from the Congregation of "Pii Operarii" and induced them to declare solemnly that the devil was the author of the recent events in the Monastery, and that Mary Celeste was deluded and Falcoia unbalanced. "Fortunately," says Mary Celeste with her usual charity, "Father Falcoia was well known and respected in Naples, where he was looked upon as a saint and a scholar, so that his reputation in no way suffered from these reports. ..."

After this meeting of theologians, the Vicar was sent to Scala to visit the Monastery and acquaint the Nuns of Father Filangieri's decision. He was to endeavor to obtain from them the promise to withdraw themselves from Father Falcoia's direction, and to expulse Mary Celeste. If they accepted these conditions Filangieri was prepared to give annually a certain sum of money for the upkeep of the Convent; if they refused he would take no further interest in the Monastery. Accordingly the Vicar called the Nuns together in Chapter and read to them a long letter in which were laid down the Father-General's conditions. He then questioned each Nun separately. All without exception refused to expulse Sister Mary Celeste, saying that they had no reason for doing so, and that their conscience would reproach them should they agree to such a measure. They also refused to be deprived of their spiritual Father, who had done so much for their souls. They said, as for the Father Superior, he might keep his money, for God would take care of the Monastery if they remained faithful to Him.

Before such a unanimous reply the Vicar had nothing more to say. The Superioress was present, but, although opposed to the views of the Community, she had not the courage to protest, except to say that Father Filangieri had done as much for the Monastery as Father Falcoia, and that the Nuns would lose much by their decision. She spoke very timidly and her words were not seconded.

This question being settled, the Vicar, acting on Father

CHAPTER VII: THE FIRST STORM

Filangieri's instructions, called Mary Celeste before the assembled Chapter and reprimanded her severely. He accused her of being the cause of all this disturbance in the Monastery and ordered her as a penance to retire to an attic where she would live apart from the Community, being unworthy to remain in the society of her Sisters. She was forbidden to assist at any of the Community exercises, except in the refectory, where she was to go every day with a rope round her neck and ask pardon for the scandal she had given. Sister Mary Celeste heard this sentence kneeling, and accepted the penance with deep humility of heart.

The Vicar then returned to Naples to give an account of his mission. Father Filangieri had not expected such an attitude on the part of the Nuns. He was much annoyed and for a time took no further interest in the Monastery, though he continued to correspond privately with Mother Mary Joseph.

CHAPTER VIII

JOYS AND SORROWS

AKING with her nothing but an old blanket and a crucifix Mary Celeste went up to her attic. It was a loft under the new wing of the building, high and solitary, the window of which looked out on to the vineyard of the monastery. Here, far from all noise, the silence broken only by the singing of birds, she was happy in her solitude and gave herself up to prayer. Her humility was too sincere, however, to admit of her rejoicing in this peace. On the contrary, her soul was troubled to find herself so calm in such circumstances. No doubt the devil took advantage of this occasion to suggest despairing thoughts to her. It seemed to her that God had abandoned her, that her whole life had been an illusion, and that she was the cause of all the troubles and disturbance in the Monastery. Thus she wept in affliction of spirit. Then in the midst of her sorrow her Divine Spouse spoke consoling words to her in the depths of her soul. "Be reassured," He said, "do not fear, it is I. Have I not told you that the devil would try to harm you, but that he could not touch one hair of your head without My permission? I have warned you of all beforehand. Confer as much as you can about your soul with your spiritual guide, abandon yourself in all humility, without any fear of what men and the devil may do."

At these Divine assurances her soul recovered its strength, and she was comforted. Nevertheless the devil again tried to trouble her, and two or three times a day her soul alternated between these alarms and divine peace and security. One morning before Holy Communion her mind was greatly distressed, and she approached the Holy Table weeping, but after Holy Communion Our Lord consoled her, saying with great sweetness: "You are My beloved and My friend; it is for this reason that I place you in the kingdom of My Cross; know that everything must be destroyed in you, so that the work of My Institute may be established."

"Such assurances," she says in her Autobiography, "gave me great peace of soul in spite of fear and suffering. Yet I still feared to be in delusion when I saw so many good and holy people suspect me and think me a visionary. Sometimes I experienced an ardent desire of suffering contempt, and this with such interior joy that my soul wished for every sort of injury both from men and from the enemy. I had also transports of love and besought Our Lord that His glory might be manifested and not hindered by my faults and sins. The recollection of my soul was so profound that Our Lord used to place me before Him and show me His work as if it were already accomplished, which gave me great peace and confidence that it would be carried out."

She remained thus in her attic, a prey to alternate sorrow and consolation, for a fortnight. Then the Novice Mistress obtained from the Vicar the authorization for her to return to her cell and to Community life. It was at this time that Our Lord made known to Mary Celeste what was passing in the mind of the Superioress, Mother Mary Joseph. With the greatest reluctance the poor Sister forced herself to speak of this. The following letter to her spiritual Father shows how much she shrank from such supernatural favors and commands:

"Reverend Father in God,

"I find myself in great perplexity and am much disturbed interiorly concerning the lights which God has given me. It seems to me that it would be better for my peace of mind to pay no attention to them, but to lean only on God, thus I should avoid the fear of being under delusion and of having deceived you in the past. Forgetting everything, I should live with more security in my painful solitude, and in this dear cross I should be wholly abandoned to God. It is impossible for me, however, to act thus, as your paternity has ordered me formally to tell you everything which passes in my soul, and this command is at present my greatest cross. One morning after Holy Communion Our Lord bade me to go to our Mother Superior, who was tempted with wrong thoughts against me. He told me all that the devil was suggesting to her about me, and wished me to make it known to her with great humility and charity. Accordingly, my time of prayer being ended, I left the Choir and went at once to find our Mother. I told her simply all that the Lord had revealed to me. What more especially displeased her was that she thought that I had advised the religious, who were her subjects, not to obey her. She opened her heart to me in all confidence and told me all she had against me. She said that what I had just told her was quite true, the devil had suggested to her that I was trying to attract the Nuns away from her with the object of becoming myself Superioress of this monastery. She also complained that I had hidden from her the graces that Our Lord had vouchsafed to me concerning the new Institute, whereas she, as Superioress, should have been the first to know of it. I was able to calm her fears, assuring her that I had never given any advice to the Sisters contrary to the esteem and veneration due to their Superioress, that I loved her very much in the Heart of Jesus and would always be her obedient subject. I added also that she need never fear my becoming Superioress of that Monastery, even if the Rule were established, as it was not the Will of God that I should be the foundress of His Work, in which I had no other part than the desire for the glory of God and for His Divine pleasure. When I had finished speaking the Superioress appeared satisfied and said that as soon as the new Rule was established she would make no objections. She then embraced me with great cordiality and tenderness. She assured me that her mind was now quite at ease, and when I left her she seemed perfectly happy. This serenity did not last. The devil once more disturbed her soul, and though more kindly disposed towards me, her expression was still severe. I beg of you therefore, Father, to pray to God for her and for me, and I beg you to bless me in the Heart of Jesus."

This letter shows us how simply and directly Sister Mary Celeste acted on the lights she received from Our Lord, however painful the duty imposed on her. Mother Mary Joseph was not to remain long at the head of the Monastery, however. At the expiration of her three years of government she was never again re-elected, although God granted her a very long life. She lived a retired and holy life and died in 1750, at the age of eighty-five.

On June 5th, 1726, Mother Mary Angela was unanimously elected Superior. The Community had lost nothing of their first fervor, and now enjoyed great peace. But Father Filangieri had been misinformed on this point. From his correspondence with Mother Mary Joseph he thought the Sisters were in a state of unrest and sent Father Angelo Criscuoli, as extraordinary confessor, to the Convent to set things right. Great was this Father's surprise to find the peace and charity which reigned in the soul of each Nun. He was greatly edified and on his return to Naples informed the Superior-General of the happy state of affairs. Father Angelo had hoped to remain in charge of the Monastery as spiritual director, for this had been the intention of his Superior in sending him to Naples. He therefore offered himself to the Nuns to take the place of their spiritual Father, saying that, as Father Falcoia could no longer be their director on account of the interdiction laid on him, it was not good for them to remain without direction. The Nuns answered that they thanked him very much for his kindness, but that they thought it better to await the moment when it would please God to give them a new election, and that then their own director would continue his office.   Thus Father Filangieri's designs again came to nothing, and, moreover, he was no longer to continue his violent opposition to the Convent. It was revealed to Mary Celeste that he would die of a serious illness before the work of God was established. Three months later he was stricken with apoplexy, he became paralyzed and could scarcely speak. Towards the end he himself said to his confessor: "The Nuns will establish the new Rule, but I shall not live to see it." Shortly afterwards he died, but before the end he evidently relented in his mind towards the Monastery, for he left them an annual income of 123 ducats.

Father Falcoia, on the other hand, had also been seriously ill, but had recovered his health. About this Father it was revealed to Sister Mary Celeste that not only would he recover from his present illness, but that after seeing the new Order established he would live for another ten years. This prediction, like the preceding one, was fulfilled to the letter.

CHAPTER IX

DIVINE DIRECTION

S Falcoia was forbidden to continue his direction of the Monastery, Mary Celeste was at this time without a guide and could only communicate very rarely with her spiritual Father by means of letters conveyed to him by the ordinary confessor. Our Lord, therefore, constituted Himself her director. One morning after Holy Communion she was a prey to great interior struggles, when Our Lord deigned to speak clearly to her in the depths of her soul. The following is the account left to us in her Autobiography of this Divine direction. Our Lord began by encouraging her, saying: "My child, do you not know that with but little human aid I shall establish My Institute, if you on your part will show fidelity? I wish you to tell everything to your spiritual Father. In all this consider only Me, and do not be anxious about yourself. Know that in contradicting your ideas about many things your director is obeying My orders, and that he is in no way blameworthy. Do you not remember how I showed you this Institute, whose aim is to transform its members into My likeness? I have revealed to you the spirit of this Work and made you partaker of the treasures of My life, that is to say, of all My works and virtues. You know how much I was despised, persecuted and humbled by those dearest to Me, and at last expired on a Cross. I passed My whole life in humiliation, hiddenness and scorn. It was thus that I glorified My Father, laid the foundations of My Church and remedied the evils of pride in men. My life was a treasure hidden in contempt and humility. That is to be the spirit of your Institute. This is why I wished that these Rules should be first of all planted in your heart by doubts, scorn and difficulties for several years, before establishing My work, so that it might have solid foundations of humility, poverty and self-contempt. You think that I do not love you," continued the voice of Our Lord, "that I do not listen when you ask for help in your needs, but it is not so. I know what is good for you, but you are wanting in conformity to My Will, committing several imperfections, not voluntarily, but in your judgment. This is a great detriment to the love you owe Me. My daughter, you think yourself to be entirely detached fr6m creatures, but you are mistaken. You do not see the depths of your heart nor all that agitates it. The highest and most spiritual part of your soul is dominated from time to time by inferior desires, such as anxiety to see creatures return your affection. You allow entrance to this feeling, not by a deliberate act of the will, but by weakness. This spoils the firmness of your soul and troubles it, for this desire does not tend solely towards Me, and can only defile your heart. I warn you of it in order that you may fight against it and not give way to it, either in regard to your director or to any other person. Be upright and follow only the impulse of equal charity towards all. Obey your director in everything, give him a sincere account of all that takes place in your soul, and desire nothing either from him or from anybody. Do not Seek either satisfaction or affection in anyone at all, act as if I alone existed for you. Do not wish for the esteem or affection of any creature whatsoever, for all that would be desiring to live in their heart and to feel them living is yours. This would be to lower your soul to childish play, and to raise obstacles to your liberty and purity. Love Me above all things. Contemplate Me as present even in the smallest action. Do all solely to please Me and to give glory to Me without occupying yourself with Creatures. Thus the devil will be unable to harm you. He knows that you are weak on this point. He always attacks on Nature's weakest side, and if he cannot conquer, at least he can trouble the soul's peace. My spouse, if you knew how jealous I am of your heart, you would proceed with the utmost diligence, running in the odor of My sweetness. Do not be guided by feelings. It is necessary for you sometimes to feel their weakness if you wish to gain the crown. You are still an exile from your heavenly country; that is why patient love is so necessary to you. Do not count on human judgments, for I love you with a perfect love and I dispose all things for your good. Know that I shower graces and blessings on all those who love you and help you. What is done to you I receive as done to Myself, for I rejoice to see My loved ones loved; see therefore how far My love for you extends. When My Holy Spirit breathes on a soul, It controls all its movements. That soul cannot fall into error unless it so desires; it produces good fruit and runs in the way of perfection. But the evil spirit simulates virtue while desiring only evil. He hides his malice when he can and clothes himself with the appearance of good. The effects he produces are darkness in the intellect and tepidity in the will, always accompanied by some error, so that the soul finds itself in fear, darkness and uncertainty. The contrary is the effect produced by the Holy Spirit."

Sister Mary Celeste understood these Divine teachings and many other things which it would be too long to include here. It was as if a most learned Master had instructed her to such good purpose that Faith seemed to disappear in sight, so clear did all these truths appear.

Another day Our Lord was urging her forward about His work, but, finding herself faced by a sea of difficulties, she hesitated to correspond to the Divine inspiration, not being willing to write what she heard. Then Our Lord sent to her an angel having in his hand an arrow, which he dipped in the Blood of the Divine Lamb, and with it he pierced her heart. This mysterious wound so strengthened her that she was transformed by it, and felt herself henceforth able to bear gladly all contradictions, contempt, and insults in the service of God.

St. Alphonsus di Liguori giving the rule to the Redemptoristines and Redemptorists.

THE MAN OF GOD—ST. ALPHONSUS

OUR years have gone by. In the Monastery the Nuns, faithful to obedience, have spoken no more of the new Rule, and Sister Mary Celeste, at the expiration of her Novitiate, confirmed the vows of profession which she had previously made at Marigliano. As for Father Falcoia, he was still under the prohibition to communicate with the Convent, yet he never ceased to pray for the spiritual daughters he had formed to religious life, and for whom he entertained a fatherly affection. He was far from thinking that the project which he believed to be buried in oblivion was now about to be realized, and that the man chosen by God to establish the new Order was close at hand.

Father Falcoia went often to the College of the Holy Family at Naples, whose founder and superior, Mathieu Ripa, was a friend of his. It was here he met a priest who was living there, although not a member of the association. The name of Alphonsus de Liguori was at that time on everybody's lips. The young nobleman, who had renounced his brilliant future, his family inheritance and his wonderful career at the Bar to consecrate himself to the service of God and the salvation of souls, was much admired. Father Falcoia looked at him with interest and quickly discerned in him one of those privileged souls whom the Divine Master loads with gifts of Nature and of grace because He intends them to accomplish great things.

On his part Alphonsus saw in the old man a saintly religious gifted with understanding above the average, a wise counselor whose long experience would be profitable to him. Thus mutually attracted towards one another in spite of the difference of age, the old priest and Alphonsus became friends. Shortly after this meeting Falcoia was nominated to the Bishopric of Castellamare, which lies close to Scala. Two years previously he had refused the Archbishopric of Lanciano, in the center of Italy. This time he thought to see the Hand of God in the fact of the new appointment being offered to him so soon after his last refusal, and, realizing that the acceptance of the bishopric would restore his freedom of action with regard to his spiritual daughters, he decided to overcome his natural repugnance and to don the miter.

At the same moment Alphonsus, worn out by unceasing work, had been obliged to seek change of air and rest in the country outside Naples. A providential circumstance led him to choose the hermitage of Ste. Marie-des-Monts, just above Scala, as his place of retirement. Certainly he could not have wished for better air or more complete solitude. Yet even here he found occasion to exercise his ministry. Though priests were not wanting at Naples and in the towns, there was no one to look after the souls of the dwellers on the hillside and country districts, and these poor peasants were left like sheep without a shepherd in total darkness and ignorance. Alphonsus at once set about remedying this, and soon found himself surrounded by goat-herds, shepherds and peasants from the mountains of Scala and the neighbouring districts, so that his "rest-cure" developed into an uninterrupted mission which produced great fruit for God. The inhabitants of Scala now desired to hear the celebrated preacher, and at the Bishop's request Alphonsus preached in the Cathedral. It was the Sunday after Corpus Christi. His sermon on the Holy Eucharist was so moving that the congregation burst into tears and sighs, which could be heard even by the Nuns in their monastery at Scala. The latter at once sent to invite Alphonsus to preach in their church. He consented, and thus the man of God entered for the first time the sanctuary where his future vocation was to be revealed to him by the lips of Mary Celeste.

CHAPTER X: THE MAN OF GOD—ST. ALPHONSUS

Bishop Guerriero, anxious to keep such an apostle in his diocese, begged him at least to return in September to preach the celebrated Novena of the Cross. Alphonsus promised to do this; he also undertook to preach the Nun's retreat at the same time.

Falcoia heard the news with the greatest joy at Rome, where he had gone to receive his episcopal consecration. To the Sisters of Scala, who, delighted at his promotion, had written to him "Make haste to return and do not leave your daughters any longer without spiritual help!" he replied that, finding it impossible to leave Rome before the month of November, he was sending them a man after his own heart, the missionary Alphonsus de Liguori, who would preach their retreat and fulfil the functions of extraordinary confessor. He begged them, therefore, to consider this priest as his second self and to have no secrets from him. Alphonsus was not ignorant of the accusations made by Filangieri and certain theologians regarding the revelations of Mary Celeste. More than once he had heard the supposed hallucinations of the Nuns of Scala condemned and laughed at by clerics and laymen; but he was more impressed by the doubts and fears of his own friend, Falcoia. When therefore, in September of the year 1730, he presented himself at the monastery, it was rather in the quality of judge than of preacher, persuaded as he was of the necessity of enlightening these deluded souls. He hid neither his impression nor his intention from the Superior and her assistants, who received him in the parlor. The worthy Superioress, Mother Mary Angela, replied humbly that she and her companions would conform to his wishes, and that all would gladly receive his counsels. She then replied clearly to the questions put to her and explained with simplicity and directness the events that had occurred during the last five years, also the artifices employed by the enemy of mankind to trouble the peace of the Community and retard the work of God. Before pronouncing any opinion on her statements

Alphonsus declared that he would study the matter fully; and in order to facilitate this he asked to see each member of the Community separately. Accordingly the next day the Nuns appeared before him one by one. Sister Mary Celeste, the chief cause of the discussion, was the first to be called. This was the first interview between the holy Doctor and the Venerable Sister Mary Celeste. She spoke to him with the utmost frankness, opening her heart entirely and relating the events of her whole life. Alphonsus quickly understood this soul and saw that God had great designs on her, but he persisted in pursuing his inquiry to the end. All the Sisters were heard in turn, including the former Superior and those who were opposed to the revelations. Finally the Sister who had been instantly cured by the application of the manuscript of the Rule was called, so that the Father might judge for himself of the reality of her cure.

After such an inquiry, made by a judge as holy as he was brilliant, the truth could not fail to come to light. From that moment Alphonsus had no further doubt as to the Divine origin of Mary Celeste's mission. Once satisfied on this point, he assembled the whole Community and made known to them the result of his inquiry, namely, the absolute certitude that the revelations in question came from God. He then exhorted the Nuns to thank Heaven for so many favors shown to them, and proved to them that their duty was to replace their present Rule by the one revealed to them by God, and that as soon as possible. Turning then to those opposed to the scheme, he made them understand the responsibility they incurred in retarding the plans of God. His words made a deep impression on the Community, and the former Superior declared that not only would she no longer oppose God's Will, but that she would be the first to embrace the new Rule.

Hearing these words, tears of joy rose to all eyes, the! Sisters embraced one another as a token of union, and gave thanks to God with hearts overflowing with happiness.

Nothing could be done, however, without the authorization of the Bishop of Scala, who alone had jurisdiction over the Convent. Without losing any time, Alphonsus presented himself at the Palace. The Bishop, Mgr. Guerriero, who held him in great esteem, made no difficulty and placed everything in his hands. "Organize the Community as you judge best for the glory of God and the sanctification of the Nuns," he said. Thus provided with frill authority from the Bishop, Alphonsus arranged with the Sisters the date when the new Rule should be inaugurated, and then commenced the retreat. He preached on the life and virtues of the Divine Redeemer. His eloquence roused the enthusiasm of the Community and redoubled their fervor. The Sisters now considered themselves his daughters in Jesus Christ, and Would never forget what they owed to him. They could not do enough to express their gratitude and were grieved over his departure. A story about this is handed down to us which, in its graceful simplicity, might be taken from the Fioretti. "When Don Alphonsus had finished the retreat and he and his companion, Jean Mazzini, another missionary, were obliged to leave the Convent, the Reverend Mother did not wish them to go without taking with them a cake to eat on their journey. The Sister cook was very busy at the moment and, having mixed the ingredients for the cake, she turned to Our Lady and said, 'Dear Mother, help me, please!' Thereupon she entered into an ecstasy, and on coming to herself found the cake nicely baked, although she had not even lit the fire. She sent it at once to Don Alphonsus with these words: 'Eat it; the Madonna has made it!' Alphonsus is said to have confessed afterwards that while eating this cake he had felt his heart inflamed with Divine love."

On his return to Naples, Alphonsus received an affectionate letter from Falcoia, in which the latter declared his joy at the good news from the monastery, for both the Nuns and Alphonsus had acquainted him with all that had happened. "I thank you, my son," he wrote, "in their name and in mine. I take the liberty of calling you 'my son,' since you are good enough to give me the dear name of 'Father.' As for the inauguration of the new Order, be good enough not to speak of it to anyone until my return." Falcoia meant this merely as a precautionary measure to guard against any further obstacles to the work.

An intimate correspondence began from this time onwards between the Nuns of Scala and Alphonsus de Liguori. Each one asked advice in order to advance in the way of perfection, and promised never to forget their new friend before God. Alphonsus replied as sweetly and gently as did St. Francis de Sales to his daughters by the following letters:

"Many days have passed since the retreat at Scala, but the memory of the hours spent with you lives in my heart as though I had just left you. From time to time my eyes turn towards your Convent, and I say: 'O souls full of divine love, yes, love Jesus. Remember not an instant passes without His loving you.' Speak to Him often, especially when you are in choir, in presence of the Blessed Sacrament. Love Jesus, love above all His adorable Heart, His holy and sweet Will. Unite your will to His and say to Him: "Lord, Thy good pleasure and Thy glory are sufficient for me. Though afflictions, abandonment, darkness and storms may come, let us accept them all, because God wishes it, for God is always good and worthy to be loved. To Him, then, throughout all ages be love and benediction!"'

Alphonsus next, taking them at their word, recommends himself with touching humility to the prayers of the Community. "Being a priest called to save souls," he says, "I should be able to procure glory to God, but pray for me always. Perhaps I may seem importunate in begging your prayers so frequently, but I fear your zeal in this cause may cease as time passes. The thought that you are praying to God for me gives me strength and courage. It seems to me that God cannot refuse to hear your prayers when you pray for my poor soul. As for me, I never forget you; you have a large part in my poor prayers." Indeed he had a special reason for asking the Nuns' prayers. "Do you know," he writes, "I am now paying dearly for the joy and peace of Scala, as I told you would be the case. I am at present in the midst of storms, and sometimes, seeing light neither in Heaven nor on earth, I am left in darkness, as in a gloomy cave. May the adorable Will of God be done! Should He wish to send me to hell I would consent, if it were for His greater glory, but I beg of you, ask Him not to allow me to offend Him, for that would not be to His glory. For the rest, Lord, I am here; do with me what Thou wilt!"

The Divine Master, however, deigned to console His servant through the instrumentality of Mary Celeste, in whose revelations he had believed. In the midst of his trials he received a letter from her in which, after having reminded him of the union established by God between their two souls, she continues: "Father, during prayer, I was asking God never to separate us from Him, when I saw the throne of glory that He had prepared for you in eternity in reward for your love of Jesus and for the work you undertake in His Cause. 'As a proof of the love I bear him,' He said to me, 'I will grant an increase of grace and of fervor to all souls under his care. Those who listen to his words shall find in them heavenly blessings. Tell him from Me that I take pleasure in the work he does to convert sinners, especially in the care he takes to lead the souls of just men in the way of divine perfection and love, for it is chiefly they who give glory to Me, and it is by such souls that I dispense mercy to the world.' Father," continues the letter, "I communicate this to you because such is the Will of God, to which I must submit." This letter gave great joy to Alphonsus, and he always kept it carefully as a most precious treasure.

CHAPTER XI

THE RULE OF THE MOST HOLY REDEEMER

N the Feast of Pentecost, May 13th, 1731, the new Rule was inaugurated in the monastery of Scala. It was a great event, and this Feast is always dear to Redemptorist hearts. The Nuns at that time had not in their possession the Rule written by Mary Celeste under Divine protection. It was in the hands of Falcoia, and as he did not wish to part with it, he ordered the Sister to re-write it. This seemed impossible to her. It was several years since she had received the Divine revelation, and she could not remember it sufficiently. "It would require a miracle to do what you ask," she wrote to Falcoia, "and I should be afraid of tempting Providence."

Fearing to fail in obedience, she nevertheless sat down and tried to make a beginning. Her difficulty, however, was increased by the attacks of the devil. The latter did all in his power to hinder the work, causing sudden and violent noises to be heard in the monastery, and one day even appearing to her under a horrible form, and trying to frighten her with threats. He declared that if she continued to write, he would torment her and cause her to lose the grace of God. Finally she went in great trouble to find her confessor, who ordered the devil to leave her alone, after which his attacks ceased. All this Sister Mary Celeste wrote to Falcoia, and an account of it is to be found in her autobiography. Even after this, the Sister could make no progress. One evening she resolved to give up the attempt and put out her light. Immediately she heard Our Lord say to her: "You are tired, rest in Me." At these words her heart burned with love, and her whole mind and body felt at peace. The Divine Master added:

"Trust in Me, do you not know that I am able to make you re-write the Rule, not only in outline, as at first, but in its finished perfection?" And in one moment Our Lord communicated to her the substance of the Rules, with so much precision and clearness that all their meaning was explained. She also understood the signification of the truths of the Holy Gospels, of which these Rules were the application, so much so that if her lamp had not been extinguished, she could have written the whole Rule. However, night was advancing, and Mary Celeste, as she tells us with great simplicity, felt tired and wanted to sleep, but could not do so because of the Presence of God. Then Jesus granted her the grace with which He had favored St. John, at the Last Supper, by telling her to repose on His Heart. The next morning she hurried to her Superior to tell her all. The latter was delighted, and blessing the Sister whom Jesus deigned to visit, ordered her to write the Rule without delay, as their Spiritual Father had commanded. Mary Celeste obeyed, and wrote so quickly that her pen seemed to fly on the paper. This important document was completed in two hours. She then began the Constitutions. Our Lord continued His assistance and she saw herself surrounded by Angels who helped her to write. When she prayed or walked about the monastery, they were still with her and a celestial light surrounded her. One day Saint Catherine of Sienna appeared and said: "Write, my daughter, for the Lord Jesus has blessed thy hand with the fulness of His grace." Her work being finished, the Sister sent it to the spiritual Father, together with an account of all that had transpired. There were, therefore, at this time two copies of the Rule, both written by the hand of Mary Celeste, the second copy being more developed than the first. Falcoia kept both copies. Each began with a declaration from the Eternal Father. The Heavenly Father recalls the immense love which caused Him to give His only-begotten Son to be the light and life of the world. It is in order that men should be mindful of this infinite charity and of the works done by His Divine Son for love of man, that He has raised up this new Order. Each of its members must be a living image of this Divine Son, the sole Head and Founder of the Order. Each Nun must walk in that newness of life and of justice taught by Him in the Holy Gospels, so that all may partake of the treasure of eternal life enclosed therein.

After this introduction, Our Lord Himself gives the Rule. He defines its aim, viz., the imitation of His life. The Choir Nuns should be thirty-three in number, in order to honor the thirty-three years of His life on earth. The spirit of the Community is that of perfect unity, charity and simplicity, which was His own spirit with His apostles. Next comes the description of the garments, and their beautiful symbolic signification. Then the order of the day with particular rules for certain days of the week, and for Sundays and feast days. Thus the 25th of each month is kept in honor of the birth of Our Lord, and all the exercises of that day are consecrated to the mystery of the Incarnation. There are three periods of mental prayer during the day, and three hours of strict silence, to honor the three hours' Agony of Jesus on the Cross.

Finally, the Divine Master speaks of the nine fundamental virtues upon which, together with the imitation of His own life. He bases the whole practice of religious life: fraternal charity, poverty, chastity, obedience, meekness and humility of heart, mortification, recollection, prayer, self-denial and love of the Cross.

To this Rule, revealed by Our Lord, Mary Celeste adds constitutions of each of these virtues, together with certain articles of monastic discipline. Both Rules and Constitutions needed to be defined and completed on many points. The Bishop of Castellamare wished to undertake this work, but the Bishop of Scala had no intention of allowing his neighbor to legislate in a monastery of his diocese. Alphonsus, in obedience to the orders of his Superior, held aloof from this discussion. The Nuns heard this news with alarm. It would mean death to the newly-born Institute, if Alphonsus were not there to defend it. In the midst of the general desolation, Mary Celeste alone remained calm.

"This prohibition will not be maintained, to help us in our affairs," she wrote to Alphonsus. "It is merely an exercise of patience for you and for us. God did not send you to our monastery without some special design. He did it for the sake of our future progress, and not only for the good that you have already done in the past, but God wishes us to suffer. Those who help us must suffer with us. When I heard of this prohibition, I complained to Our Lord in prayer. He then made me understand that nobody can take away from us the man whom He has given us for our support. That is why I am quite peaceful about everything."

Mary Celeste was right. Bishop Guerriero finally allowed Falcoia to elaborate the constitutions, on condition that Don Alphonsus should revise and correct them. Thus God providentially arranged for His servant to work at the Rules and Constitutions of the Order, as He had brought him to Scala so that the revelations upon which that Order is founded might be approved.

The editing of the Rules and Constitutions lasted two years. The text written by Mary Celeste was in the form of exhortations addressed by Our Lord to the Nuns. Falcoia wished to retain this form, thinking it more forcible than any other. He quoted as an example, the "Imitation of Jesus Christ," in which the teachings are almost always placed in the mouth of Our Lord. Alphonsus, more experienced in legal matters, insisted on a prescriptive form, which being clearer and more traditional, would more easily obtain the approbation of the Holy See. The form desired by St. Alphonsus was therefore adopted. As for the Rules and Constitutions themselves, the part taken by the saint in compiling them was absolutely preponderant. For this reason the Very Rev. Father Murray, in speaking of the Rules of the double Order of Redemptoristines and Redemptorists, defines it thus:

"Our Rule and our Capitulary Constitutions such as they have always existed almost without change, as well as the Rule of the Nuns of the Most Holy Redeemer, tinder the form approved by the Holy See, were composed on the whole by our Father Saint Alphonsus. He has followed for the greater part the Rule and Constitutions written by Sister Mary Celeste, while taking into account the corrections introduced by himself and Falcoia; nevertheless, this double Rule, such as it exists to-day, has St. Alphonsus for its author."

It is the text thus revised and transformed by St. Alphonsus which obtained the episcopal approbation, and later on that of the Holy See; and it is of this text that a Bishop, speaking to the Redemptoristines of his diocese, said: "I have read your Rules carefully, they are the most divine, the most perfect, the most marked with the seal of the Holy Spirit, among all those that I have read."

It is to be noted, however, that this third edition of the Rules did not differ substantially from the two preceding ones, written by Mary Celeste under Divine inspiration. It contained all that they contained. For this reason, Falcoia said later in a letter to one of the Sisters: "It is useless to dispute as to the choice of these three Rules, as they are in reality all alike." Mary Celeste also, in her autobiography, owns that the Rule which she received from Our Lord is maintained in its entirety in the edition made by Falcoia. The holy Sister complains, however, of two additions made to the revelation she received: that of the theological virtues added to the nine virtues mentioned by Our Lord, and the wearing of a scapular having been added to the holy habit. To-day we have good reason to believe that Alphonsus, and not Falcoia, added the virtues of Faith, Hope and Charity to the nine virtues indicated by Mary

Celeste. Truth itself seemed to require this addition, since the theological virtues are the foundation of all the others, having for their object the Divine Model Himself, and uniting us to Him. There is also the advantage of being able to attribute to each month of the year a special virtue, and thus to complete a regular cycle of holy exercises. This is the tree of life of which the Apocalypse speaks (22:2). It bears its twelve fruits, producing one each month. As for the scapular, it is the habit brought from heaven by Our Lady, and symbolizes the sweet yoke of Jesus. It seemed, therefore, natural and conformable to the intentions of Our Lord that the new Order would take this holy livery of that sky-blue colour required for the mantle.

Besides, Mary Celeste did not ignore the fact that all revelation must be admitted to the judgment and interpretation of the confessor. God wishes it to be thus, so that souls whom He favors with His Divine communications may have the merit of faith and of humble submission to the Church. When the Rule with its additions was finally drawn up, she declared herself willing to accept blindly all the prescriptions of the Rule given to the Community. The action of St. Alphonsus at this period was not confined to the revision of the Rules and Constitutions, he also undertook the task of imparting to the Nuns that interior spirit of constant application to the imitation of the life of Our Lord, which was to be the essential feature of their sanctity. For this purpose, he went often to Scala to preach retreats, novenas, and to hear the Nuns' confessions. In fact, in the month of August, 1731, he seems to have made a sort of canonical visit to the Convent, treating of matters both spiritual and temporal.

Mary Celeste, on her part, did not fail to communicate to him the lights she received from God. She wrote to him on one occasion: "Jesus has given all the members of this Order to His beloved Mother Mary, confiding them to her as most dear daughters, and the Holy Virgin has received them with tender love. It was also granted to me to hear that the prayers of Our

Lady have caused this new Order to come to life, in spite of all the efforts of the evil spirit." In this same letter, she says that the habit of the Order symbolizes the mortification of Jesus Christ, and she adds: "It was shown to me that the spirit of this Order consists in two things; scorn of self and ardent charity towards God and our neighbor."

We also read in St. Alphonsus' diary this encouraging thought, probably communicated to him by Mary Celeste: "The devil curses all that I do for the monastery, but the Lord blesses it."

Besides, after the year 1730, on account of his advanced age, Falcoia could rarely come to Scala; also for a time he was not on good terms with the Bishop of the place. Mgr. Santore, and therefore refused to enter his diocese, while St. Alphonsus, on the contrary, often stayed at Scala between the years 1730 and 1738. In 1738, the relations between Falcoia and the Nuns themselves were rather strained, and ended in a rupture, which was however only temporary. In the month of May, 1731, the Sisters had inaugurated the new Rule. In the following month of August they were to be clothed with the new habit. The Sisters procured material for the habits and mantles, and were careful to make them exactly like the model which Our Lord had shown to Mary Celeste. The habit of deep red to denote the infinite charity of God towards the human race, the cincture of the same colour and material, to be worn as a symbol of the bond of love uniting all in the Heart of Jesus, the mantle of sky-blue colour to remind them that their life and thoughts should be raised above earth and fixed on heaven. They sent to Naples to obtain the picture of the Most Holy Redeemer which the professed Nuns were to wear on their breasts. When all was ready, Mary Celeste wrote to St. Alphonsus begging him to come for that important and solemn day, for they considered him as their father and founder. Falcoia himself was not able to be present.

The ceremony took place on August 6th, 1731, Feast of the

Transfiguration of Our Lord. This day can therefore be considered as the birthday of the Redemptoristine Order.

The Superioress, Mother Mary Angela, first clothed herself and then her Sisters in the red habit and blue mantle, with the utmost joy and fervor. It was no vain symbol, but a sign of the transfiguration of their souls. "From that day," writes Mary Celeste, "they began to run with fervor in the footsteps of their Divine Master. Their mortifications, both corporal and spiritual, were extraordinary. Their fervent prayers before the Blessed Sacrament or in their cells, were prolonged far into the night, and their conversation at recreation was so full of devotion, that all were as much inflamed with divine love as though they had been at prayer. After so many storms, peace reigned once more, both within and without the monastery." The world, always changeable, attracted by the reputation of Alphonsus now praised the Convent and admired the Nuns it had been so ready to deride.

Falcoia wrote of his appreciation of all that had happened and justly gave the credit to Alphonsus. The Nuns of the Most Holy Redeemer can, therefore, in truth, claim the saint as their founder, for although he certainly did not conceive the idea of the Order nor compose the Rule (the Redemptoristines have the unique honor of holding their Rule from Our Lord Himself, through the instrumentality of Mary Celeste, which is what distinguishes them from other religious Orders of the Church), yet it was St. Alphonsus and he alone who, in spite of universal opposition, had the revelations of Mary Celeste recognized as divine, and by this means brought to life the Order of the Most Holy Redeemer.

It was Alphonsus also who inaugurated the change of Rule, obtained the Bishop's permission and fixed the day. It was he and he alone who, when revising the Rule, obtained the approbation of the Bishop, and finally he never ceased to infuse into the souls of his daughters the spirit of their Order. Therefore the Church has not hesitated to say in the Office of

St. Alphonsus: "He instituted in his episcopal town a monastery of Nuns of his Congregation." By doing this, Alphonsus was the first to spread abroad the Redemptoristine Order, for, from the Convent of St. Agatha, founded by him, they have spread throughout the old world and the new.

CHAPTER XII
THE FULL REVELATION

N the Divine plan the tree planted by the Heavenly Father in the garden of the Church was destined to bear two branches. The Redemptoristine branch had been the first to grow, before that of the Redemptorists, as contemplation precedes action and the hidden life precedes the public life. Both were to imitate the life of Our Lord, the one by prayer, the other by works. Again, it is Mary Celeste whom Our Divine Lord chooses as the messenger for the completion of His Work.

The following is the account given in her Autobiography: "It was on the vigil of the Feast of St. Francis of Assisi, October 3rd, 1731. We were in the refectory when I was suddenly drawn into contemplation and saw Our Lord with the Seraphic Father, St. Francis, and Father don Alphonsus de Liguori. Pointing to the latter. Our Lord said: 'This soul is chosen as the head of My Institute, it is he who will be the first Superior of the Congregation of men.' At the same time I saw a vision of this work, as though it were already established; I was filled with joy and could take no food. During the whole of the meal I remained thus lost in contemplation."

Nothing further was revealed to her at that moment, but the next day, the Feast of the Holy Patriarch, to whom she had a great devotion, she went to Holy Communion absorbed in the thought of what had happened on the previous night. Suddenly her soul was illuminated by God, and she understood that she was to write as motto of the Institute of men those words of the Gospel: "Go and preach to all nations that the Kingdom of Heaven is at hand;" She also received light on the spiritual exercises, on the work, and especially on the poverty of these apostles, who were to be raised up by God to seek out and help abandoned souls. She wrote down all that had been said to her, and then sent a detailed account of what had been revealed to her to her spiritual Father. Falcoia, as was to be expected, feigned to disbelieve all. "According to what you say," he wrote, "you seem to be in continual conference with Our Lord; I cannot believe your revelations, and I counsel you to do likewise. We cannot regulate our conduct on these imaginations, and if I wish to know in detail all you think you see and hear, it is in order to be able to direct you better." He then forbade her to tell Alphonsus anything of what happened. Yet in spite of his affected disbelief Falcoia went to Scala to question Mary Celeste. Experience had taught him that God deigned to favor this soul with supernatural gifts, and he was not long in realizing that the revelation came from Our Lord, Who was about to complete His work.

Twenty years before this, when Falcoia was living in Rome, as he was one day walking along the banks of the Tiber, he had an interior vision and saw in the light of Divine Truth this new Order which God intended to create in His Church, and whose aim would be to imitate the virtues of Jesus Christ. This vision had in view only a society of priests, as is stated in the "Analecta C.SS.R.," p. 256. There is no reason to suppose that Falcoia had ever thought of a congregation of women before Mary Celeste's revelations.

The humble religious had said nothing at the time, but he had long been seeking a zealous soul to undertake this work, and now in the revelation of Mary Celeste he saw the hand of God. Without delay Falcoia wrote to Alphonsus, saying that he had important news to communicate to him. On hearing what Falcoia had to say, Alphonsus was not surprised, as he had suspected for some days that Sister Mary Celeste was in possession of a secret concerning him, which obedience forbade her to disclose. He had gathered this from a letter written to him by the Superioress, Mother Mary Angela. The Saint naturally wished to hear for himself what Mary Celeste had to say; he therefore went to Scala accompanied by Mazzini and Mandarini, his two friends, to whom, however, he did not disclose the reason for this visit. The day after his arrival he heard the Sisters' confessions. When Mary Celeste presented herself in the confessional, he urged her to give him a detailed account of what she had seen and heard. The holy Sister obeyed. She then declared to him with great clearness that it was God's will that he should leave Naples, where there were plenty of priests, and that he should found a Congregation of Missionaries whose special vocation would be to preach the word of God to the hitherto neglected and abandoned souls in the country districts. Alphonsus replied that he knew himself and felt his incapacity for such a work, and that her revelations on this subject must be imagination. Mary Celeste, however, continued to insist that God intended to provide for the salvation of abandoned souls in the country districts, and that He had chosen His servant Alphonsus to found this work. Thereupon an altercation ensued, so that Mazzini, who was in the chapel at the time, wondered what could have upset his friend; and when, after the confessions, Alphonsus shut himself up in his room and was heard sighing and groaning, Mazzini knocked at his door to ask what was the matter. As it was not a question of a sacramental secret, Alphonsus told all to his friend. "Just imagine," he said, "Mary Celeste insists that I ought to leave Naples and found a new religious Society at Scala, whose aim would be to preach to the country folk, She tells me that this is the Will of God for me. It is an undertaking beyond my strength; besides, you know my work at Naples, the missions in which I am obliged to co-operate, all the business, in fact, in which I am engaged. This is the cause of my trouble. I cannot see the means of undertaking this work, yet if I refuse I fear to resist the Will of God."

Mazzini endeavored to console his friend. "Courage," he

said. "We do not yet know the Will of God; wait until it is more manifest."

"Besides," continued Alphonsus, still following out his train of thought, "where should I find companions to join me in such an enterprise?"

"As for that," replied Mazzini, "I will be your first companion. Come, let us dine, since it is time for our meal, and leave God to arrange all!"

These words restored Alphonsus' peace of mind, and the two friends were soon joined by Maudarini, who, on hearing of the proposed Institute, at once offered himself as novice. This generosity on the part of his friends restored hope, and even joy, to the heart of Alphonsus.

The next day he again interviewed Mary Celeste and questioned her more closely as to her vision. The two friends, who were made acquainted with all that was said, declared themselves ready for any sacrifice for the sake of such a holy enterprise. They then all returned to Naples with the intention of making a beginning as soon as they could obtain permission to do so from their directors. For this reason, St. Alphonsus required Mary Celeste to write down a detailed account of what she had heard and seen, so that he could submit it to the judgment of his director. Father Pagano. From the evidence given at the process of beatification of St. Alphonsus we see clearly that the foundation of the Congregation of the Most Holy Redeemer was made as a direct result of the revelations of Mary Celeste. Yet Alphonsus did not act on private revelations only before following the call of God. However sure he was as to the divinity of what was revealed to the holy Nun, he acted only under obedience to, and on the advice of, his directors. He could not doubt the Divine Will in this matter after the decisions of such enlightened priests as the Venerable Father Fiorillo, O.P., Father Vincent Cutica, Superior of the Lazarists, Father Dominic Manulias, Provincial of the Jesuits, and Father Pagano, of the Oratory, who had been his guide for so many years, and finally Mgr. Falcoia, under whose direction he was soon to place himself altogether.

The sacrifices made by the Saint to follow so clear a call from God are well known. Who does not remember the moving scene when his old father held his son in his arms and for three long hours implored him not to leave him? Alphonsus overcame all obstacles. On November 9th he left Naples and went to Scala with a few companions, for it was at Scala, according to Mary Celeste, that God willed the new Institute of Missionaries to begin. The Inauguration was fixed for November 9th. It took place in the poor guest-house of the Sisters, which was the first temporary convent of St. Alphonsus and his companions.

It was at this time that the new Bishop of Scala made his entry into his diocese and showed himself full of kindness for the religious whose house he considered a sanctuary for the parish. Between the Bishop, the Brothers and the Sisters admirable union, concord and charity reigned. Seeing these good beginnings, the devil sought by every possible means to persecute and frighten the religious. Again, as when the Rule was being written, terrifying noises were heard, Sisters were struck by invisible hands, etc., but, on the other hand, signs of God's guidance and protection were not wanting. One night, when the Sisters were in adoration, the Monastery was suddenly illuminated with a brilliant light from Heaven; so much so that the Fathers in the neighbouring guest-house came running to the Convent, thinking it was a fire. They called several other secular priests of the neighborhood and showed them the splendor that shone over the Monastery. One of these latter, who was a great servant of God, said: "There is no necessity for us to go to the Monastery, for it is the night which the Nuns spend in adoration, and that light is most certainly the fire of the Holy Ghost." Two months after this, on September 11th, while the Blessed Sacrament was exposed in the Nuns' chapel, the Holy Cross was seen to appear in the Host, at first black, then red as blood, then as white as snow. After this the image of Jesus crucified appeared, and then the instruments of the Passion, and red rocks, were seen in the foreground, also white clouds and other signs. This spectacle was clearly visible in the Sacred Host, not only to the Nuns, but also to several priests and members of the congregation who were present. This vision was renewed many times, notably on November 6th, 7th and 8th. Doubtless by these signs God wished to set the seal of His approbation on the Order and to prepare its members to bear the Cross, which is never wanting to the followers of Christ. From this apparition the arms of file Order of the Most Holy Redeemer have been formed, viz., a Cross surrounded by the instruments of the Passion. The Cross, indeed, was about to weigh heavily on the shoulders both of St. Alphonsus and of Sister Mary Celeste.

CHAPTER XIII
THE RAGING OF THE TEMPEST

HE STORM RAISED BY SATAN TO DESTROY THE WORK OF GOD, is the title given by Mary Celeste to the sad events which we are about to relate. In receiving the full revelation of the Divine plan, she does not separate the Brothers from the Sisters. Together they form what she calls the Institute, or the work of God. Following the example of Jesus Christ Himself, she employs both expressions indifferently to denote the double branch of the Order. That is why we have stated that Our Lord, in His revelations to Mary Celeste, named St. Alphonsus as head of the Sisters as well as of the Brothers, pointing to him and saying: "This is he whom I have chosen to be the head of My Institute." Our Divine Master was not only thinking of the Sisters but also of the Missionaries, when He said: "Fear nothing regarding the Institute, your desires shall be fulfilled; in order to establish it, I will raise up great souls who will do great things for My glory."

Redemptorists and Redemptoristines form but one soul, having the same Rule in its entirety, founded on the imitation of the virtues and the example of the Redeemer. This one Rule for the two branches of the Institute needed explanations, additions and adaptations. It is precisely this necessary work which caused the division of opinion among the companions of St. Alphonsus. Of these companions Marini had not as yet obtained permission from his director to join the new Order. The others, Mandarini, Donato, Romano and Silvester Tosquez, remained at Scala. Vincent Mandarini was a Doctor of Theology and had been dismissed from the College of the Holy

Family for his adherence to Alphonsus. John Baptist Donata was a clever and zealous priests He had belonged to a society for the propagation of devotion to the Blessed Sacrament, but on hearing from Mandarini of St. Alphonsus' plans he did not hesitate to seek admission to the new Institute. Peter Romano, a Canon of Scala, was the ordinary confessor of the Nuns. It was natural that he should resolve to join the Congregation, the divine origin of which he knew better than anyone. Finally there was Silvester Tosquez, whom Mary Celeste in her Autobiography speaks of as "the pious gentleman." A lawyer of great eloquence, very much appreciated at the Court of Vienna, where his brother held a high position, Tosquez had a brilliant future before him, as he was both virtuous and talented. He had higher ambitions, however; his soul, touched by grace, found the greatest happiness in meditation and prayer, and to this he consecrated all his free time. Well versed in mystical theology, he was singularly competent to speak of spiritual things. His vivid imagination and large heart led him to admire and prefer the extraordinary ways of prayer granted to certain privileged souls. He himself aspired to the height of perfection and resolved to leave the world. But he had not as yet discovered the Order which corresponded with his ideal. One day Tosquez related to his friend Mandarini a vision he had had while at the Court of Vienna, of an institute whose members were vowed to the imitation of Jesus Christ, who wore a habit like the Savior's, and like Him also preached the Gospel to the poor. "Strange to say," continued Tosquez, "this same vision of eight years ago has just been granted to me again at Pentecost while I was praying earnestly for light to know my vocation. When such an institute comes into existence I shall enter it without delay." Mandarini was much moved on hearing these words, for he recognized the description of the evangelical society which Alphonsus wished to establish. He explained all this to Tosquez, and added: "I have promised to belong to this Society; why should you not join us also?" The ardent young man was overjoyed. He accepted at once, and a few days later, on St. Alphonsus' advice, went to submit his vocation and desire to Mgr. Falcoia. Such a brilliant personality as that of Tosquez was hardly suitable for the role he was authorized to play in the beginning of the Institute, for he had the defects of his qualities and was wanting in common sense, as also in that prudence and reflection so necessary in any council. But in one short interview Falcoia could not discover his weak points, and saw in this young man, besides his undeniable virtue, a favorite at Court, and in consequence a protector sent from Heaven to support the new Congregation against the inevitable attacks of people of the world and of statesmen. He therefore suggested that Tosquez should visit the Monastery of Scala and talk things over with the Nuns, especially with Mary Celeste. He would thus be able to study at its source the holy life he wished to embrace.

Don Silvester, having visited the Convent at Scala, could hardly tear himself away. The Nuns seemed to him to be leading the lives of angels, and their spiritual conversations transported his soul with joy. Being friendly with the Bishop of Scala, Mgr. Santoro, Tosquez was easily able to obtain permission to renew his visits, and it was even through his instrumentality that the new Rule was authentically approved, as the former Bishop, Mgr. Guerriero, had died suddenly before according this authorization.

On their part the Sisters were both charmed and edified to find so much piety in a man of the world. They were also grateful for his devotion to the Institute. They were loud in his praises; Mary Celeste in particular was deeply grateful for his services regarding the approbation of the Rule.

Such were the first companions of St. Alphonsus, who now met together to deliberate on the Constitutions of the Institute. All were unanimous in declaring that the basis should be the revelations of Our Lord made to Mary Celeste, and that therefore the daily exercises must be copied from the Nuns'

Rule; but there were many other questions to be decided, such as, for example, whether they should keep schools, whether their houses were to be founded in solitary places or in towns, whether the Divine Office should be recited in common, etc. Opinions were divided, and the only way out of these difficulties was to appoint a head to whose decision all would submit. The Fathers would gladly have chosen St. Alphonsus as arbitrator, since he had been designated by Providence as head of the Institute, but, besides the fact that his absolute dependence on Falcoia annoyed his companions, he himself absolutely refused to take the lead, alleging his youth and inexperience. He was then only thirty-six years of age and had been ordained but six years. To Alphonsus' mind one arbitrator alone seemed possible—Mgr. Falcoia—on account of his age, his holiness, his experience and his episcopal authority, which would give ballast to the new Institute; besides, argued the Saint, being the spiritual Father of the Nuns and of Mary Celeste, it was for him to interpret the latter's revelations. Romano shared the same opinion, being himself a spiritual son of Falcoia. But the three others would have nothing to do with the prelate, whose authoritative character they disliked. According to them Falcoia, being Bishop of another diocese, had no reason to interfere with this business; moreover, they complained of the additions he had introduced into the Rule.

Don Silvester proposed to seek Mary Celeste's advice, saying that, as she had received the revelation of the Rule, it was for her to explain it. We know the end of these sad discussions and how St. Alphonsus was abandoned by his companions, just as Jesus was abandoned by His apostles in the Garden of Gethsemane; but also, like the Redeemer, he cried in the midst of his trial: "Oh, my God, may Thy Will be done!" He then made a vow to persevere with the work even though he should remain alone. In such circumstances this vow was heroic. The work owes its preservation to him. This disunion among the Fathers could not fail to have a distressing effect on the monastery of Nuns. The Superioress, Mother Mary Angela, and most of the Sisters felt it their duty to submit to Falcoia as being their spiritual Father, but Mary Celeste, having received the divine revelations and instructions, felt bound to defend them. "All the time that the Fathers were deliberating as to whether the revelation came from God or not," she says, "I felt obliged to be silent, but once the work was declared to come from God I thought it my duty to resist any suggestions which appeared to spoil or change God's designs for His work, and this I did out of respect for Truth."

In spite of these difficulties, all might have been arranged peacefully, thanks to St. Alphonsus' influence, if the devil had not interfered to sow further trouble and discord. The evil spirit loves to counterfeit all good. At Lourdes several people had false apparitions of Our Lady, for Satan hoped thus to negative the effects of the true apparitions vouchsafed to Bernadette. He acted in the same way at Scala. There was in the Monastery a very young Sister who tried to mix herself up in this affair, and the devil made use of her to serve his own purpose. Mary Celeste does not name this Sister, but we know from other sources that it was a certain Sister Mary Columba. She professed to be in constant communication with Our Lord, and gave out many things about her so-called revelations and visions. Unfortunately she was thought a great deal of, both by the spiritual Father of the Nuns and by the confessor. Falcoia considered her a simple soul to whom God communicated Himself, and he approved of all she did. She even wrote to St. Alphonsus that he had been elected by Our Lord as head of the Institute, but that he must submit in everything to Falcoia, whom God had chosen to be the principal head. This naturally pleased the humility of the Saint, and therefore he followed her advice.

During many years this young novice continued to speak of the graces she had received from God, and wrote letters to various people saying that Our Lord commanded her to tell them to go and preach to the heathen. Moreover, she gave herself out as having received the stigmata and as possessing the gift of prophecy. All this time Mother Mary Angela, who had been this Sister's Novice Mistress, and knew her to possess all the faults and frivolities of her age, was most anxious about this state of affairs and could not believe in the visions, etc. She feared, however, to discredit the Sister by complaining to the confessor, who evidently believed in her. She therefore spoke privately to Tosquez and asked him to talk to the young Nun, and to endeavor to make her see the error of her ways. Tosquez accomplished his mission as delicately as possible. He warned the Sister against illusion and error, as he was experienced in spiritual theology. Unfortunately this interview was the prelude to disaster, for the young Sister would not listen to reason and was indignant at the advice given her. She thought that Mary Celeste had asked Tosquez to speak to her, and from that moment did all in her power to stir up the Community against Tosquez and against Mary Celeste. Thus the powers of darkness were successful in spreading strife and trouble where formerly peace and charity had reigned. It was truly an infernal machination to ruin and destroy the work of God.

At this time also Sister Mary Celeste, prompted by serious reasons of conscience, which we shall hear later, ceased to allow herself to be directed by Falcoia and simply made her confession to the ordinary confessor of the Monastery. It was then, the Venerable Mother tells us in her diary, that she began to be persecuted by the Nuns her companions. Those who had formerly been her intimate friends now became severe and rigorous judges. "But," says the holy Sister, "God allowed it all, and in all they did they only acted in a spirit of zeal and for a cause which, in their eyes, seemed justified; for devils so clouded their minds that the smallest action performed by this Sister was severely judged and condemned. In consequence they wrote a great number of letters to the spiritual Father speaking against her, and in particular concerning her intercourse with the pious gentleman. The latter, indeed, ignoring the troubles which had arisen in the Monastery, continued to write at length, not only to the Sister in question, but also to the other Sisters." The Bishop of Castellamare, in the meantime, distressed at all this dissension, endeavored to establish peace. He began by demanding that Mary Celeste should make a vow to be directed only by him; that she should also sign the Rules such as he had presented them to the Community, and finally that she should cease all intercourse with Tosquez. Before hearing of this injunction, however, Mary Celeste had herself realized that silence was better than discussion. She therefore secretly wrote to Tosquez, begging him for the love of God to cease writing to her, as the letters were only intercepted and caused further trouble. His letters were criticized and censured by the other Sisters, and all that he wrote concerning his soul they looked upon as hypocrisy.

This letter, written by Mary Celeste with the very best intentions, in the hope that once the correspondence with Tosquez ceased the Nuns would be satisfied, only seemed to add fuel to the fire. Intercepted like the other letters, it was sent to Falcoia. The latter ordered Mary Celeste to be imprisoned and severely punished. Then he sent don Alphonsus to the Monastery with orders to speak severely to the Sisters on the great danger of illusion, and on the number of souls who deceive themselves and thus lose the way of prayer and salvation. Alphonsus obeyed, and after the instruction he asked for Mary Celeste. The latter begged to be excused, as she was ill and unable to come downstairs. She was indeed very ill, as future events will prove.

It is important to remember that this was the occasion of the two famous letters of Alphonsus to Mary Celeste. The Venerable Sister's reply was the letter which she, in her turn, wrote to the confessor of the Monastery. These three letters, while enlightening us as to the sad events which caused them to be written, reveal also the depths of these two great souls. It is therefore important to analyze them with the greatest care. This we shall endeavor to do in the three following chapters.

CHAPTER XIV
THE FRIENDSHIP OF SAINTS

 HE law of sanctity imposes many a sacrifice on the human heart, but it never fails to repay a hundredfold what it has taken. "You shall no longer converse with men, but with angels," said Our Lord to St. Teresa when He granted the favor of her first ecstasy. Like unto angels are souls raised above the things of sense, divested of all self-love, celestial spirits living only for the love of God. The friendship of saints obeys the laws and participates in the prerogatives of divine charity, which is its principle and its aim. Between Alphonsus and Mary Celeste the grace of Jesus Christ and providential events had created one of these spiritual friendships of which St. Teresa so often extols the advantages.

Although many letters must have passed between St. Alphonsus and the Nun, those only which we are about to analyze have been preserved. We have described the events which led to their being written. They date from March, 1733, at the time of the trouble and dissension which was to end in the departure of Mary Celeste from Scala. In those hours of anguish God did not permit St. Alphonsus to be a consoler in the human sense of the word: the trial for both of them would have been softened. The role reserved to the Saint was a higher one, more befitting the heroic friendship which united those two souls. To a superficial observer these letters might seem harsh and cold, but to those who remember the circumstances which gave rise to them they show the heights to which these two friends had resolved to attain by mutual help, regardless of the rough toad they would have to traverse. This double document furnishes us with a proof of the union which existed between Alphonsus and Mary Celeste, while at the same time it reveals to us the quality of these two souls. Only a saint could speak thus, only a saintly soul could understand his meaning. That Mary Celeste did fully understand future events will show.

One striking detail in this correspondence is the fact that St, Alphonsus uses the familiar second person singular when speaking to Mary Celeste. Although this was customary at that time in Naples, yet it does not fail to denote both paternal condescension and great intimacy on the part of St. Alphonsus. He very rarely addresses a person as "thou" in all his voluminous correspondence, except perhaps to one or two of the first Redemptoristines of Scala. Another still more significant detail may be found in the terms he employs when addressing the holy Sister: "Celeste ... my Celeste ... my dear Celeste ... my beloved Sister in Jesus Christ." We have no need to seek for further proofs of the affection which St. Alphonsus bore for Sister Mary Celeste, for the Saint himself describes the strong bond of union which existed between them. When Mary Celeste in anguish of soul felt herself abandoned and persecuted by all, she may for a moment have wondered whether Alphonsus, in obedience to Falcoia, had not turned from her, and she wrote to him, saying: "How is it that my soul can interest you so greatly?"

"Ah, Celeste," writes Alphonsus, "do not say that; it is too ungrateful. To what depths of union have not our souls attained in Jesus and Mary? Do you not know that the interests of your soul have become mine? God has brought this about, not I; it is impossible for me not to desire your perfection as greatly as I desire my own. I wish to give myself truly and entirely to Jesus Christ, and I desire and ask that of you too. From this day onwards mortify me in any way you wish, rather than let me suspect for a moment that there is a cloud between us. All that I have written to you, my Celeste, I have written because I love you in Jesus Christ; if you were offended by it you would be wronging me."

Finally Alphonsus, excusing himself for the rather excessive sharpness of his words in a previous letter, explains them thus: "It is always profitable to humiliate a soul overwhelmed with favors from God, and I have used this method with you all the more on account of the intimate bond which exists between us through the providence of God."

It was indeed the providence of God, Who, to realize His eternal plans, had associated these two souls in the same work of redemption to which for the future they were to devote themselves entirely. For this reason also St. Alphonsus was right in saying that his union with Mary Celeste's soul was not, a question of personal choice, but the outcome of the Will of God: "God has done this, not I!" he would say. Jesus the Redeemer had placed between these two foundation stones the indestructible cement of His charity. Such a friendship must be accompanied by profound esteem and respect based not on natural qualities, which remain in the background, but on the progress made in the soul through its own good will, aided by Divine grace. The letters we are at present studying clearly demonstrate the esteem in which St. Alphonsus held Mary Celeste.

Now it is important to remember that both letters are addressed to Mary Celeste, and that praise is naturally restricted out of discretion when speaking to the person in question. Besides, the object of these letters is to inculcate in a very special way humility, and not ordinary humility, but that perfection of the virtue which God demands of souls who enjoy His particular favor, and whom He calls to the heights of sanctity. It is true that according to a favorite doctrine of both St. Alphonsus and St. Teresa a knowledge of the gifts of God is not contrary to humility. It is even favorable to it, while being indispensable to a soul who is to undertake great things for God. Nevertheless it is necessary to warn souls not only against the slightest shadow of self-complacency, but also against those illusions which the evil spirit and self-love can always mingle with Divine graces and communications, even the most authentic, and above all they must be warned against over-confidence in their own judgment. Souls such as these, so greatly favored by God, need more than others the spirit of perfect and docile humility, both in order to avoid the snares of the devil and to respond fully to God's designs for them. Moreover, friendship is often anxious, especially a friendship whose ambition soars beyond human aims. Alphonsus was anxious in his supernatural affection for Mary Celeste, especially as regards the point of humility; indeed we might say only on this point; for, provided she remained humble, he had no other fears for this soul whom God had made of purest crystal. Therefore we must expect to find in St. Alphonsus' letters everything calculated to maintain Mary Celeste in deep humility. Moreover, St. Alphonsus knew to whom he was writing, and that to a strong soul he need not measure his words. His manner of acting in circumstances which to souls of weaker mold would have been so cruel, so disconcerting, proves the esteem he had for his penitent, and also that he knew this great soul to be already grounded in humility; otherwise he, who was usually so prudent, would never have dared to praise her thus.

"I do not say," he writes, "that I deserve to have you humble yourself before me. I confess myself unworthy to kneel at your feet, because I know what my life has been and what yours has been." And he, whose own love for Jesus was so great, adds: "I never for an instant lose hope of loving Jesus as much as you do, through His infinite mercy." Could he have given greater praise to this true spouse of the Redeemer? When St. Alphonsus speaks of the virtues she had practice up till then he does not consider her guilty of an ordinary fault of pride, but he fears that by an involuntary illusion a shadow may have fallen across her idea of holiness. In his eyes it would be a catastrophe, and he is right. He therefore exclaims: "Oh, Celeste of former days, where are you? How has this ruin come to pass? It breaks my heart to think of it. Where is your former beautiful obedience to your Superiors? Where is that humility which made you desire the scorn and opprobrium of all?"

It is to be noted that all through the anxious trial through which Mary Celeste was passing, if the Saint thought or feared her mistaken in anything, he never suspected her of a wrong attitude of mind and will. "I know that you do not feel angry with me," he said; and again, regarding the question of total submission, "As I have already told you," he wrote, "I have never blamed your will." If he so ardently desires and asks of her perfect humility it is because humility and union with God go together. "Union implies humility, therefore I would wish," he said, "to see a different foundation of humility in a soul so united to God and so overwhelmed with divine favors as you are." Let us end with a consideration which explains much. Sister Mary Columba had communications regarding Falcoia which she believed to be divine and which Mary Celeste very justly suspected. St. Alphonsus admits the possibility of illusion in Mary Columba. He admits it also in the case of Mary Celeste as far as the light which she thought to have received about Falcoia's direction was concerned. This possibility of illusion in souls very dear to God is explained, as St. Alphonsus observed, by a special permission of providence; and he adds this affirmation, which leaves us no room for doubt regarding his impression of Mary Celeste: "For my part, I truly believe you both to be saints."

Human friendships are often indulgent and accommodating to one another in a way which would be impossible in the saintly friendships of great souls. A saint united by the divine Will to another holy soul cannot help but demand great things of her. His exactions are in proportion to the sanctity which each is called to.

Alphonsus, as the letters we are now analyzing will prove, does not fail in this duty which belongs 'to every supernatural friendship, to the friendship of saints.

CHAPTER XV

WHAT ST. ALPHONSUS REQUIRED OF MARY CELESTE

 HE first and fundamental demand made by St. Alphonsus concerns, as we have already made clear, the question of humility. Humility, the virtue most necessary to a soul seeking after perfection—humility, the condition of Divine grace and union with God—humility, the mother of docility and of obedience, and in consequence the only safeguard against the illusions of self-love and of the devil, which are possible to all. Whence came the Saint's anxiety? In the first place from his solicitude for this soul so dear to God. Besides, every human being is open to attack on some point. For a proud nature like that of Mary Celeste, for a strong mind like his own, the danger most to be avoided was that of confidence in their own judgment. A life of rare innocence and of shining virtue, a providential and important mission, a widespread reputation, much admiration often imprudently shown and exaggerated—all this constituted a danger to be avoided. Don Silvester's folly had caused trouble in the Institute, both among the Redemptoristines and among the followers of St. Alphonsus. Was Mary Celeste in league with Tosquez? In the community it was thought so. Did she not take his part when she believed him to be unjustly attacked? Did she not constantly recall the services he had rendered to them, and the high opinion they once had of him; also the many virtues of which he had given proof? All this was enough to cause her to be accused of supporting him. Many complaints reached the ears of St. Alphonsus, complaints regarding Don Silvester which were partly justified, and complaints about

Mary Celeste which seemed to be not entirely without foundation. Was there no reason to fear, when Don Silvester was heard to declare on every possible occasion that he depended entirely on Sister Mary Celeste, that the lights granted to her and the divine communications should —interpreted by himself, of course—constitute, down to the smallest details, the only Rule of the new Institute? Don Silvester was exaggerated in his praises of the Nun, placing her without hesitation above St. Teresa. Alphonsus anxiously asks himself whether the incense of all this praise was not likely to turn the Sister's head? Don Silvester had declared himself plainly to be opposed to Falcoia. Mary Celeste on her part had renounced Falcoia's direction. Was it not in order to escape from the state of humiliation and annihilation in which this director kept her? Had she not come to this decision at the instigation of Don Silvester, and hoping to find in the latter a guide who would unmistakably be a most insecure one? Another thing troubles the Saint's peace of soul. The intensity of this trouble, which seems to be out of all proportion to its cause, reveals to us his one preoccupation: that Mary Celeste should place no obstacle in the way of her perfect sanctity.

"There is," he writes, "a thorn piercing my heart; last night, my Celeste, it deprived me of sleep. Is it the difficulties of my Institute which thus torment me? No, this anxiety is on your account, my Celeste. ... I search my mind for reasons to excuse you and to calm my fears ... but the thorn continues to torment me." Alphonsus had written to Mary Celeste somewhat harshly, yet with good intentions. "Perhaps," he says, "in my indiscreet zeal I have gone too far; but," he adds, "if you feel that I have offended you, I ask and will always ask, your pardon. I particularly wish you to pardon me. I would be ready even to kiss your feet, if that were allowed, in reparation for having so treated a beloved spouse of Jesus Christ, and if Father Falcoia permits it I will ask your pardon publicly before the Sisters."

CHAPTER XV: WHAT ST. ALPHONSUS REQUIRED

Is that, however, Alphonsus' sole anxiety? No! the Sister had replied to him rather coldly. He complains of it.

"In your last letter, especially, I have noticed how you address me, how you sign yourself, how little you care whether I believe you or not. You do not even say that you are praying for me, as though I were already beyond forgiveness." He particularly notices the cold termination of the letter, in general the manner of writing so different from the usual style employed between them. It is not susceptibility which makes him speak thus, nor yet wounded friendship. Saints forget themselves and accept personal wounds in silence, even with joy. Their holy affections do not attach exaggerated importance to such details as these. What grieves Alphonsus is not to have discovered clearly in Mary Celeste's letter any expression of humility such as would formerly have risen spontaneously from her heart, even when confronted with still harder treatment. He would have liked to see in her not only humility in words, but that true humility which consists in having a low opinion of oneself, and of knowing how to be humble before those whose despise us. "It is this humility," he adds, "that I wish for you; I do not see it at present; this is what torments me. You will understand now the cause of my grief, the reason why I could not approve of you, as I wrote in a letter to your Mother Superior before receiving yours." He adds: "For my part, I promise to pray specially for you each morning at Mass, as long as I am worried about you. I began this morning. I prayed so much for you that Our Lord may grant you perfect humility. On your part, ask Jesus Christ the same grace for me, that I may no longer resist the voice of God, Who wishes me to belong entirely to Him. I have resisted Him enough up till now, I must no longer make any resistance; I wish truly to give myself utterly and entirely to Jesus Christ, and that is what I wish and ask for you also. But without humility neither you nor I can do anything."

In the eyes of St. Alphonsus everything depends on the

humility of Mary Celeste; both the continuation of God's graces and holiness itself are to be bought at this price. To this fundamental question of humility belongs also that of direction; added to this there was the question of Falcoia and the question of Tosquez. True obedience, particularly obedience to a director, is the daughter of humility. It attacks and kills in its germ the principal and most noxious fruit of pride, which is that of wishing to be our own masters and to depend on ourselves for the government of our life. Supported by the teaching of the saints, Alphonsus recalls that this independence constitutes the greatest danger in the spiritual life, that a saint who relies on himself runs a greater risk than an ordinary soul who follows the path of obedience; that there is no need of devils to tempt a soul who trusts in its own guidance; finally, that a hidden life lived in obedience is worth more than the greatest work done to satisfy our own will. Only God's Will is of any value, obedience alone is the sure guarantee of God's Will, such is the order established by Jesus Christ. Revelations do not dispense us from this universal law; on the contrary they double its necessity and obligation. By themselves and without the control of obedience they can never be relied on, nor can they constitute a sure rule of conduct. It belongs to the domain of authority, of the authority established by the Church, to distinguish the divine element in revelations from that human element which may be unconsciously added by the spontaneous working of the mind. Moreover, divine communications are often obscure and incomplete, because God does not wish to suppress the role of his intermediaries, nor to take from His privileged servants the trial and the merit of patient labor and humble subjection. An independent spirit opens the door to illusion and causes presumption founded on illusion. Then illusion itself, from whatever source it springs—and God has allowed this hard trial in very saintly souls—loses its dangerous character for an obedient soul; for in case of conflicting opinions all revelations, even the most

certain, must yield to obedience. The example and teaching of
St. Teresa's life confirms this doctrine. Alphonsus never desired
any other rule of conduct for himself but to seek to please God
by the accomplishment of the Divine Will, and to seek the
Divine Will in obedience. Doubtless he does not forbid just and
holy initiative, but he submits it, and will always submit it, to
obedience. He fully believes in the revelations of Mary Celeste
regarding the Institute; yet they in themselves, apart from
obedience, did not determine his entrance into the Institute.
Should a doubt come to him, it would be enough for his peace
of mind to have obeyed. Even at this time he would not hesitate
to leave the Institute rather than do anything against
obedience. Besides, he realizes that God will know how to keep
him in the Order whatever happens, and whatever man may
do, if such be His Will. Even when in the Institute he does not
aspire to be the leader nor to exercise any authority, but only
to fulfil the Divine Will as interpreted by obedience. Formerly,
in spite of Falcoia's persuasions, he refused to occupy himself
with the question of the Rules of the Scala monastery, because
his director at that time forbade it. Later on this same director
placed himself entirely in Falcoia's hands, and from that
moment Falcoia's will was for him the Will of God. He declares
that by following this path of obedience he is sure of becoming
a saint. Outside this path he warns Mary Celeste that she can
only fall over a precipice, or at least fail to attain sanctity, that
sanctity which is the sole object of all their desires and
aspirations. But to whom should Mary Celeste entrust the
guidance of her soul, her eternal destiny in fact? Would
Silvester Tosquez be the right person to direct her? Certainly
not. St. Alphonsus had nothing against Don Silvester, no bitter
feelings at all. Like Falcoia, like all of them, he had been pleased
to see him join the Institute, and had expected great things of
him. Tosquez had fallen short of their hopes, yet Alphonsus had
not even now given up all idea of reconciliation with this
impetuous spirit who was sincerely desirous of good. In his first

letter to Mary Celeste the Saint dwells with pleasure on the fact that the clouds which had gathered between himself and Tosquez seemed to be dispersed, and union between them to reign once more. He writes: "My Celeste, it is not true that I spoke of Don Silvester as being deluded; I do not remember ever to have said so." Even after the separation Alphonsus is convinced of the fundamental honesty of his former companion, who on his part always had for the Saint the greatest admiration and devotion. Nevertheless, Tosquez is not the right spiritual guide for Mary Celeste. It would be great imprudence on her part to entrust him with the direction of her soul. Even if she believed herself to be divinely enlightened, these lights must be controlled, and Silvester was not qualified to do this. Besides, when Mary Celeste received these revelations, Falcoia was her spiritual Father; he therefore, and no other, should be the judge of them. Added to all this, Tosquez's doctrine was not sound. He had fallen into error on more than one occasion. Mary Celeste, above all, should mistrust his judgment regarding herself, for, as St. Alphonsus says: "You know he thinks you greater than St. Teresa; he has sung and published your praises everywhere, he approves of all you do and depends entirely on your judgment, which is a thing, as you know, to be avoided by all spiritual directors in order to lead a soul in the way of humility. Oh, my Celeste, how greedy Don Silvester has made you lose your humility and helped you to rely on your own judgment!"

At the end of this second letter St. Alphonsus makes a further demand. Not only can Tosquez never be Mary Celeste's director, but also the Sister is asked to consider whether she cannot make a still greater sacrifice. "I have nearly finished writing," he says, "but I feel obliged to add a few words. My Celeste, forgive me if I speak plainly; do you not see how attached you are to Don Silvester, and he to you?" Certainly there is not the slightest fault, and Mary Celeste may be under the impression that the attachment comes from God, because she herself is seeking God alone. Yet is this altogether true? Is she quite sure that there is no shadow of anything human about her attachment? Even the slightest thread would be enough to bind her to earth, and to prevent her close union with God. It might also imperil, if not her salvation, at least her holiness. Therefore Alphonsus concludes thus: "Celeste, leave Don Silvester, give that sacrifice to God. I know it will be hard for you to do so, but the greater the sacrifice the harder, the swifter will be your flight towards perfection."

There now remained the most difficult and most delicate question of all, the question of Falcoia. This man of God was destined to fulfil a triple role, whose importance can neither be exaggerated nor diminished; he had become the spiritual director of St. Alphonsus; he had been Mary Celeste's director at the time of the revelations regarding the new Order; in consequence of this he had exercised, and still exercised, the right to control and direct the work which God had decided to accomplish by means of these two holy souls. In order to prevent any mistake we must bear in mind that throughout these difficulties and misunderstandings the perfect loyalty of all concerned never once failed, and this is apparent to anyone who studies attentively the documents, circumstances, etc., relating to the beginning of the Institute of the Most Holy Redeemer. There is no instance of wrong done in the moral sense of the word. God was not offended. His law was never broken, all were solely occupied in seeking His greater glory, and in the present instance this was sought by Falcoia as much as by Mary Celeste. God's designs must be fulfilled. His elect must suffer. The law of God was to be applied in all its rigor to those whom He had chosen as His instruments to found the Institute of the Most Holy Redeemer. Mary Celeste herself said: "God willed to establish His work on a foundation of crosses, trials, humiliations, scorn and suffering on the part of all those who should help in the beginning of the Institute." Alphonsus would reach his Calvary later, after passing through innumerable trials. Mary Celeste's Calvary was already at hand. Regarding the question of Falcoia, Alphonsus makes a clear distinction between the Nun's own personal direction and that of the Order. Concerning personal direction, his one desire is to see Mary Celeste return to her former guide. "Tell me, Celeste, why have you left Mgr. Falcoia?" Let us note carefully that Alphonsus' anxiety is as to the motive which resulted in this decision. Regarding the actual choice of a director he is not immovable, as we shall see later.

Certainly there is much to be said in favor of Falcoia. "He is holy," continues Alphonsus, "he is enlightened, as you yourself have often said. You are certain that he was sent to you by God, and he has guided you so well for so many years that you ought to thank God for him on bended knees. The reasons for leaving such a spiritual Father must indeed be serious ones. What evil have you discovered in his soul? What harm has he done you?" The reply is obviously in the negative; therefore Alphonsus is forced to conclude that Mary Celeste has left this spiritual Father because she could no longer bear the crushing state of humiliation in which he kept her. Yet to his mind this state was necessary, and should be an additional motive not to leave a director, but to remain faithful to him. Alphonsus' second preoccupation, closely connected with the first, is that Mary Celeste should be guided by the laws of Christian prudence in her choice of a director, and in fact in all her conduct. What presumption, what want of correspondence to grace, what a risk would it not be to trust only in her own judgment! Her great penetration of mind would enable her to find a hundred arguments to justify herself in her own eyes, and to defend her personal feelings in the matter. "You will give yourself thus a lot of trouble," says St. Alphonsus, "and all to no purpose, for it will not help you to attain sanctity. What will all those fine arguments be worth before the tribunal of Jesus Christ?" But supposing Mary Celeste to have received special lights from God, and that God Himself is guiding her. Supposing that the present peace of her soul proves the Divine origin of these lights? "Even so," replies Alphonsus, "all that may be an illusion; history furnishes us with many such examples, even in the case of truly holy souls. There is every ground to fear illusion when the supposed lights meet with the disapproval of the spiritual Father. The approbation of the latter does not necessarily prove the Divine origin of the revelations, but it renders them harmless, whatever be their origin. Neither is the disapproval of the spiritual Father a certain proof that the communications are not divine, but it constitutes an unfavorable supposition and obliges the soul to suspect the communications and not to allow her life to be governed by them. Obedience remains the only sure road, the only path approved by Jesus Christ." Such is the law of which Alphonsus insistently reminds Mary Celeste. And how does the Saint conclude?

First of all he demands from his correspondent humility and submission. Here it is a question of the entire problem not only of personal direction, but also of the government of the work, of which latter we shall speak later. "My dear Celeste, listen to me, humble yourself. If you consent to humble yourself, God will enlighten you. Obey your Superiors; thus you will be sure of not going astray." He then spoke of his great desire to see Mary Celeste return to Falcoia for direction, yet always provided that she has no legitimate and serious reasons for leavening him. "Falcoia is holy, he is good. Do not imagine that he bears any ill-feeling towards you," says Alphonsus; "if you submit humbly to him you will surely be dearer to him than before." But this solution seems impossible to Mary Celeste; what is she to do? To give up all desires, all preconceived ideas, and to accept blindly God's Will. Then she must pray, ask advice, and without hesitation act on the advice given. This is the road of Christian prudence, in which all are safe. Let us quote the Saint's own words: "At least resign yourself to accept God's Will, whatever it may be, and in this spirit of resignation pray earnestly, otherwise your prayers will be of no avail. All your reasoning will come from passions and all your revelations and lights will be illusions. If you believe neither me nor Falcoia, at least ask advice of some other disinterested person. Seek help, do not walk on blindly towards your own ruin. Take counsel, not in order to be confirmed in your ideas, but to learn the truth and to follow it loyally."

"The truth!" Alphonsus was therefore certain that the road he had first indicated was the right one, and if Mary Celeste would follow it she would meet with his approval. From the question of personal direction Alphonsus passes to that of the direction of the work. Here he is on familiar ground. He is treating of a problem the full scope of which is known to him. It is not therefore surprising that he should speak with absolute authority regarding its solution. St. Alphonsus does not deny the outstanding part played by Sister Mary Celeste's revelations in the foundation of the Institute, nor the fact that these revelations have formed the basis of the Rule, both for the Nuns and for the missionaries. Only he affirms, and Mary Celeste agrees, that the revelations, like all revelations, must be freed from every human element, and that the Rule required explanation and completion. How therefore was the legislation of the Institute to be established in the present and secured for the future? It would be perfectly just for each member of the Institute to write down his personal opinion regarding the points under discussion. But by what means was unity to be brought out of this diversity, so that one law be established and accepted by all? Let us hasten to say that later on, when all discordant elements had been eliminated, Alphonsus' ideas, built on the revelations of Mary Celeste, which he faithfully respected, alone prevailed on every point. He therefore remained the sole legislator of the Institute, as he is also its divinely appointed head and founder, as Mary Celeste had prophesied. Could a stronger proof be given in favor of the method of obedience followed by Alphonsus? Its results are assured of the divine blessing, for God's Will triumphs over all difficulties and thus brings His works to perfection. But we have not yet reached that stage, and in the meantime there were conflicting opinions to be reckoned with. How were they to be reconciled? Alphonsus refuses to arbitrate himself, urging his inexperience of community life. The others, with one exception, have all had a certain experience. Should they then, as Sister Mary Celeste suggests, each give their opinion and make mutual concessions? This would be lawful were it only a question of honor or personal comfort and convenience, but in matters concerning the glory of God, the form of government in which to establish for ever His new Order and assure its vitality, there could be nothing but obedience and the consent of all to abide by the decisions of one arbitrator; nothing less than this can induce one person to yield to another in consideration of the grave and sacred interests involved. "But why," says Mary Celeste, "in that case do you not have recourse to him whom you chose as Superior?" Now this was the very man whose ideas regarding the new Institute were false, and who was soon to leave it. His slight experience of Community life had caused him to be named provisional Superior. For the time being the others could obey him in all that had already been agreed upon, but to accept new rules manufactured by him was out of the question. Alphonsus declares that such a thing had never been thought of. "Thus," says the Saint, "the sole means of establishing everything on a solid basis is to place ourselves in the hands of one person to whom we can expose our ideas with the firm intention of following his decisions blindly in the future." This sole arbitrator must be a man of experience, who understands community life, missions, and other spiritual exercises and has a knowledge of apostolic work; an enlightened and spiritual man, who has sufficient authority to decide all points of discussion. "This is also," continues Alphonsus, "the best and only means of maintaining among us that spirit of union and holy charity without which our work cannot advance. You have said so yourself, and I have preached it by every means in my power." Where is the Order or Congregation which has not been established thus: by the dependence of all on one director? One single example to the contrary had at first struck St. Alphonsus, that of the Teresian reform, but there again it had become necessary in the end to have recourse to Father Jerome Gratian, who finally drew up the Constitutions which were accepted by all.

"Necessity therefore obliges us to have recourse to one arbitrator, who shall decide every question. That," says St. Alphonsus, "is a recognized truth for any reasonable being." "But," he continues, "there are people who say, 'Yes, let us have one arbitrator, but not Falcoia.' Why this exclusion?" asks the Saint; and he adds rather pointedly, "Has there been some special revelation from God telling us to depend on anybody rather than on Falcoia?" Alphonsus, having clearly defined the line of conduct from which they ought not to swerve, and having denied the right of the provisional Superior to make new rules, declares: "For my part I shall obey Falcoia in all that he decides. He is my director, and also the only possible director for our work." He then develops his ideas on this subject and brings unanswerable arguments to support his opinion. "If we do not wish to act by passion," he says, "why should we seek any arbitrator other than Falcoia?" The Saint then brings forward the supernatural reasons which point to Falcoia as being providentially intended for this role. In the first place there are the revelations of Sister Mary Columba, which go as far as to call Falcoia "the principal head of the work"—according to her Alphonsus is also the head of the Institute, but under the direction of Falcoia. Mary Celeste questions the reality of Mary Columba's revelations. St. Alphonsus does not formally deny them, and in the present circumstances this fact is significant. Mary Columba was not nearly so level-headed as Mary Celeste; this, however, in St. Alphonsus' opinion, need not prevent her from being a saint.

Not wishing Mary Celeste to exaggerate the importance of her role as intermediary between Heaven and earth, Alphonsus reminds her that other people besides herself have had divine revelations concerning the new Institute, notably Falcoia himself, who on this account had tried for so many years, both at Naples and at home, to establish this Institute. Nevertheless Alphonsus assigns to Mary Celeste's revelations a place apart, not only as being certain compared with those of Mary Columba, but also as being more important than those vouchsafed to others. Although his own conduct was not based on these revelations, but rather on the foundation of obedience, yet it is none the less true that these revelations were the providential starting point of his vocation, and also the foundation of the union of his soul with that of Mary Celeste—a union to which, as we have seen, he attaches great importance. Now these revelations constitute an unanswerable argument in favor of Falcoia. They both establish and define his role, as St. Alphonsus with marvelous precision proceeds to demonstrate.

"In the first place," he says, "the fact that Falcoia was your director would be sufficient indication that God intended him to bear the responsibility of the work. He therefore, and no other, should approve and explain the lights you have received; just as St. Teresa's confessor, because he was her director at the time when she received the revelation of the reform, became in consequence the director of the whole work of the Reform."

Mary Celeste was not of a contrary opinion. In a letter which St. Alphonsus had providentially kept, and which he offered to return to her, she said to him: "Be at peace and abandon everything to the judgment of our Father, whom God has placed in the work, and let us all depend on him."

"But," continues St. Alphonsus, "even were there no supernatural indications, since we must choose one head as being the only sure way of establishing our Rules and preserving harmony among us, why not choose Falcoia as this sole arbitrator? Besides, it is not a question of choosing him, but of not leaving him. The choice was made long before the arrival of don Silvester on the scene. At that time we thought only of Falcoia and relied on him in everything. This choice was, and still is, a wise one. Falcoia has in his favor age, experience, knowledge and an enlightened mind, practical experience of community life, of mission work, of studies, and even worldly knowledge. This choice was, and is, necessary. Where could we find another priest uniting so many qualifications, all of which are indispensable for the direction of our work?"

Therefore what great responsibility Mary Celeste would incur if she opposed this union with Falcoia, especially should she persist in her opposition! It might even cause the ruin of the work which came from God, not from her. It is true that God could easily save His Order in spite of her, in spite of them all; He could even use her desertion as a means of advancing the work, for where there is no question of revelation? the road to Rome becomes smoother and pontifical approbation is more easily obtained. In the meantime, however, what would become of her soul if before the tribunal of Jesus Christ she has to bear the heavy burden of having opposed the Divine plans? As for himself, Alphonsus declares that if they should exclude him from the Institute, as had been suggested, he would only have merited it, and would be quite resigned as long as he be not excluded from obedience. Besides, his fate depends on God, not on men, and he believes himself truly called to the Institute, because the voice of obedience told him so.

"But you," he cries in a final exhortation, "I see you on the edge of a precipice, and from the depths of my heart I grieve for you if you do not change your mind."

Then he implores her to cease all resistance to Falcoia, and to submit to him at least as general director of the house. Total humility, total abnegation of her own judgment, a return if possible to Falcoia's direction, in any case complete submission to Falcoia in all that concerns the direction of the work, such are the demands made by St. Alphonsus. He knew them to be hard in themselves, hard also in the terms in which he proposes them. He thought himself obliged, however, to speak thus. Besides, his heart was so torn with anguish in the face of the dangers which he believed to threaten the soul so dear to him that, in spite of his great self-control, his words from time to time bear the stamp of the vehement supernatural emotion which gave rise to them.

We are now about to hear the reply of one saint to another.

CHAPTER XVI
MARY CELESTE'S REPLY

T. ALPHONSUS neither expected nor desired a written reply to the two letters he had sent to Mary Celeste. Fortunately for us, however, she answered the first letter; and it is to this circumstance that we owe the admirable epistle we have just analyzed in the preceding chapter. Perhaps the Venerable Sister saw in this second letter merely an echo of the persistent and unkind reports of which she was the victim. However that may be, she only replied by a short note, thanking Alphonsus for his charity, having fully determined to respond to his appeal in the one way he desired—by actions rather than by words. This indeed was the response for which the Saint longed; only thus could he have the certainty that this great soul was not straying from the path of holiness Let us hear what he said to her at the very beginning of his second letter:

"Celeste, my very dear Sister in Jesus Christ and in Mary. ... I beg of you to read these lines, and do then whatever God may inspire you to do. But read them with an open mind, without seeking a reply to what you are reading; because if you are all the time wishing to contradict, you will easily find many arguments with which to answer me, but in this way you will never find the truth. Therefore read these pages, then pray for three days, but with a mind wholly resigned and detached, and without writing to me or preparing in any way to do so; then act as you think best."

Mary Celeste replied as St. Alphonsus desired, by actions. This is proved by a document which is in itself an act; a letter written by Mary Celeste three weeks later. It is not addressed to Alphonsus, but to don Peter Romano, one of Alphonsus' companions, a faithful adherent of Falcoia, and confessor of the Monastery of Scala.

In all probability, the Sister prayed over St. Alphonsus' letter not only three days, but those three whole weeks, before writing the letter we are about to quote. She begins in a somewhat dramatic striking manner. This is not surprising, considering the tragic circumstances in which it was written. We must not see in this introduction either pose or affectation. Mary Celeste was sincerely herself, and the courage and serenity she shows in the midst of the troubles which surrounded her are sufficient proof of the reality of her words:

"Praised be the Name of Our Lord Jesus Christ!

"Very Honored Father in Our Lord,

"In the Name of the Father and of the Son and of the Holy Ghost. After much prayer, I take up my pen in the name of God, in order to give expression to my last thoughts; from henceforth I shall never again open my mouth on this subject, nor allow any further ideas about it to enter my mind. I call God to witness, it is in His Presence, and in the presence of all creation, that I bear true witness to the state of my own conscience."

This opening is not intended to be theatrical. It is a serious testimony to truth, for Mary Celeste has realized that the total resignation to the will of God, so much insisted on by Alphonsus, and which he considered more important than anything else, must be a true death to self, particularly death to her own judgment, because that is the rock on which even the greatest efforts towards sanctity are liable to suffer shipwreck. For this reason, Mary Celeste looks upon this letter as a sort of "will"—hence the expression, "my last thoughts"—not only her last wishes, for she has no intention of having any personal wishes. She goes even further, and says, "her last thoughts," for it is a question of reaching down to the root of self-will, which is one's own judgment; this she intends to uproot entirely. She will say what she feels herself obliged to say, to her confessor, after which she will retire into silence—silence both exterior and interior, as if she were already in her grave. Not that she no longer wishes to think, but her thoughts will be of Jesus Christ alone, as He is her only Love.

In order to understand what follows, we must realize that in all the renunciations of which Mary Celeste is about to speak, she intends that renunciation to be made to the uttermost; to give up all personal attachment, self-seeking, personal pleasure, all interior joy or outward manifestation of self. She intends to die to herself, but not give up living in Jesus Christ and by Jesus Christ. She rejects everything that could in the slightest degree impede her flight towards Jesus, every obstacle to her own death in Jesus Christ.

Mary Celeste continues:

"Therefore before Our Lord Jesus Christ, my Judge and my Creator, I reject and detest all illusions that I may have had, either lights, spiritual visions, revelations, whether general or particular, regarding the new Institute or Rules, or concerning the Brothers of the Congregation, or the Sisters of this Community, and I wish to have no further knowledge of anything, whether good or bad. I renounce my own judgment, even when reasonable, I renounce also my will and all interior lights. I renounce my very self and all that belongs to me, and all the things of the world. I make this resignation both interiorly and exteriorly, with the intention of never again caring for these things, however strong may be the inward or outward impulse I may experience. I will neither accept such impulsions, nor notice them nor make them known. From this time forward, the sole object of my thoughts and affections shall be Jesus Crucified, the Holy Gospel and our Holy Faith. I wish to imprint this doctrine on my heart, to take Jesus Crucified for my guide, my rule of life and pledge of security.

With all my strength, I shall meditate on this night and day, for that is the sure way to heaven. My sole desire is to attain to my last end, which is to unite myself as far as possible to my only and sovereign God, and to please Him alone."

This is indeed the total indifference, the absolute detachment from creatures, particularly from herself and her own judgment, and from all that could nourish pride and self-will, this is the heroic abnegation of self, which St. Alphonsus required and expected of Mary Celeste.

She then goes on to make an examination of conscience on certain points. She announces two, and treats of three, from which all her words and actions proceeded. What is the meaning of this examination? "I solemnly declare," she says, "that my intention is not to explain the motives by which I have acted, but to speak thus openly in order to bear witness to the Truth." In other words, she does not seek to justify herself in the opinion of others, but she declares simply that she has acted uprightly according to her conscience. She was certainly justified in saying this to her confessor, so that he could judge of the state of her soul. First comes the important and serious question of Falcoia's direction. "The first point is concerned with the motives which induced me to leave my former director, the most worthy Mgr. Falcoia. Apart from the lights which I received for the past year, and of which I took no further notice, neither allowed them to influence me during the whole of that time, there were three motives and causes which led to this decision, making me act in accordance with the lights received, not because of these lights, nor though I have believed them, but because of certain reasons which, quite apart from these lights, I had in the depths of my soul.

"The first motive was that, for many years, in spite of the frankness with which I laid bare the state of my soul to him, this Father always remained in a state of uncertainty and perplexity regarding the paths by which I was being led, and this prevented me from being sure of the way I had to follow.

Therefore I judged that Our Lord did not wish to enlighten me by means of this director, as to whether I was progressing in the right way or not.

"The second motive is as follows: By reason of a certain infusion of spiritual grace, or in consequence of an extraordinary impulsion of pure simplicity, which came from God, I was sometimes moved to speak without realizing that I did so and without weighing my words. Any words or actions such as these were taken by my director in the wrong sense. God evidently allowed him to misunderstand the spirit from which they proceeded, therefore his replies and reflections, being contrary to this spirit of simplicity, hindered the freedom and simplicity of my intercourse with him, and caused me much disturbance, and, because he had all my confidence and all my esteem, I suffered on this account. Above all, it seemed clear to me that a director who, by God's permission, could not penetrate into the inmost recesses of my soul, would be unable to lead me along the path marked out for me, where alone I could find peace of soul. I felt that he forced me to do what was beyond me, and this state of effort and strain, in which, with the best intentions, he kept me, placed an obstacle between us, causing me great sorrow.

"Third motive: Seeing him always in a state of perplexity regarding me, I told him the thoughts I had had on this subject, and asked him to allow me to seek the advice of some other priest, particularly in important matters. He disapproved of such a desire, however, attributing it to pride. Thereupon I had to resign myself to live always in a state of sorrow, because of the things he said to me, but I never dared to transgress his orders nor infringe them in the slightest degree. Then, when it pleased Our Lord to inaugurate the work of the Institute, my affliction of soul increased. Because of certain lights which were granted to me regarding this work, I was publicly censured by the Father before the whole Community, and among the Brothers of the Congregation. At a time when the greatest possible peace and concord were necessary, in order to inspire confidence and esteem for the work, in the hearts of those who were about to associate themselves with it, he went about raising doubts, difficulties, and opposition, which gave rise to disunion and mistrust among those who were to enter the Institute. Therefore, because the work had already been approved as coming from God, I resolved for my own peace of soul, and also to ensure liberty of action to the Brothers of the Congregation, to leave this director, although he was a holy man, and to have recourse in future to some other guide. I did this after much consideration, and with the pure intention of seeking God in peace of soul.

"Now, however, I renounce these same judgments and reasons, no longer desiring to bring them forward, or to speak of them; and if the above-mentioned motives were wrong, although I thought them to be right, nevertheless I now detest and repudiate them. Henceforth my only guide will be pure faith, together with the evangelical virtues which faith inspires, and I will no longer think of anything else."

We can hardly believe that St. Alphonsus was not satisfied with this reply. Mary Celeste did not leave Falcoia out of caprice, nor through motives of pride or insufficient humility. In making this decision, she did not take into account the supernatural lights received. She prayed loyally to know God's Will. The motives which dictated her decision are just ones, or at least she believes them to be so, and this is what matters most, for neither directors nor those directed can pretend to infallibility. All that is asked of us is to do our best and leave the rest to God. All who act thus can be at peace. Again we say, as before, that this principle of conduct justifies Falcoia in the present case as well as his penitent. In the face of Mary Celeste's strong arguments, let us hope that Falcoia remembered what he himself had written concerning Mazzini, on July 9th of the preceding year. "There comes a time when a change of director becomes necessary. Several times St. Teresa made use of this privilege, and I myself would never have entered the Society of 'Pii Operaii' had I not followed her example." He demanded that Mary Celeste should make a vow to address herself to him only for the direction of her soul. This demand finds its excuse in Falcoia's desire to establish unity and peace of mind, for the general good of the work. Nevertheless, Mary Celeste's conduct in refusing to bind herself thus can only be commended. An illustrious example of a similar case springs to our mind. St. Jane Chantal had for her first director a holy and clever religious, who, nevertheless, wished to bind her to his direction by four vows of this kind, one of which was to speak of her conscience only to him and never to leave him. In her inexperience, the Saint made these vows, which created difficulties in her first relations with St. Francis de Sales. The latter, when he was informed of the state of affairs, brushed them aside, the vows, as being of no account, saying: "Promises of that kind only destroy one's peace of conscience." St. Teresa was certainly of the same opinion, for, anticipating the decisions of the Church, she protests against those Superiors who consider it a breach of regularity and almost an insult to the Community should a Nun ask for another confessor, or even to speak to a priest other than the one appointed as regular confessor.

Mary Celeste's decision, in any case, was not of a nature to diminish the esteem in which Falcoia had always been held as a director. For, again to quote St. Teresa: "God leads souls by many different paths, and a director cannot be expected to know them all." As for the desire to take as guide, or rather Rule of life, the Gospel, pure faith, and the evangelical virtues, Alphonsus could do nothing but commend this: for, in a letter which he himself had written to Mary Celeste, he praises Falcoia for having "followed the light of the Gospel, which" adds the Saint, "is worth more than all your lights and his own." In doing this, the Sister was but conforming to the advice given by St. John of the Cross. "He who would obtain visions or revelations would, it seems to me, insult Our Lord, if he did not keep his eyes fixed solely on Christ, and God would have the right to say to him, 'You have here My beloved Son in Whom I am well pleased,' listen to Him, and do not seek new modes of learning, for in Him and by Him I have told and revealed to you all that you can desire or ask, giving Him to you as Brother, Master, Friend, as Ransom and Reward."

Falcoia will himself write later to St. Alphonsus, advising the Sisters to take no account of revelations, but to be guided solely by the maxims of Faith (letter of March 17th, 1735). Finally, Mary Celeste was not without a guide. She spoke freely to the confessor of the Community, who was a friend and follower of Falcoia, thereby proving that she was in no way prejudiced. Besides, St. Alphonsus teaches in his book: "The Holy Religious" (c. xviii), that a Nun can, in all security, follow the direction of the confessor of the Monastery, being at the same time free to make use of any other help granted to her by Providence. In the tragic circumstances which we are about to relate, Mary Celeste will consult her own brother, a prudent and holy religious, and the choice will be a wise one; in the first place because it is necessary, she having no one else to consult; in the second place, because, judging by the counsel given and accepted, this was certainly not a case in which to apply the Gospel maxim: "A man's enemies are those of his own household." The question may arise as to what would have happened if Mary Celeste, before the crisis of this trouble, or in the midst of it, had placed herself under the direction of St. Alphonsus. To our mind such a question is useless. Alphonsus would not have accepted without Falcoia's consent, and who can say whether the latter would have accorded it? Alphonsus would not have wished to step into Falcoia's shoes, as it were, and Mary Celeste would never have asked it of him. Moreover, a little reflection will give us the key to this enigma: all concerned were seeking only the Divine Will, therefore this Will was accomplished, not only in the sense that God's Will must always be done, but in that perfect fulfilment of the Divine Will which takes place when no obstacles are raised in its path; and the Will of God was, in this case, that those taking part in this work should suffer, and suffer again and again. Sister Mary Celeste's second declaration concerns her own course of conduct during the difficulties which had arisen regarding the new Institute. "I believed that the orders revealed to me by Our Lord were authentic, therefore, urged on by a clear interior light, I thought myself obliged to make known the communications I had received, and to explain these things to him whom God had appointed for the execution of His work. I did not think it pride to cooperate with God, as it would have been in the beginning, when it was not a question of supporting the work, but only of finding out whether it came from God or not. Therefore, just as formerly I believed myself bound to be silent, I now considered myself bound to speak, to show zeal for God's honor without being afraid, and to make God's interests my own, not for my sake but for His. In consequence, I felt obliged to resist and protest against all that might prevent, hinder, or spoil the free accomplishment of God's work. For this reason, I showed what I felt and expressed my opinion to those persons whom with good intentions, no doubt, but without sufficient reason, were opposed to it; the more so, as it was easy to see in this opposition the work of the devil, who did all in his power to raise obstacles and to cause disturbance. I have never sought esteem or honor for myself, for thanks be to God I have had a horror of such things all my life. At present I repudiate and detest all the motives and acts just enumerated. I efface from my memory all these reasons which I formerly thought to be right. I look upon them as so many errors on my part, and will think of them no more."

Let us note here that Mary Celeste gives due honor to Falcoia's providential mission for it is evidently he to whom she refers by the words: "whom God had appointed for the execution of His work." Moreover, we shall see that she fully submitted on this point to the decisions of the Bishop of Castellamare. It might be of interest also to recall, that in 1743, when St. Alphonsus sent Father Villani to Rome to beg the approbation of Pope Benedict XIV for the Rule of his Congregation, the arrangement of certain articles in the Rule had to be changed, in order to obtain this approbation. In consequence, quite unintentionally, the first order of things, as indicated by Mary Celeste was re-established; and thus the Redemptorist Rule, in the form approved by the Holy See, was rendered more conformable to the original version made by the Venerable Sister.

Mary Celeste's third declaration has reference to the attitude of the Community towards don Silvester. "I was opposed to their behaviour on certain points," she says, "because I thought it neither just nor right, for reasons which I shall explain fully here, and in all Christian sincerity I could not approve of their attitude, because:

(1) It proceeded from troubles and contention raised by the devil;

(2) Because it was too violent and contrary to prudence. They did not reflect on the consequences it might have on the work, or on certain people;

(3) All this was not the work of disinterested persons;

(4) Because the actions of those same people were governed by passion, at every instant they spoke unkindly of the person in question. Such cannot be the effect produced by zeal for God, which engenders charity towards one's neighbor. True zeal would extenuate rather than exaggerate even the serious offences of others.

(5) Because even his simplest words and actions were interpreted in the worst possible sense; words and actions which had been said and done in my presence and with quite another meaning from that ascribed to them.

(6) Because these rumors were spread abroad indiscriminately out of anger, and far more than was necessary to attain the end these people had in view, and which they said to be a just one.

(7) Because they sought to penetrate the depths of this soul and its

motives, which should be left to God, Who alone is able to judge. Man cannot judge another without sinning.

(8) Because they who tried to judge thus were poor ignorant women, like myself; we cannot possibly discern what is evil, what is sin, and what is virtue, and this man whom they were judging was a learned man.

(9) Because these criticisms were made concerning faults of weakness and inadvertence, from which no man, however perfect, is exempt in this life.

(10) Because between this man and ourselves, communications regarding things of the soul had taken place; he told us frankly what was good in him and what was bad. He expressed clearly what was in his mind, because he thought himself to be dealing with sensible people, to whom one can tell everything without giving a wrong impression. He told us all, even the favors he had received from God, while always protesting that they belonged to God alone; in the same way he told us his faults, his weakness, his misery, and we have seen him weep over his sins, we have also seen him overcome with fear, and that before us all. On our part, we treated him in the same frank way, speaking of our faults and of our virtues.

(11) Because the attitude of these people resulted in trouble, anxiety and suspicion. They caused disunion in the monastery and provoked discussion. Those who tried to excuse what the others exaggerated were treated as rebels, and as being deluded; from hence arose persecution and scandal.

"Therefore, having examined all these things, my soul condemned them as not coming from God. While others acted freely, in the supposition that they were doing justice to the truth; my soul, on the contrary, looked upon these things as being against my conscience, and in consequence I was not able to share in their feelings. Many a time, withdrawing myself before God from all attraction, inclination, interest, prejudice and personal satisfaction, I have weighed these things in the balance of Truth, praying in order to see how I ought to act in conscience, and I have never found that I would do well to share in such feelings.

"Finally, I noted this, that while they suspected their neighbor of not following the right path, they did nothing to help him, not even recommending him to God in prayer as they had formerly done when they considered him a benefactor. Moreover, they pronounced his name with horror, as if speaking of an excommunicated person, they always spoke of him scornfully, and went so far as to say that God may have helped and enlightened His Church by means of the lights granted to these Nuns regarding the character of this man. This seemed to me to be the height of presumption on our part, to place so much trust in our ignorant ideas, without fearing in the least to have made a rash judgment against our poor neighbor, who was perhaps more pleasing to God than we. From all these reflections which I made in order to regulate my conduct, and not to allow myself to fall into illusion, I concluded that these dissensions were purely the work of the devil to overthrow the work of God and to bring confusion on us all by sowing quarrels and disunion among us. I thought it necessary to examine what was true and what was false in all these things, so as not to err on one side or on the other. I was anxious to do nothing prejudicial to God's honor, nor to people, nor to the work of God. These are the motives which have influenced most of my actions and resolutions up till now."

Sister Mary Celeste judged it necessary to examine what was true and what was false in the passionate accusations made by her companions against Tosquez. She acknowledged, or at least implied, that don Silvester had been wrong, but she was opposed to what was said against him on certain points. Who can find fault with her reasoning, and her conduct? Falcoia himself wrote to Alphonsus: "Celeste's letter is very reasonable, I have read it and return it to you." It is more than probable that the heated arguments of the Community had done much to cause St. Alphonsus' anxiety. This letter must have reassured him, and the Nun's conduct still more so, for on being asked, she promises to break off all communication with Tosquez.

There still remains to be considered in Mary Celeste's letter an heroic act of total self-abnegation and an heroic act of humility.

The act of abnegation is as follows:

"From this day, however, I repudiate all these motives, all this reasoning, all my actions. For love of God, I renounce my own judgment, my will and all that belongs to me. I renounce all lights both natural and supernatural, without seeking to know whether they come from God or from the devil. I renounce also that interior peace and security which I experienced in the spiritual favors granted to me. I renounce all supernatural light, in spite of the fact that my path and the revelations I received were always founded on the light of holy faith. Now I do not even accept these lights, I renounce them with my whole mind. Certainly I never desired lights nor visions, nor spiritual consolations. I did not seek them. On the contrary, I sought to avoid them when it was possible to do so. I even begged Our Lord not to send me consolations and satisfactions, either spiritual or temporal, and now with all my heart I renounce and detest them; I renounce all the revelations and visions I may have received, either of things in general or particular, whether they came from God, the devil, or from my own mind."

After the act of abnegation follows the act of humility:

"I am sorry and regret to have been displeased that Mgr. Falcoia and other people should have discredited my words in public and treated me as being deluded at a time when I thought it unwise to do so. Although this displeasure did not come from any desire for my own honor of grief at my dishonor, but because it seemed to me that they were acting against God's interests; but now I detest and repudiate an erroneous zeal where, under good intentions, self-love may have been concealed. I confess that I have been wrong, for I ought to accept whatever comes to me, which is only just and right. As regards the honor and glory of God, He is able to defend what is His. He has no need of me and can do all Himself. If He used me as His instrument. He did so for His own unfathomable ends. This instrument, because it is very imperfect, weak and full of evil, can only be an obstacle to His mercy and His honor. Let this bad and unworthy instrument be shamed, let it be punished, let it be crucified, so that the honor of God, stolen by the instrument, may be re-established in that degree of purity which belongs to God alone. For this reason, as you are my confessor, I lay on your conscience the duty of imploring Mgr. Falcoia and the Community, also the Brothers of the Congregation, to be good enough to grant my request by making known to all my imperfections and my sins, by publishing everywhere the fact that I am deluded and mistaken, also by making known any other faults of mine they may see, such as want of virtue. I beg them to do this task out of charity and love of Our Lord Jesus Christ, also in order to make restitution for the glory and honor of which He has been deprived through me. I shall take pleasure in hearing myself thus spoken of until my death, and even on the day of judgment, may they only know these things of me, for I seek to please God alone. My mind is already in peace and I fear nothing more, following with love, by means of the precepts of the Gospel, in the steps of my Savior.

"Please make this letter known to everybody, particularly to Mgr. Santore, to Mgr. Falcoia, and to the Brothers of the Congregation. I wish for nothing and renounce all. I shall no longer fear illusions nor deceptions, as I seek only Jesus and Him crucified. Seated at the foot of the Cross, I shall weep over my faults, yet with great peace of soul, because the infinite beauty and mercy of Our Lord will cover my infirmities. My heart will always sing, and my sorrow shall be changed into joy when reflected in the true light of God. I desired the perfection of others, but unless I can remove the beam that is in my own eye, how can I take away the mote that is in my brother's eye, as Our Lord Himself has said? I desired God's glory and I have mourned and wept because others hindered it, but blinded as I am, I did not first desire that His glory should be realized in me. I shall no longer act thus, I will follow Him and will glorify Him solely, in myself, and what belongs to Him will never be taken away from Him.

"Pray for me and bless me. I respectfully kiss your feet.

"Written on April 20th, 1733.

Your very humble servant in Our Lord,

Sister Mary Celeste of the Holy Desert."

Again we say, these are not empty words, but true words. St. Alphonsus' letter to Mary Celeste is that of a saint, Mary Celeste's reply is the reply of a saint. Alphonsus can console his anguished heart. Mary Celeste is now more than ever on the road to the highest sanctity.

CHAPTER XVII
THE SUPREME TRIAL

ARY CELESTE'S supreme trial is now at hand. Sad though it is to relate the events which follow, we cannot suppress them.

The friends of God would be too happy in this world if the wicked alone were allowed to cause them suffering. A generous soul could not be saddened by such persecution, for it is both logical and honorable, even at times consoling. But the suffering which comes from good people, from servants of God, from our own loved ones, is what causes the bitterest sorrow and affliction. Mary Celeste was to drink this bitter chalice to the dregs. This will not surprise any except those who are ignorant of human nature and of the ways of God's Providence. Our Lord Himself has predicted to His faithful servant that this very suffering was to be the condition of her resemblance to Him, and the pledge of the success of His work, of which she was to be the instrument.

First of all the spiritual Father ordered the Superioress to forbid Mary Celeste to receive Holy Communion, which was the Life of her soul, and also to forbid all the Nuns to speak to her. This last injunction was formulated because there were in the Convent several Sisters who, following the dictates of their conscience, defended Mary Celeste, and they were not to be allowed to encourage her with their sympathy.

Finally, as had previously happened, she was banished to a distant part of the Convent, so that she should be isolated from everyone, and particularly from her own two sisters. Moreover, she was forbidden to write to anyone or to go to the parlor, even to speak of spiritual matters. All this was done in order to force her to recognize herself in the wrong and to bring her to repentance.

The Sister, believing her imperfections to be the cause of all the trouble in the Community and an obstacle to God's work, humbly submitted and cast herself at the feet of her Lord. Her interior desolation was still further augmented, as she no longer heard the voice of her Divine Spouse, which had so often supported her through previous trials. In her Autobiography she says: "In my former tribulations I had still the encouragement of Our Lord, of the Nuns, and of my spiritual Father; whereas now, not only did God fail to enlighten me, but my soul was plunged in darkness and aridity. The most painful thing of all was to see myself persecuted by those dear to me, by my most intimate friends, and thwarted by real servants of God, who did it out of zeal, thinking they were working for His glory."

A physical weakness resulted from all this suffering of mind, so that she fainted several times and was consumed with fever. Unable in this state to take any food, she grew weaker and weaker, until she was too feeble to rise from her bed. The Infirmarian was not sent to her, nor did the Superior, who did not believe her to be ill, visit her. Her own sisters were forbidden to come, and she lay there, sick and ill, without help of any kind. To add to her misery, one or other of the Sisters who were opposed to her would visit her from time to time in order to threaten her with severe penances if she should still refuse to return to her former director.

Seeing herself abandoned by all and a prey to anguish of body and soul, the poor Sister cast herself into the arms of Divine Providence, resolving to cling to Our Lord by faith alone, and to wait patiently until it should please Him to disperse the dark clouds which surrounded her.

Oh, holy Mother, henceforth when we think of Scala, it will not only be to see in spirit the apparitions in the Sacred Host, or the grotto in which Our Lady spoke such beautiful words to

St. Alphonsus, but to contemplate these two Gethsemani: first, the poor hermitage where St. Alphonsus saw himself abandoned by all; and secondly, that lonely cell in which you were kept prisoner, deprived of all help and consolation, and from where out of the depths of your annihilation, and through your prayers, the double Institute of the Most Holy Redeemer was to rise triumphant!

It entered into God's designs, as Mary Celeste herself assures us, that she should leave Scala. To bring this about God made use of her youngest sister, who, to quote Mary Celeste's own words, "was not as yet very far advanced in the virtues of her holy state; so that when she saw the sufferings and ill-treatment inflicted on her sister she became frightened and upset, especially so when some of the Sisters imprudently told her that still more severe penances would be imposed on her sister should the latter persist in her refusal to be directed by Mgr. Falcoia." On hearing these words poor Sister Mary Evangelista, who could not go to the help of her imprisoned sister and saw herself surrounded by spies to prevent her doing so, sought out her eldest sister and informed her that she would no longer remain in the Convent and wished to return home. Mary Illuminata did all she could to calm the young girl's fears, telling her that suffering must be borne for the love of God, Who would help Mary Celeste now as He had done in the past. Nothing, however, could turn the youngest sister from her purpose. She went to the Superioress and told her that she would rather live in the world than remain in a convent where such things were allowed to happen. She was so insistent that the Superioress was obliged to write to Don Crostarosa informing him of his daughter's desire to return home. On receipt of this letter the old man naturally wished to know the reasons which had dictated it. He therefore sent one of his sons, who was a Jesuit priest, to the monastery. This latter was a man of great learning and virtue and much esteemed in the Society of Jesus. His father was anxious above all that he should find out what motive was urging his youngest daughter. He desired his son to speak first of all to the two elder sisters and find out from them the cause of so sudden a resolution on the part of the youngest.

Don Crostarosa tenderly loved his daughters, but he was now over eighty and very infirm, so that, unable to go himself to the Convent, he thought the next best thing was to send his son to make a thorough inquiry into the matter.

On arriving at Scala the Jesuit went straight to the parlor and asked for the Superioress. He told her that, as the brother of the three Nuns, he had been sent by their father to inquire into the reasons which made his young sister wish to leave the Monastery. In consequence he asked permission to see each of his sisters privately. The Superioress and her two companions refused his request, saying that he could not see his sisters in private, as the Rule obliged two witnesses to be present at such an interview. The Father then began to suspect that there was some hidden motive for this refusal, and said that in his quality of confessor he considered himself dispensed from this point of the Rule. The Nuns, however, would not agree to this, and the Jesuit left the Monastery saying that he intended to go straight to the Bishop in order to obtain the necessary permission. On hearing this the Superioress immediately wrote to Mgr. Santoro imploring him not to grant this permission, as in the present circumstances it would not be expedient for the Nuns to speak to their relatives.

Father Crostarosa went, as he had said, to the Bishop and explained to him the object of his visit to the Monastery, stating also that it was absolutely necessary for him to see his sisters in private, since his father had sent him from Naples to find out why his youngest sister, a professed Nun, wished to leave the Monastery. This, he added, was a serious matter, and he begged the Bishop to allow him to go to the confessional, where he could speak to his sisters, and they to him, with perfect freedom. The Bishop, however, having received the

CHAPTER XVII: THE SUPREME TRIAL

Superioress' note, refused this request, saying that it was not the custom for a strange confessor to go to the confessional, and that they could not give special privileges to particular sisters. The Jesuit now saw that some grave motive lay behind this refusal, and answered promptly: "Very well, then I shall start for Naples and address myself to Cardinal Pignatelli and obtain his permission." He then withdrew. Hardly had he left the room than the Bishop, fearing the consequences of this step, had him recalled. He then wrote to the Superioress, ordering her under obedience to allow the Father to go to the confessional and to speak to his sisters there. This was done.

The first to present herself was the youngest. She told her brother everything, and ended by saying that she would not remain another hour in the Monastery, because she was full of fear and anxiety and was not allowed to see her sister any more. Then came the second, Mary Celeste. From her Autobiography we learn that she told her brother, under obedience, all that had happened, including her doubts, her fears and interior suffering. The Father consoled her, telling her to wait for Our Lord in patience, for He alone could remedy what now seemed hopeless. She then consulted him regarding the three promises which the Nuns wished to exact from her. He answered that, for the first, she should no longer write to don Silvester; as to the second, the signing of the Rules as revised by the spiritual Father, she should tell them that in all things she would follow the regulations of the house without any resistance, being the last in it, and that she wished only to serve God and observe the Rules like her Sisters, without in any way interfering with the affairs of the Community; regarding the third promise, however, which would bind her to Falcoia's direction, he told her never to make it, because such a vow was contrary to all justice. He advised her to tell the Nuns that she would be satisfied with the ordinary Confessor, and not make known the state of her soul until it should please God to send her another guide. He added that she ought to have left the spiritual Father long ago, and that she had done wrong to allow herself to be directed by him during such great trials.

He then examined Sister Mary Illuminata, and asked whether the two elder sisters also wished to leave the Monastery. They replied that they had no such intention, for it could not be the Will of God that of their own will and through cowardice they should run from the cross and from suffering, but they would await the help of God, trusting that He would make His Will known to them. The Jesuit then left them, saying that he would inform his father of the youngest sister's determination to return home, so that he could send to fetch her. On arriving at Naples he informed Don Crostarosa with great prudence of all that it was necessary for him to know, and urged him to take his youngest daughter out of the Monastery because the observance there was too strict for her, and it would be better to place her in another convent, where her health would allow her to follow the Rule and work at her sanctification in peace of soul.

In consequence of this the old man told his son to go and fetch his young sister who was as yet so weak in virtue, and to bring her home so that he could then arrange with her what was best for her future happiness. The Jesuit returned to Scala and informed the Superioress that he had come to fetch his youngest sister, who was determined to leave the Monastery. The Nun at once sent an express courier with letters to Mgr. Falcoia, informing him that Sister Mary Evangelista was about to return to her home. On hearing this news the spiritual Father set off in haste for Scala, in order to be present at what was going to take place. He feared that after her departure this young Nun would tell her father all that had been done to her sister, and the trials through which the latter was still passing. Knowing how highly Don Crostarosa esteemed his second daughter, he was afraid that the old man might resort to violence and insist on his daughter leaving the Convent. He therefore thought it more prudent to forestall such an event by having Mary Celeste sent away from the Monastery unless she would consent to make the three promises already mentioned.

The Chapter was accordingly convoked, and Mary Celeste was called. We can picture to ourselves the innocent victim standing modestly and yet sadly before the assembly who are about to judge her, and in imagination we seem to see at her side the Figure of Our Lord, in Whose Divine Footsteps she is so faithfully treading. The Superioress proposed to her the three conditions:

(1) That she should no longer write to Don Silvester.
(2) That she should sign the Rules as revised by the spiritual Father.
(3) That she should make a vow to allow herself to be directed by this Father.

If she should refuse to submit to any one of these conditions she would be expelled from the Monastery.

The Venerable Sister replied calmly and simply in the way her brother had advised her to do. On hearing these declarations the Superioress, on the part of the Chapter, expelled her from the Monastery and ordered her to leave at the same time as her sister, Mary Evangelista.

In spite of the intense grief which this decree caused her the Sister knew it was the Will of God, and accepted her dismissal without a word. She had prayed so much, she tells us, during this terrible trial, that she was convinced Our Lord would have shown her clearly had He wished it to be otherwise. Moreover, she had that very day concluded a novena to St. Vincent Ferrer, to whom she had prayed to obtain from God a cessation of this terrible trial. But, in His mysterious Wisdom, Our Lord arranged that on the very day she finished the novena she should be turned out of the Monastery.

When Sister Mary Illuminata heard that her sister was to be sent away she declared her intention of leaving the Convent also, as she did not think it could be God's Will for her to leave her sister to suffer alone. Thereupon Mary Celeste asked permission to write to her father in order to inform him of these decisions, for he had been expecting only his youngest daughter to return home. The permission was given, and she wrote the following little note:

"Sir, My Very Dear Father,
"I write to tell you that the good Nuns have expelled me from the Monastery on account of my imperfections, and wish me to leave immediately. God has willed it thus. I beg of you to find a monastery where I can stay until God shall make known His Will to me, for it is not good for us to live in a secular house. I beg of you not to distress yourself, for God will find a remedy. Deign to bless your daughter, who respectfully salutes you."

The Jesuit Father who had come to Scala to take home his youngest sister was in ignorance of the recent events at the Monastery. When he heard what had transpired he was very much upset and grieved. He sent off a courier to Naples with a letter to his father, informing him of the further complications and enclosing Mary Celeste's note. He awaited his father's reply with great anxiety, for Don Crostarosa, now over eighty, ill and in bed, could not fail to feel keenly this distressing news. Thus the effects of Mary Celeste's trials were felt by every member of her family. After the Chapter she was ordered to retire to her cell and to remain there until she left the Monastery. The other Sisters were forbidden to visit her. Ail this was carried out with great rigor. Nevertheless, after having obeyed punctually the orders of the spiritual Father, the Nuns were stupefied at what they had done, and even those who had been the cause of all the trouble were frightened at what they had accomplished, and they showed this by their manner. Those who had only obeyed the orders of the Superioress and the spiritual Father wept bitterly, and these were by far the greater number. On the other hand, those who were to leave suffered still more, and particularly Mary Celeste. What agony must have overwhelmed this great and devoted soul during those last hours spent in the house she had loved with all the affection of her loving and sensitive heart! This house which already was hers no longer! Memories of the years spent in the beloved Monastery filled her mind; memories both sweet and bitter, memories of graces received, of sorrows borne, of prayers and struggles, of hopes and fears, of supernatural joys and griefs. The flood of souvenirs must have swept over her like the waves of the sea, leaving her spent and broken against the cruel rocks which had wrecked her life. The following morning Father Crostarosa, desiring to put an end to this sorrowful situation, came to take his sisters from the Monastery. After much reflection, he had decided not to await the return of the messenger from Naples, deeming that his father would prefer the three sisters to leave immediately. Accordingly he informed the Superioress of his intention. She replied that, since he was charged with escorting the travelers, he would have to provide clothes for them, as they would not be allowed to take away the habit of the Order.

At this fresh complication the poor Father knew not where to turn, for he knew nobody at Scala, and it would have taken too long to send to Naples for what was necessary. Great was his relief when the chaplain of the Monastery took pity on the three sisters and promised to procure habits for them, which he could borrow from one of the convents in the town. The priest was a kind old man, fully acquainted with all that had been suffered by Mary Celeste. Not only was he willing to procure habits for the sisters, but he also invited them to remain in his house until the messenger should return from Naples, and in fact for as long as might be necessary. He also offered to accompany them to whatever monastery they were to go. This charity and sympathy brought a ray of consolation to the afflicted hearts of both brother and sisters.

The following morning therefore, about nine o'clock, the Jesuit came to the Monastery accompanied by this good priest.

It was Ascension Day, May 15th, 1733. They brought with them three habits borrowed from the Benedictines of the Monastery of St. Cataldo, at Scala. The three sisters took off their own habits and put on those which had been lent to them. They then went to the chapel to pray before the Blessed Sacrament. Mary Celeste abandoned herself entirely into the Hand of God, offering herself utterly to Him so that He might dispose of her as He willed.

At last came the moment when they were obliged to go to the enclosure door. The Superioress and nearly all the Community were already assembled there. The three sisters kissed the hand of the Superioress and embraced all the Nuns without exception, recommending themselves to their prayers. All were in tears ... they then quietly left the Convent. Mary Celeste, heartbroken, crossed the threshold over which she had passed ten years ago full of joy and hope, believing herself about to enter Paradise. The heavy door closed behind them for ever like the gate of a tomb, shutting them out from all they held dear and vibrating with a melancholy clang which was echoed in the hearts of the exiles.

The Sisters retired to the good priest's house, where they remained secluded. On the following morning they received a visit from the Vicar-General, who had been sent to them by the spiritual Father. He came to make the proposition that they should return to the Monastery on condition of asking pardon of the spiritual Father and of the Community. Here again Falcoia gives proof of the contradictory spirit with which he acted in his relations with Mary Celeste. The sisters had the good sense to reply that it was now too late, and that in any case they believed their departure from the Monastery to be the Will of God. Thereupon the Grand Vicar replied, still speaking in the name of the spiritual Father, that if they would not return to the Convent they must leave the town at once. Doubtless the prelate feared that a prolonged sojourn in Scala might arouse sympathy for them, which would be to the detriment of the Monastery.

We read the following important note in Canon Mansi's book: "The Nuns had not the courage to own that they had expelled Sister Mary Celeste. They merely inserted the following notice in their Chapter book: 'On May 14th, 1733, the Chapter met to send away Sister Mary Evangelista, who had no vocation and troubled the Community by not conforming to the prescriptions of the new Rule. By the Divine Will her two sisters, Sister Mary Illuminata and Sister Mary Celeste, left the Convent at the same time.'" And Mansi adds: "In order to establish the true facts which the above note might obscure we have a document drawn up by the public notary of Scala, Francis Verone." This document is quoted in full by Mansi, and serves to show that Michael Crostarosa, on May 24th and 25th, 1733, lodged a complaint with the aforesaid notary, in the name of his father, brothers and sisters, against the Nuns and against the Bishops of Scala and of Castellamare, for having forcibly expelled the three sisters from the Monastery against their will, and without returning their dowries or the clothes they had brought with them.

No action was taken as regards this complaint, because Mary Celeste refused to sign it. Mansi concludes: "By opposing this request made by her family for restitution the innocent victim proves that she was a saint who, in the words of Holy Scripture, 'suffered in peace her bitterness most bitter'" (Ps. 38:17).

St. Alphonsus was absent at the time of these sad events. Had he been there it is possible that he might have averted the tragedy. When he returned to Scala after a long absence Mary Celeste was no longer there. He wrote to Falcoia, his director, asking permission to visit his holy friend at Nocera. The permission was refused. The following year Alphonsus renewed his request, which, when one knows his blind obedience, shows how deeply he must have felt on the subject. Falcoia replied that he would leave it to his conscience. Did

Alphonsus ever go to see Mary Celeste? A certain passage in the latter's Autobiography leads us to believe so. There is, however, no reliable document to prove this.

Many years later St. Alphonsus was to undergo the same trial as Mary Celeste, who, together with him, had been the instrument chosen by Providence to found the new Order. He also, through the complaints of some of his brethren, found himself excluded from the Congregation which he had founded, and that by the Pope himself. But, just as this canonical exclusion did not prevent him from being a member of the Institute in God's sight, so Mary Celeste, although expelled from the Monastery of Scala, will always remain a member of the Order whose habit she wore and whose Rule she observed until her death with the approbation of her Ecclesiastical Superiors.

But, to continue our story. Don Crostarosa, on hearing of his daughters' trials, was deeply grieved; but his spirit of faith made him see the Hand of God in all that had happened, and he endeavored to come to the help of his dear children. He thought of a way out of the difficulty and, sending for his eldest son, told him to go to Nocera dei Pagani, about twenty miles distant from Naples, where he had many friends, and to seek in that town some monastery where his daughters could be received for about three months until he could think things over and have time to look for a convent where they could pass their lives in peace and consolation. In the meantime he wrote an affectionate letter to his daughters telling them of his plans for them, and asking them to come and spend a few days with him before they were accompanied to their destination.

But Mary Celeste thought it better to sacrifice this consolation of seeing her old father and to proceed straight to a religious house. It was therefore decided that for the present the three sisters should go to Amalfi, to the Convent of the Holy Trinity, whose Community was composed of the nobility of the town. These Nuns were not only willing but anxious to receive them for a few days. They decided to leave Scala the next morning. Accompanied by their brother and the priest who had befriended them, they descended the mountain side—this beloved hill, which had been Mary Celeste's Tabor and was now to remain for ever her Golgotha! The words of Our Lord to His spouse had been fulfilled; denied, abandoned by her sisters in religion, expelled from the monastery which was to owe its future glory to her, she went her way in borrowed clothes, divested of all—for neither her dowry nor her trousseau had been returned to her, and she refused to sign the request for restitution—with a heart full of sorrow, she walked towards the unknown future, too humble to feel any bitterness at human injustice and lovingly resigned to God's guidance.

The principal part of Mary Celeste's mission had now been accomplished.

PART III

NOCERA AND FOGGIA

CHAPTER I
STRENGTH IN WEAKNESS

"When I am weak, then am I powerful" (1 Cor. 12:10).

HESE words of St. Paul might justly serve as an epigraph to the third stage of the life of the Venerable Mary Celeste. St. Paul had asked God to deliver him from the painful and humiliating trial which, so it seemed to him, was an obstacle to his ministry. God had replied: "My grace is sufficient for thee, for power is made perfect in infirmity" (2 Cor. 12:9). When the Apostle was tortured by his infirmities, calumniated, persecuted and reduced to utter weakness, almost annihilated, then it was that God's grace was given to him abundantly, and that God used him to accomplish great things. In very truth, then, could St. Paul exclaim: "When I am weak, then am I powerful."

How many other servants of God have since repeated these words—missionaries, founders of Orders, promoters of charitable works? For has it not been at the very moment when they have been forced to recognize their own powerlessness, when all the world was against them and all hope seemed lost, that God crowned their struggles with victory and used them to promote some of His great designs?

On leaving Scala, Mary Celeste surely reached her hour of complete powerlessness, of extreme humiliation. It need not surprise us, therefore, to see multiplied in her and by her the effects of God's strengthening grace. Let us follow her first to Amalfi, where the good Nuns had offered to receive her in her distress. In addition to placing the guest-house of the Monastery at the disposal of the three sisters, the steward of the house was sent to meet them and to act as guide, and they were given a warm and sisterly welcome on their arrival.

The Nuns gazed curiously at Mary Celeste, this descendant of a noble race, whose face retained its dignity even under the weight of suffering!—The mystic whose extraordinary and much-discussed reputation had penetrated even the cloister walls! On her countenance, pale and worn by grief, in her words, in her whole attitude in fact, shone the Divine light of outstanding virtue. This was so obvious that the Nuns were awed and fascinated and curiosity gave place to veneration. Very soon the Nuns, and in particular the Superioress, became so much attached to Sister Mary Celeste that they did not wish to let her go. They begged and implored her to become their Superior, saying that they would adopt the new Rule with pleasure and be clothed in the habit of the Most Holy Redeemer. They were indeed already taking steps to refer the matter to the Holy See in spite of the fact that from all parts rumors had reached them treating the new-comer as deluded. All this only caused the good sisters to hold their visitor in still greater veneration, and they continued to implore her to guide them in the way of perfection.

Mary Celeste, however, would not hear of it. To many, indeed, it would have been a temptation to rest quietly in this haven after the storm; to secure for herself religious life and at the same time recognition of the work for which she had suffered so much. ... And had she been an ordinary soul what a revenge would it not have been on those who had persecuted her! Needless to say, such considerations did not enter her mind; one thing only mattered—God's Will. Let us hear what she has written on this subject; it shows her deep inward humility: "It seemed to me that for the time being I was to live in contempt and humiliation unless some certain sign to the contrary were granted to me from God; and that, therefore, it would not be good for me to accept the charge of Superioress, or any office of government. That is why I refused so absolutely." Nevertheless she had much difficulty in preventing the Nuns from writing to Rome.

Mary Celeste and her sisters lived quietly in the guesthouse which adjoined the Convent chapel. Thus they had every facility for their daily devotions. They desired, however, to take advantage of their sojourn in Amalfi to make a pilgrimage to the Church of St. Andrew, where lies the Apostle's body, from which a sweet-scented and precious liquid flows. They visited this sanctuary, made their confessions, and received Holy Communion there; and it was there that Mary Celeste received a great consolation, of which she gives the following account in her Autobiography:

"In this church Our Lord deigned to console me, granting me an interior light in the depths of my soul. For a long time I had been plunged in complete desolation and abandonment, a prey to painful doubts and fears regarding my way of prayer, besides the exterior sorrows which have already been mentioned. Our Lord, therefore, wished to console and strengthen me a little. Whilst hearing Mass in the chapel of the glorious Apostle, He showed me a beautiful and pleasant road which led from earth to Heaven. At the beginning of it were many crosses and thorns, but at the end was a splendid aureole of light, through which I seemed to see Paradise. Not only did I walk along this road, but flew, supported by the strength of God and accompanied by many predestined souls who followed me. I understood that these souls would be saved by means of me, for Our Lord told me that He would make use of me for the salvation of many. At this sight I once more took courage and went on my way in spite of abandonment and desolation."

At length their eldest brother, Michael Crostarosa, arrived from Nocera and told his sisters that their father had been seeking in that town a monastery without enclosure which would receive them for three months. His search had been successful. There were many convents in the town, and one in particular seemed suitable, as it was in a flourishing condition.

It was an orphanage kept by a community of twenty-four Nuns. The building was beautifully situated and very convenient and was governed financially by three administrators. One of these was the venerable parish priest, and the other two, Nicolas Villani and Francis Salvati respectively, were personal friends of Don Crostarosa and were highly respected in the country. When these two learnt the object of Michael's journey to Nocera they were delighted and begged him to bring his sisters to this convent at once in spite of the more or less fantastic stories which had been circulated concerning Mary Celeste.

The servant of God and her sisters remained ten days with the Nuns at Amalfi, and the latter not only gave them hospitality free of charge, but also provided them with every comfort. Moreover, by God's Will the air of the sea near which this convent was situated had a strengthening effect on Mary Celeste's health. She had left Scala weak and ill, prostrate after all her trials, but the good air of Amalfi, together with the kind treatment and rest, restored - strength to her body and peace to her mind. It was with expressions of the deepest gratitude for all the kindness shown to them that the sisters bade farewell to these Nuns, who on their part felt the most sincere regret at their departure. Mary Celeste never forgot the generous hospitality she received at Amalfi. The Nuns traveled by sea to Salerno, and from thence drove to Nocera, a distance of several miles. There, by permission of the Bishop, they were received into the convent chosen for them by their brother and were cordially welcomed by the Nuns. All were most favorably impressed by the apparent holiness of Mary Celeste, and exclaimed that God must have sent her and her two sisters to their convent, for it seemed to them that they were receiving three angels sent from Heaven to help the community. Their hopes were fully justified, as future events will prove.

CHAPTER II
AT NOCERA

 HE charming city of Nocera dei Pagani is situated in the beautiful and picturesque valley which lies between the Apennines and Mont Saint-Ange; the mountain rises at the back and overshadows the town like a protecting angel, while before it is spread the vast plain of Vesuvius with its varied and ever-changing scenery.

The Christian history of the town goes back to the time of the Apostles, since its first bishop. Priscus, gained the palm of martyrdom under the Emperor Nero. Its destiny has been far from peaceful. Pillaged again and again by the conquerors of Naples, or destroyed by earthquakes, the brave little town has risen up after each successive storm without losing anything of its charm. Kings and princes have dwelt and died there, and within its walls St. Gregory VII and Urban VI took refuge from their enemies. Many a larger town could be proud of such memories, but for the inhabitants of Nocera one glorious souvenir stands out above all others. It is that their town was for many long years the chosen residence of St. Alphonsus; it was there he breathed his last sigh and gave up his soul to God in the convent of his Order, which still exists and in whose chapel his venerated remains are buried.

What consolation would it not have been for Mary Celeste if on her arrival in that town she could have foreseen the future. If she could have known that the Institute of which she was the sorrowful Mother would for more than a century have its principal site there, until the day when, by reason of the extension of the Congregation throughout the universe, the

Holy Father should decree that the Mother house of the Most
Holy Redeemer should be installed in the capital of the
Christian world! Already, by her heroic submission to Divine
guidance, and by the good she was to accomplish in that
country, Mary Celeste, unknown to herself, was the pioneer at
Nocera of St. Alphonsus and his sons.

A few days after her arrival Don Silvester came from Naples
to see her and to bring her the copy of the Rules written by
herself, which he had received from the hands of Monsignor
Santoro, and which he had refused to give up to the spiritual
Father of the Nuns at the beginning of the troubles in the
Monastery of Scala. Mary Celeste assures us that this action on
the part of Don Silvester was permitted by God, for these Rules
were to be used later on for the foundation ordained by God
Himself.

"The pious gentleman" was much surprised to see Mary
Celeste and her two sisters dressed in the habit of St. Benedict
instead of in that of the Most Holy Redeemer. He asked the
reason for this change, and the sisters told him in all simplicity
how, before leaving the Monastery, they had been despoiled of
their habits by the Nuns of Scala and obliged to borrow those
they were wearing from a convent in the town. She added that
the habits of this convent had been lent to them in all charity,
but that they must be returned; and at present there was no
possibility of this, as they were entirely without resources with
which to procure others.

Don Silvester could not refrain from expressing his surprise
at such poverty, for he knew the high rank the Crostarosa
family had held in the kingdom—Mary Celeste therefore
explained that her old father had lately met with many troubles
and financial difficulties, which had left him in real distress, so
that he was quite unable to give his daughters any further
assistance. This was the reason of their present poverty. Added
to this, the Nuns of Scala had not returned their dowries, nor
the furniture, beds, linen which they had brought to the

Convent from their home. "But," said Mary Celeste, "in all this they were glad to resemble their Divine Spouse."

On hearing this sad story Don Silvester was deeply moved. With all possible delicacy he offered to come to their assistance so that they might provide themselves with what was necessary. The three sisters, as becomes the true poor of Jesus Christ, accepted humbly a few gold pieces from him. With these they at once set about procuring red and blue material with which to make their habits, and we can imagine with what consolation they found themselves able once more to don the beloved livery of the Most Holy Redeemer. As Mary Celeste says, they seemed now to be more than ever the disciples of Jesus Christ. What was most surprising in all these events was that no obstacles were placed in the way of the sisters, either by the Nuns or the administrators of the convent at Nocera. Even the Bishop not only gave his consent to their entering that monastery, but also came to visit them and showed them every kindness. However, they were still without beds or linen. These were lent to them at first by the community; then little by little, without having asked for anything, they were provided with all they needed. So lovingly did the Providence of God watch over them that everything necessary was given to them by charitable people. This was a great consolation to Mary Celeste, for she says that thus the life of Our Lord was being established in her not in words, but in deed and in truth. The holy Rules which Jesus had formerly dictated to her were now being worked out in her life, as she was experiencing poverty, contempt and persecutions. Added to this, she felt great loneliness of soul and abandonment, besides being stricken with bodily infirmities and troubled with doubts, fears and temptations which the devil did not fail to suggest. She felt as if she were finally abandoned by God in her misery. Fully resigned to this state of suffering and humiliation, she lived quietly in this monastery, spending her days either in her cell or in choir, praying and asking God to give her His Divine light. Although frequently receiving the Sacraments, she was not able to open her heart to anyone, not knowing whether there was any priest in that town capable of understanding her spiritual needs. As so many people thought her to be a visionary, she feared to be plunged again in doubts and fears. Therefore in confession she did not speak of her spiritual life, preferring to wait until such time as Our Lord should deign to make known His Will in the matter. In the midst of this darkness and silence the holiness of the venerable Sister shone forth as it had done in the Convent of Amalfi. It was as apparent as a pure flame in an alabaster vase. Therefore God did not delay in manifesting the merciful design for which He had brought her to Nocera.

CHAPTER III
THE REFORMER

HE monastery in which Mary Celeste now found herself stood in great need of reform. The Nuns, with the exception of two, lived in an appalling state of laxity. They no longer observed their Rule in the slightest degree, and what was worse, they carried on particular friendships with seculars. Obedience did not exist among them, and the Superior was no longer respected. This Superior herself had introduced the bad habit of visiting secular friends outside the monastery, therefore it was not surprising that her orders were now ignored and she was openly, treated with contempt. "God allowed this as a chastisement," says Mary Celeste, "for although the poor Nun may be excused on the grounds of simplicity and ignorance, yet she should have shown more zeal for her responsibility as head of an orphanage." The convent itself was not in want, and the Nuns had no need to beg. Poverty was forgotten, and buildings were year after year added to those already existing. That the orphanage should be in such a flourishing condition, made the disorders within die convent all the more reprehensible.

The administrators did not know how to remedy this state of affairs, until the providential arrival of the Venerable Sister opened the way for them. At their very first interview with her, hope filled their hearts; and the more they observed the humble refugee, the more this hope increased. Before long they endeavored to convince Mary Celeste that God had sent her to this convent in order to help the souls of these Nuns, and to bring them back to regular observance. The poor Sister was very much perplexed at hearing this proposition, for she could not be sure if it were really the Will of God. She hesitated to accept the charge of Superior in that convent, for these Nuns were of another Order, and she felt herself called by God to the new Order of the Most Holy Redeemer. She therefore excused herself to his Lordship and the administrators, reminding them that she had only come there for three months, and meant to retire into some other monastery when God should make known His Will to her. However, they would not listen to her objections.

The Bishop and the Administrators came together to the Convent and gave Mary Celeste such overwhelming proofs and reasons in favor of what they wished her to do, that she was obliged to yield. Moreover, the Prelate commanded her by virtue of holy Obedience, to accept the charge of Superior without demur, as such was the Will of God. He added that he would only oblige her to remain in charge for three years. After that she would be free to undertake the work which God inspired her to do, or to remain for ever in the monastery. He then authorized her to keep her own habit, while exercising her charge, and to Practice the Rule of the Most Holy Redeemer.

Matters being thus settled, the Community were called together. In their presence the Bishop invested Mary Celeste with the office of Superior, and gave her power to imprison those who were disobedient and insubordinate, or to send them out of the Monastery if they resisted. The Venerable Sister had already acquired such ascendency over the hearts of the Sisters, that all accepted her willingly as their Mother and promised her obedience. The Superioress then in office had for some time intended to leave this house where, by God's permission, she had suffered so much from the Community. She now knelt down before Mary Celeste and begged her, for the love of God, to accept her charge, as she was going to retire to another convent. There was nothing for Mary Celeste to do, therefore, but to bend her back to the burden of Superiority, and from all these circumstances she was able to recognize the Will of God.

CHAPTER III: THE REFORMER

Having thus established her in charge, the Bishop gave her as Vicar her eldest sister, Mary Illuminata. From that day a wonderful transformation took place in the Monastery. God allowed that all the Nuns should become much attached to their Superior. She began by endeavoring to win their confidence with great prudence and gentleness, seeing each one in private, and examining the state of their souls with the tenderness of a mother. All without exception opened their hearts to her, and spoke to her willingly of their frivolities and their faults. With a heart burning with charity she tried to help and strengthen each one. Not knowing whether she would find in the town a priest experienced enough to speak to them in the way she felt to be most necessary, she undertook to give them spiritual conferences herself.

She spoke to them of the eternal truths, and exhorted them to do penance. By degrees even the hardest hearts became softened, and they asked for an extraordinary confessor. The wise Superioress then asked for a priest to be sent who should possess all the necessary powers and be a great servant of God. The Bishop sent to them one of the Fathers of St. Francis of Paula, who was much esteemed and led an exemplary life. Each Nun purified her conscience by a sincere confession, and, as Mary Celeste tells us, they began to live in the fear of God.

She therefore chose this moment to replace all the officeholders who were in charge when she arrived. At the turn and the door, she placed Mary Illuminata, her Vicar, and the two Sisters who had always led edifying lives in the Monastery. She then closed the grilles which had so long been unused and named auditrices to accompany the Sisters when they went to the parlor. All friendships with outsiders were forbidden. This was the most difficult to obtain. However, by the grace of God, all difficulties were eventually overcome and excellent order established in the Monastery. Common life and regular observance were perfectly and admirably practice, and to this day all is most religiously observed, "thanks to Our Lord Jesus

Christ" as Mary Celeste does not fail to say. The Monastery which had once been a scandal to the whole country, soon became a model to everyone, and on all sides it was spoken of with admiration.

Such a transformation could not fail to attract many people towards the Superioress, and many ladies of the town and others came to consult her on the affairs of their soul. They followed her counsels and she was thus the means of bringing many souls back to God. One of the administrators sent to her a young man who, after listening to her words, abandoned his disordered life, went to confession, and became a man of prayer, leading henceforth an exemplary and pious life.

In the midst of these remarkable happenings, an event occurred which came as a painful surprise.

The Bishop of Nocera received a letter written by the spiritual Father of the Nuns at Scala. In this letter the Bishop of Castellamare stated that having learnt that certain Nuns had arrived in the diocese of Nocera, he thought it better to warn his colleague that they were lazy and worthless people, so that in order to prevent harm, he might turn them out of any monastery in which he had placed them. He added that he wrote thus out of respect and from a good motive. It is impossible to understand such a document coming from such a man. For the previous misunderstandings between Mary Celeste and the Bishop of Castellamare, there may be explanations and excuses. In the present case, all one can say is that such a letter is unworthy of the great soul of Falcoia. Fortunately the Bishop of Nocera was in no way impressed on the perusal of this letter. He simply said that he now saw that these good Nuns had indeed been tried by the Lord and persecuted by the devil and those whom he made use of to carry out his evil purposes. Then, wishing to prove his confidence in Mary Celeste, he sent the letter to her. It was brought by his secretary. The Venerable Sister merely smiled when she saw how he had written the letter, and after reading it, handed it back to the secretary without a word.

The Bishop of Nocera, replying to Falcoia, said that he thanked him for the advice given in his letter, but that the experience he had had with the Nuns in question was quite contrary to what had been written: "It is very easy to see," he added, "that these are calumnies, for Our Lord says: 'By their fruits you shall know them' and the works of these Nuns are only productive of good." Therefore he considered that the Lord Himself confirmed him in his judgment.

Indeed Mary Celeste's works spoke for her. Whilst inconsiderate people made rash judgments against her, and in their unconscious cruelty overwhelmed her with blind condemnations. Our Lord glorified His faithful spouse by communicating to her His saving Power, by allowing her to work a greater miracle than the resurrection of the body, namely that of the resurrection of souls.

CHAPTER IV
THE MESSAGE OF PEACE

ARY CELESTE was still without a director, which caused her to suffer much in the midst of the darkness in which her soul was plunged. She prayed unceasingly to God that He would make known to her the priest who was to be her guide. At length her prayers were answered.

The young man whom she had been the means of converting went, on her advice, to make a general confession, choosing for his confessor a distinguished ecclesiastic from the Seminary of Nocera. This priest was a man of great virtue and endowed with a supernatural gift of prayer. He lived in the seminary, leading there a very retired and contemplative life. The renown of this priest, by name Bernadine Sommantico, was so great that the young convert wished to remain under his direction. After having made a general confession, he told the Father of his resolution to serve God and to lead a virtuous life. Don Bernadine was delighted at these dispositions, but knowing that his penitent had been the scandal of the whole town, he asked by what means the Lord had enlightened him. The young man then related his interview with Mary Celeste and told of the good she had done to his soul, and asked permission to continue to visit her to seek her help. The good priest gave him permission to consult this Nun from time to time while remaining under his own direction. Don Bernadine had heard the story of Mary Celeste and knew that she was considered by some people to be a visionary, but seeing all that God was accomplishing through her—the reform of the monastery, the conversion of this young man, the help given to many souls—he concluded, as the Bishop had done, that the

Sister in question was a saintly soul traveling along the royal road of the Cross. He therefore desired to know her.

At the same instant, as if to confirm his desire. Our Lord deigned to enlighten him concerning the soul of this religious. He saw as in a flash all her doubts, her fears, her trials, and patient suffering. He had no further hesitation, therefore, in charging his new penitent to inform the Superioress that he wished to come and see her, as God had revealed to him that she needed consolation.

One morning shortly after this, Don Bernadine came to the Monastery and asked for Mary Celeste. As soon as he saw her, even before she had had time to speak, he said to her: "Take courage, for God has not abandoned you as you think, but in His Divine Providence has disposed all things for your good." The poor Sister's joy and astonishment can be imagined at seeing her secret sorrows understood, and that by a priest whom she did not know, for she had not disclosed the state of her soul to anyone since leaving Scala. Realizing at once that the Divine Master had sent him to her, she had no hesitation in confiding to him all her doubts, fears, and temptations. She told him also of the profound state of abandonment in which God had left her. She went on to speak of the anguish of mind she had gone through when under her former spiritual Father and asked if she had done wrong to leave him. Don Bernadine reassured her on all these points and told her in God's name that all that had happened had been allowed by Divine Providence, for God was leading her by the hand. As regards the former director, he said that there were very few people to whom God gave the grace of understanding souls, and the guidance of the Holy Ghost in their regard. She was therefore to keep her mind in peace, and in the name of obedience to forget the past.

Mary Celeste then begged him to accept her as his spiritual daughter, since God Himself in His goodness had sent him to her. Don Bernadine consented, and for her own peace of mind, he ordered her to refrain from mentioning her interior difficulties to anyone without his special permission. From that time forward, Mary Celeste tells us, she recovered that peace of soul and security of mind of which she had been deprived during this time of interior and exterior troubles and sorrows. The trial had lasted five years.

St. John of the Cross, that great doctor of Mystical Theology, explains to us the reason of such suffering: "Just as the blacksmith cannot fashion the iron into the desired shape, without placing it in the fire and striking it many times with the hammer, so God cannot transform a soul into His likeness without casting it into the fire of suffering, striking it with temptations, and taking from it part of its very being. There are, of course, different forms of suffering. In the case of some souls the pain is greater and of longer duration than in others, according to the degree of union to which God has destined them, and according to the strength or weakness of the vices from which they are to be delivered. ... After having recognized Job as His faithful servant before the good and bad Angels, God allows him to sink into a sea of physical and moral suffering. He then raises him to the height of spiritual and temporal well-being. It is thus God acts with those whom He wishes to lead to the highest perfection. He plunges them into a torrent of suffering which cleanses them from all sin, and from which they emerge pure and beautiful; he then unites them to Himself and transforms them into His likeness."

Moreover, the same doctor speaks of the sufferings, griefs, anguish and inexplicable annihilations which God sends to His friends, "until the soul, submissive, humbled, and pacified, has acquired by detachment from all things that unworldliness, simplicity, and delicacy by means of which it becomes one with the Spirit of God according to the measure of unitive love granted to it by God's mercy. The trial will be more or less severe, and more or less long, according to the degree of this union."

CHAPTER IV: THE MESSAGE OF PEACE

This teaching Our Lord deigned Himself to give to Mary Celeste, whilst He granted her a favor which clearly shows the high degree of union to which she was called. We quote without commentary the account left to us by the Venerable Sister in her "Entretiens." It reveals to us the rigorous exactions of infinite purity, beside which even Angels are not perfect, and at the same time the humility of Mary Celeste herself.

"THE SOUL: This morning, June 29th, 1737, on the Feast of Thy holy Apostles, Peter and Paul, Thou didst show me in an ineffable manner in Holy Communion that Thou art a vast ocean of Infinite Goodness, and I am a drop of water falling into this immense sea and becoming immersed in it. I see myself absorbed in that ocean of Infinite Good, wherein is endless strength and majesty. Oh, what treasures Thou dost show me, my God. Thy mercy is infinite and my soul will sing of Thine endless glory. May all the Spiritual beings and all Heaven praise Thee for me, because Thou art my Creator and Thou hast delivered me from eternal confusion and from Hell. For the last five years the devil has had power to afflict me in all ways, as Thou dost know, but particularly in the three following ways:

(1) By the tongues of men;
(2) By interior temptations of all kinds;
(3) By excessive fear of having been deceived all my life by the devil, fear that all the graces received from God were but illusion and falsehood.

"This has caused me such great grief that my soul has been crushed under the weight of it. Knowing this, O my God, Thou didst speak to my soul this morning in the following manner:

"THE SPOUSE: Write what I shall say to you. Why do you doubt my mercy after so many graces which were My work in you. It was necessary that for five years you should be deprived of those gifts and graces which belonged to Me, and that you should be abandoned to your own weakness, so that you should learn what a miserable result your own nature would produce, without My special grace, for the latter only is what I took from you. If I had deprived you of ordinary grace, what harm you would have done! It was necessary for you to feel your weakness during the whole of that time, in order to make you know the truth, and that is one of the greatest mercies I have granted you. Know that you were under a delusion regarding an inordinate, though spiritual, affection for a creature. You were dazzled by it, and this obscured your thoughts in many cases. It was necessary for you to expiate your fault before receiving further light. Now that that is done, all will become clear. You will be with Me in the fullness of love, and there you will see your past mistakes and imperfections; also how you have judged things which I had ordained for your good, how many words and judgments concerning your neighbors have clouded your mind, how much time has been lost in this useless occupation! And all this separated you from My purity. At present remain in humility and love, giving thanks to Me for having, in the excess of My love, delivered you from your many miseries. This gratitude will make you bless Me for My goodness. I am enthroned in peace in your heart, and there I order and command that no creature shall ever more have dominion in the city of your soul."

CHAPTER V

THE CALL TO FOGGIA

ARY CELESTE had spent three years at Nocera. Years of quiet work for souls. The good accomplished by her was apparent to all, and she received many requests for foundations from different parts of the country. Among others, she was asked to make a foundation at Aversa, near Naples; also at Roccapiemonte—this latter request being made by the duke and duchess of that name. Again, at Perouse, in the Roman States, she was invited to found a house of her Order, and this would have been an important foundation on account of the privileges attached to it; for the Bishop had already obtained from the Sovereign Pontiff the permission for Mary Celeste to visit other monasteries in his diocese and to reform any want of observance or relaxation. No greater mark of esteem could have been given her, but the holy Nun did not feel called to make any of these foundations, to which there were many objections, and waited to know the Will of God in the matter. Her director advised her to wait, saying that she could not leave the souls she was guiding in the Monastery of Nocera, and who were still weak in virtue. Later on, he assured her, God would make His Will known; but for the present her duty was to continue to direct the souls of these Nuns and to lead them in the way of perfection. Humble and submissive as usual, therefore, Mary Celeste continued her charge for more than three years, being herself directed by God as she tells us.

At this period there was at Foggia a canon, a native of Nocera. His name was Joseph Tortora, and some years before he had been appointed to the diocese of Foggia by Bishop

Cavallieri, a man of great virtue. The good priest had since been made a canon, and enjoyed the full confidence of the succeeding bishop, Monsignor Fraccoli. The latter consulted him in his difficulties and in all important questions, for he recognized Tortora's worth and capability. Moreover, the Canon was esteemed by all and had friends among the most distinguished people of the country. At the time of which we are writing business called Canon Tortora to Lucera, a little town near Foggia, and while there he heard of the reform which had taken place in the Monastery of Nocera. The Superior, Mother Mary Celeste, who had effected this reform was spoken of in terms of the highest praise and gratitude. On hearing all this the Canon felt a desire to see her and to speak to her of his own difficulties. It so happened that one of the Administrators of the Convent, Francis Salvati, was present when the Canon expressed this wish. Seeing the interest the latter took in the matter, Salvati gave him an account of all the difficulties and sufferings this holy Nun had undergone in defense of a Rule dictated to her by Heaven. "Fortunately for us," he added, "her tribulations have led her to Nocera, where she has done so much good for souls." All this increased the Canon's desire to visit the Servant of God, and he begged the Administrator to arrange an interview for him on his next visit to Nocera. Salvati willingly agreed and spoke to Mary Celeste of the matter. As soon as she realized that it was not out of curiosity, but to speak of spiritual things, that the Canon wished to see her, she consented. Moreover, she obtained the permission of her director.

Canon Tortora came to the Monastery shortly afterwards. He first asked Mary Celeste to tell him, for his own consolation, all the good the Lord had accomplished in that convent. He then questioned her concerning the trials and sufferings she had had to endure on account of the new Rule. Deeply touched by all he heard, he quoted and commented on the words of the Psalmist: "*Viriliter age et confortetur cor tuum, et sustine*

Dominum" ("Expect the Lord, do manfully, and let thy heart take courage, and wait thou for the Lord."— Psalm 26:14).

He then spoke of his own difficulties of conscience. In her turn the venerable Sister reassured him, and thus a holy friendship was established between them from this mutual interchange of the lights granted to them by God. Before leaving the Canon said to Mary Celeste: "As you are not living in a community of your own Order, you ought to come to Foggia and found a house there; we have there a monastery for the daughters of the nobility, also one for penitents and one for orphans, but nothing at all for the middle class of professional people, merchants, or government officials, which compose the larger part of the population. I myself have a niece, the daughter of my late brother Dominic; I would willingly entrust her to you if you would consent to make the foundation."

Mary Celeste replied that if God willed it she was ready to go to Foggia, but that for the moment she could not leave Nocera. Such was the opinion of Don Bernadine, her spiritual director, without whose consent she could do nothing.

Don Tortora quite understood that her duty was to finish the work which God had entrusted to her, but he added: "When you are ready to leave Nocera, write to me, and I will do all in my power to obtain the necessary permissions for a foundation at Foggia."

On his return home the Canon told his sister-in-law, Donna Gaetano Roselli, who was a widow with three children—two boys and one girl—all that had happened at Nocera, and said that he hoped in time to help to found a convent for the middle classes at Foggia where his niece would be able to enter. His sister was delighted and was constantly urging him to fulfil this pious project.

CHAPTER VI
THE FOUNDRESS

URING the whole time that Mary Celeste was quietly working at the reform in Nocera she had been praying to know the Will of God regarding the future, but keeping her mind in perfect peace, knowing the way would be made clear to her in God's own time. Now, however, the second three-year period of her Rule as Superior was drawing to a close, and it became necessary to consider the various propositions which had been made to her.

She gave her attention first to the foundation asked for at Perouse. This, as we have said, would have been an important one, entailing great responsibility. Mary Celeste prayed much over it. The obstacle to it came from her parents' opposition. They considered Perouse too far away from Naples, and had no intention of giving up the consolation of seeing their daughter from time to time.

Next came the proposal from Roccapiemonte. The duke and duchess were insistent in their demands for a foundation on their estate. They had even gone so far as to order carriages for the journey. But the venerable Sister was not in favor of this foundation. It would have meant establishing their convent on the baronial lands, and her experience at Marigliano made her fear a repetition of the same difficulties which had caused the dissolution of that convent.

There were less serious objections to the other proposed foundations, but the great difficulty was to know which to choose. Mary Celeste continued to pray earnestly that God would make His Will clear, and one morning after Holy Communion she heard these words: "Go to Foggia, that is the foundation I wish you to make. Write to Canon Tortora and tell him that the time has come to fulfil his desire in the matter."

The holy Nun was overjoyed at last to know God's Will; but out of prudence and mistrusting herself she waited to make sure of the Divine origin of the words she had heard. Without mentioning this experience to her spiritual Father, she asked his advice as to what he believed to be God's Will concerning the proposed foundations. By an inspiration from Heaven, Don Bernadine replied: "Go to Foggia, that is God's Will." She then told him what had happened after Holy Communion that morning.

Assured now of the Divine Will, she wrote to Canon Tortora to tell him that God had deigned to approve of the proposed foundation at Foggia which she was now to make. As soon as he received the letter the Canon told the good news to his sister-in-law. They then both did all in their power to facilitate the necessary negotiations. Donna Roselli set about recruiting future postulants, whilst Don Tortora interviewed the Bishop, the nobility and governors of the town, and in particular a clever and influential lawyer, Francis Ricciardi. In order that none of the other monasteries might oppose his plans the Canon meant to begin the foundation without asking any financial help either from the town or from private individuals. The convent would thus be founded in that evangelical poverty and humility beloved of Our Lord. He decided, moreover, to rent a house in which the Nuns could live on the incomes of the young girls who would enter as postulants. God allowed his plan to be approved by all, and in less than one month twenty-five young ladies, including his own niece, had promised to enter. The good priest found a house belonging to the Jesuit Fathers of Orla and rented it. Rejoicing in his success, he wrote to Mary Celeste at Nocera, assuring her that it was much wiser only to rent a house, for they would then be free to move elsewhere should the exigencies of the future require it. He told her all that had been done, and that they now needed only the authorization from the Bishop to begin the foundation. She would therefore make all preparations for her departure.

By God's Will this letter only reached Nocera a fortnight after it had been written, so that in the meantime the Canon had gone to Troia, interviewed the Bishop, Monsignor John Fraccoli, and obtained from him the necessary authorization on January 17th, 1738. Every week the Canon wrote to Nocera relating all that was being done. At this time a charming episode occurred which showed that the foundation at Foggia was approved by God. It seemed as though the miraculous events of the first days of the revelations were to be renewed. In Mary Celeste's own words the facts are related: "During all this time," she says, "the Lord was pleased to manifest by certain external signs His Will and approval. Every Thursday the Canon's letters came to Nocera by a courier from Foggia; and on the previous Wednesday a little bell was heard ringing through the Convent as if for a feast day. All the Nuns heard it without being able to understand what it was for, or from whence it came, and they set about trying to find out the source of this ringing. They soon discovered that the sound came from the Superior's cell, close to her bed, where there was a parchment picture of the Most Holy Redeemer. A picture of St. Paschal Baylon also gave out little sounds, and although these were very faint they could be heard in the adjoining rooms."

At first Mary Celeste could not understand the reason for these joyous sounds coming from the holy pictures, although she herself experienced a great interior spiritual joy from them. At last she perceived that the ringing began on Wednesday evening, and continued until the arrival of the letters from Foggia, on Thursday, after which the bells immediately ceased. It was like a heavenly warning of the arrival of the Canon's letters, and evidently a sign of God's blessing on the foundation to be made at Foggia. "Such was the goodness of God," continues Mary Celeste, "that this continued until we left

Nocera. When once the foundation was accomplished, these holy pictures never again gave out any sound. The Nuns of the new monastery, however, keep them with great veneration."

A work so obviously protected by Heaven could not fail to provoke a reaction on the part of the eternal enemy. Indeed it would have been extraordinary had contradictions been wanting to the new foundation. Just as all was prepared for the reception of the Nuns and the twenty-five young girls, the parents of the latter seeing that there was no income or capital to ensure the existence of the house, drew back. They were urged to do this by people who, at the instigation of the devil, spoke against the Convent; so that they ended by withdrawing their consent to their daughters' entrance into the monastery. The poor Canon, in great distress of mind, wrote all this to Mary Celeste. The wise Superior immediately recognized the work of the devil, and wrote to the Canon to hasten the preparations, as they would secretly advance the date of their journey, since God willed it so.

On her part, she warned the Bishop of Nocera and the Administrators that the time had come to replace her, as God had shown His Will in regard to her future. The Prelate, who was deeply grateful to Mary Celeste and held her in great esteem, immediately came to the Convent to consult with her about the new appointment. He asked her advice, and she begged him to choose a Superior from the Community, and not from outside the Monastery, otherwise even worse things might happen than had before occurred. The Bishop then told her to point out to him whom he should choose for Superioress, and whom for Vicar, saying that she knew best who was capable of these important charges. He would then be at ease regarding the spiritual welfare of the community. Mary Celeste proposed two Nuns who had always led an exemplary life, and whose virtue and prudence were well known to her. The Bishop confirmed them in their respective charges, in which they maintained the reform and regular observance, to the edification of all. At the same time, the Nuns were inconsolable at losing the holy Mother who had done so much for their souls. Mary Celeste and her sister, Mary Illuminata, on their part were deeply moved by the tears and affection of the Community. The majority wished to accompany them, and they had hard work to pacify them. It is noticeable that for some time there has been no further question of the young sister, Mary Evangelista. Very probably after the three months' sojourn at Nocera demanded by her father, she had returned home according to the resolution she had taken in an hour of trial. We do not know that she ever again entered a convent as a religious.

The departure of the two elder sisters from Nocera was a subject of grief to the whole town. Seeing the general consternation, the Bishop and his Administrators implored them to remain, and the whole Community renewed their prayers and tears. All this grief was a source of suffering to the sensitive heart of Mary Celeste, and only the thought that God called them to Foggia gave her courage to resist to the end.

On March 3rd, 1738, Canon Tortora and his sister-in-law, Donna Gaetana Roselli, set out for Nocera to escort the two sisters from thence to Foggia. While at Nocera they stayed with a relation in the town, and sent word to the Sisters to make all preparations for their departure. The day before leaving, Sister Mary Celeste received a visit from her spiritual Father, Don Bernadino. He gave her his blessing and forbade her to reveal anything concerning her soul to anyone whomsoever without his permission. He said that if she had any difficulties, she was to write to him; and that she could go on without any fear, guided by God Who would continue to direct her. She agreed to this, because she knew by experience that everything this holy man said to her was ratified by God in a wonderful manner, and that his words brought peace to her soul. Lastly he told her to go joyfully, because God willed her to be at Foggia.

On the following day the two sisters left Nocera. They were

accompanied by their brother Michael, by the Canon and his sister-in-law, also by a young girl from Nocera who wished to enter the new Order. There were three carriages for the travelers. It had been raining for some days past, so that the roads were in a very bad state, but in spite of the weather they set off, and hardly had they left Nocera than the sun shone out as though to help them on their way. Nevertheless, the journey was not accomplished without difficulty. The rivers were swollen and several times the horses were up to their necks in water. The mud gave them no less trouble. The carriage wheels sunk into it up to the axles, and the horses could not move. All had then to get out while the wheels were dragged out of the mire. However, with the help of Heaven they got safely through to their journey's end.

During the whole time, Mary Celeste was absorbed in contemplation. The difficulties just related were unperceived by her and must have been told to her afterwards by others. To her, it seemed as if she were journeying towards Heaven, for Our Lord had drawn her into that state of deep recollection in which He spoke to her soul, and, to quote her own words: "Made known to her things so admirable that they cannot be told in human language." She seemed to see an immense road, so wide that it contained all creatures and things created. She was, as it were, carried along this road by the spirit and strength of God, in a swift but gentle flight towards heaven. During this flight she saw around her the inertia and insensibility of creatures who remained indifferent, although they felt also within themselves this flight towards the Divine Being, His immensity and His greatness. Thus the first two days of the journey passed. Mary Celeste never forgot this ecstasy and its effects lasted for several days.

When the travelers drew near to Foggia, certain gentlemen of the town sent out carriages to meet them, as was the custom in those days. Donna Roselli and two other ladies who wished to place their daughters in the Convent also accompanied them.

The two Nuns were invited to enter a special carriage which had been reserved for them. The Sisters were dressed in the manner prescribed by the Rule for those who go to make a foundation; they were wearing their mantles, had their faces veiled, a crown of thorns on their head and a crucifix on their breast. Thus veiled, they entered the town and were conducted to the monastery of which Canon Tortora was chaplain. A great crowd followed them, for their habit, to which the citizens were unaccustomed, caused a great sensation.

It was the Canon's wish that the Nuns should rest in this convent for several days, so that they could assemble there and go in procession to their new abode, accompanied by the principal citizens of Foggia. Had the sisters consulted their own wishes, they would have preferred to go straight to their own house and be at once enclosed. They deferred to the Canon's wishes, however, as the latter thought a solemn entry would rouse the interest of the town on their behalf. For two days the poor Nuns had to receive countless visitors. All the well-known people of Foggia came to pay their respects and to ask questions concerning the new Order. Finally, on March 9th, 1758, they were allowed to proceed to their own monastery.

Mary Celeste has left us an account of this in her autobiography: "At the head of the procession," she tells us, "walked all the canons of the Collegiate Church, followed by Don Antonia Manerba, a Bishop who was just then staying in Foggia, his native town. Next came all the clergy and foremost citizens of Foggia; then the children who were to enter (for of the twenty-five promised, only six remained). These children walked two by two, and were preceded by a priest carrying a crucifix. Lastly came the two Nuns, with the two Archpriests of Foggia at their side. The Sisters were dressed as on their arrival, with their faces veiled and wearing their mantles and crown of thorns. The priests sang the *Te Deum* alternately, and thus, in good order, they were conducted to the Cathedral, in which was a miraculous picture of Our Lady of the Seven Veils. Here they offered themselves to God, and placed themselves under the special protection of Mary. During all this time the bells were ringing and there was a dense crowd of people of all classes, who surrounded the Nuns with sympathetic attention, and shed tears of devotion.

From the Cathedral they went to the house prepared for them, and where the Convent was to be founded. The Superior and her companion stopped at the foot of the stairs, as had been fixed beforehand by the Ceremonial. There they knelt down, and asked Monsignor Manerba's blessing, and thanked him for having honored them by accompanying them in the name of the Bishop of the town. Mgr. Fracolli, who was just then at Troia. The Nuns kissed the Bishop's feet. He then blessed them and congratulated them, after which he withdrew, promising to visit them the following day.

After the Bishop's departure, they entered the house, and found there two titled ladies of the town, who were waiting to receive them and present their good wishes. Finally all the visitors retired. The Convent was thus founded under favorable circumstances, and the future seemed hopeful.

CHAPTER VII

THE FOUNDATION

HE solemn procession to the Convent had been brilliant; it seemed as though at last all obstacles were removed and the way made clear before them. Alas! how many deceptions Mary Celeste was still to meet with in the course of her work. To begin with, the Convent was completely bare. On entering the house, the Nuns found nothing but the four walls. Such forgetfulness on the part of the Canon seems inexplicable! There were no chairs even, and with the exception of a few benches and tables for the refectory, there was absolutely nothing. Kitchen utensils had to be borrowed, and only a very small quantity of provisions was found in the house. God helped them in their poverty, however, in a wonderful way, for with only the small pension paid by the children they managed to meet all expenses and provide for ten people. There were in the house besides the two Nuns and the six postulants (or *Educandes*, as they are called in Italy) two old servants who on account of their age were incapable and useless, yet they had to be kept, for they were in the house when the Nuns arrived. There was also furniture to be bought and the high rent of one hundred ducats a year to pay for the house. The expenses of the journey and installation had likewise to be met, for it had surprised the Nuns not a little to discover that Canon Tortora and his sister-in-law, although in comfortable circumstances, expected to be repaid for every expense they had incurred, and which they had carefully noted down, even to the price of the torches used for the night journey. Mary Celeste, however, closed her eyes to this avarice, and remembered only the zeal with which the

Canon and his sister-in-law had worked for the foundation. It is indeed little short of miraculous that, with so many expenses and so little resources, the house was able to exist without contracting any debts. The holy Foundress does not hesitate to see in this a miracle of God's love.

Another trial at the beginning of this foundation was the renewal of persecution from the powers of darkness. "The enemy of mankind," says Mary Celeste, "was enraged against the new Convent, to such an extent that it is difficult to relate it here." First of all the parents who had not placed their children in the house went to those who had done so, and told them that they had acted foolishly, for the Bishop had not given his approval to the new Convent, that their daughters would die of hunger, and the foundresses would soon be obliged to leave. Other people took pleasure in spreading not only these rumors in the town, but also that the Nuns had already gone back to their own country. Not knowing what; to believe, people came to the Convent door to make inquiries, questioning the servants as to the real state of affairs, and whether it were true that they were dying of hunger. In consequence of all these rumors, the parents even refused the modest sum asked for, as dowry, not being willing to risk their money under such circumstances.

The hardest trial of all to Mary Celeste, however, was the gradual withdrawal of the postulants, until only two remained. She had begun the formation and instruction of these young souls with such care. She gives us the following account of their order of day: "They began by making half-an-hour of mental prayer; after which the Superior and the Mother Vicar said the Divine Office, privately, because the children were incapable at first of reciting it in Choir. Next came Holy Mass, and they remained in the chapel while two more Masses were being said; then followed study or work of some kind until the hour of noon; after which came the Examen of conscience, and then dinner. During dinner they listened to the reading, as the

Rule ordains. An hour's recreation followed, then the bell was rung for silence. During the silence, half-an-hour of spiritual reading was made, followed by half-an-hour of prayer. Then came manual work and practical lessons. In the evening the Superior herself gave the Meditation, reading out the points, so as to teach the postulants how to make mental prayer."

This seems a very strenuous life for little children—but evidently it was not considered excessive for little Italians at that time. The chief trial for the Nuns was that they had not the Blessed Sacrament in the house, as the Bishop would only give his consent when they should be in a house of their own. "Without the company of Our dear Lord," says Mary Celeste, "we felt like bodies without a soul." This order of the day shows us how much time the Superior consecrated to prayer, and to the spiritual formation of the postulants. She does not tells us, however, with what light, unction and strength she communicated the religious spirit to these young souls and led them to God. This can only be seen later, when the parents finally consented to allow the fruits of this education, given by a saint, to ripen.

In the meantime, Canon Tortora and a certain Don Joseph Angelis who, together had charge of the Monastery, seeing that people continued to speak with contempt of the place because it was only rented, resolved to buy a house. For this reason they consulted the chief lawyer of the town, Don Ricciardi. The latter, promised to procure one, and discovered a suitable building still in the town, but with a beautiful view over the surrounding country, and with ground belonging to it on which they could build later. This house was the property of the Poor Clares; and as the lawyer was one of their protectors, he was able to conclude the contract under favorable conditions. Some small houses round the building were pulled down and a pretty little garden made. The church was then arranged, also the necessary conventual rooms. "It seems as though Our Lord Himself had chosen this place for a monastery," writes Mary

Celeste.

When everything was ready, on 4th October, 1739, the transfer took place. The Nuns had been in the temporary convent exactly one year and seven months. All was in perfect order in their new home, and to their great joy they found that it was possible to place the Blessed Sacrament in their little Chapel at once, and to begin the Offices in public.

Within the Convent, the Superior caused the Rules to be put in practice precisely as Our Lord had revealed them to her in the monastery of Scala, and of which, as we know, she had a copy. The observance was kept in every detail, except that it was not possible at this time to put up the Enclosure as prescribed by the Rules. Tortora and Angelio were both opposed to it, saying that such strictness might cause the parents to take away their children. Mary Celeste was much grieved at this, and implored God to find a remedy. She made many appeals to the Canon on the subject, and he invariably replied that he would consent as soon as there were the requisite number of Nuns.

Now that the house was acquired, the rumors against the Convent, instead of ceasing, seemed to increase. As soon as anyone heard that strangers wished to place their children there, they went to them and spoke so much evil against the Convent, telling so many falsehoods, that people knew not what to believe. "It seems incredible," says Mary Celeste, "that so much should have been done to destroy the work of God." Finally, in one last effort, the devil hoped to break it down. The following account is taken from the foundress' autobiography:

"... Six months after the Nuns had been settled in their new monastery, on 23rd April, 1740, during the afternoon silence, a little uninhabitated tower belonging to a neighbouring house collapsed. It was the hour of the noonday repose, and the postulants were lying down. The tower, which had already been much shaken by an earthquake in 1731, fell on to one of the rooms in the Monastery, where two of the postulants were on their beds. Both were buried beneath the debris. One was the niece of Canon Tortora, and the other the youngest child of Don Angelis. The roof of the attic above and the wall of the tower crashed down on these poor children. All the inhabitants of the town rushed to help remove the ruins under which the young girls lay buried. The niece of Canon Tortora was brought out dead; Don Angelis' daughter was alive, but badly injured. Her father had her carried home at once to be nursed, and when she was well again, she returned to the Convent.

Poor Canon Tortora was in great grief, and had also to console his sister-in-law, who was broken-hearted, having only this one little girl. It seemed hard that those who had worked so much for the foundation should be thus cruelly tried, "but such are the unfathomable yet always adorable ways of Divine Providence," concludes Mary Celeste. It can be imagined what consternation and sorrow this misfortune caused on all sides. As soon as the parents heard of the accident, with the exaggerated rumor that many of the postulants were dead, they hastened to the Convent to take their daughters away. Mary Celeste recognized in this the work of the devil, but full of sublime courage and confidence in God, she told the parents that they might take their children as soon as they pleased, for God had no need of men for His glory, and He would know how to raise up other generous souls to be His chosen spouses.

By this generous resignation she had conquered the powers of hell, and Satan was about to abandon a useless struggle. A priest who happened to be present at that moment recognized also in this the work of the devil. He persuaded the parents to entrust their children to God, and convinced by the sincerity of his words, they allowed their daughters to remain in the Monastery.

The devil had reached the limit marked by God in his persecution of the Nuns. After this tragic event, which one would have expected to have had a prejudicial effect on the fortunes of the monastery, many people of the upper classes came to present their daughters as postulants. As the number of vocations increased, it became necessary to build, to enlarge the church and to make various improvements. Thus, after so many trials the clouds were lifted, and the future seemed hopeful. During the Octave of Easter, March 26th, 1742, eight postulants, five Chorists and three lay-Sisters were clothed. Canon Tortora was delegated by the Bishop to preside at the ceremony. The first postulant was the daughter of a merchant. At her clothing she received the name of Sister Mary Angela of the Cross. The three others were sisters and were given the names of Sister Mary of the Crucifix, Sister Mary Emmanuel, and Sister Mary Columba. The last postulant was called Sister Mary Rose of Saint Mary. The three lay- Sisters were called Sister Perseverenta, Sister Fortunata, and Sister Baptista. This newly-planted little garden became for the Lord one of sweet perfumed flowers, so great therein was the love of

retirement and of a hidden holy life in imitation of the Savior practice therein. Their perfume was wafted abroad to the great edification of seculars, so that the work which had once been held in contempt now enjoyed the admiration and respect of all.

God raised up another benefactor for the Convent, in the person of one of the Canon's friends. This gentleman, hearing of the new Order, and of the virtues of the Superioress, asked to speak to her. The Canon accompanied him to the monastery, and he talked much to the holy Sister about the state of his soul and of prayer. After this he became much attached to the Convent and when, later on, he became a priest, he bought a house next to the monastery Church, and gave it to the Sisters. Every year he also gave them large alms and saw that they were in want of nothing. The Bishop seeing that God had evidently sent him to assist this new foundation, made him a protector of the monastery, and he remained its firm friend to the end of his life.

Such were the obscure and painful beginnings of the Convent of the Most Holy Redeemer at Foggia, which was later, by God's grace, to become a great and glorious monastery.

CHAPTER VIII
THE PRIORESS OF FOGGIA AND MONASTERY OF SCALA

 HILST Mary Celeste, in the midst of so many trials, was continuing her providential mission of reformer and foundress, what was happening at Scala?

Let us return in thought to that sad day which-witnessed the expulsion of the Venerable Sister in 1733, and hasten to say that the work of God, of which she was the instrument, was preserved intact from the storm which had threatened to annihilate it. Indeed, soon after her departure, a ceremony took place at Scala, which stands out in the history of the Order, and which we must consider one of the first-fruits of Mary Celeste's sacrifice.

We read the following account of it in the Chapter book: "After having observed the Holy Rule of the new Order for nearly two years, the Community sent a petition of Mgr. Santora, Bishop of Scala, asking to be allowed to make their religious profession according to the new Rule. The Bishop came to the Monastery on the afternoon of June 18th, 1733, and all the Nuns, both Chorists and lay- Sisters, ratified, under the form prescribed by the Rule of the Most Holy Redeemer, the vows made formerly according to the Visitation Rule. An act was drawn up by the Apostolic lawyer and consigned to the episcopal archives of the town. Each Sister signed this act of profession and kept a copy of it, so as to be able to renew it every month according to the Rule."

The fact, however, that this Rule was revealed to Mary Celeste by Our Lord was passed over by the Nuns in silence. In the awkward situation they had themselves created, it would have been difficult to mention it. They had sent away their holy Sister against their better judgment, and out of obedience to their spiritual Father. They did not doubt her Divine mission, and still considered the Rule revealed to her from Heaven as their greatest treasure. Yet, how could they speak openly of this Rule when Mary Celeste, from whom it emanated, had been treated as delusioned and rebellious? Such a contradiction would have excited public opinion and provoked their Bishop to opposition. Already at the first sign of trouble. Monsignor Santora had withdrawn the act of approbation granted to them at Tosquez' request. He had even expressed a desire, on this occasion, that they should return to the Visitation Rule. For all these reasons, therefore, the Sisters felt obliged to draw a veil over both Mary Celeste's mission and St. Alphonsus' providential role which was inseparable from it, and to attribute to Falcoia the work which in reality came from them.

We can hardly blame the Nuns, when we know that Falcoia himself, the preceding year, in order to avoid certain difficulties, had wished St. Alphonsus, in speaking to his Superior, Canon Tomi, to feign to believe that the whole project of the Institute emanated from the Bishop of Castellamare. Moreover, in order to quiet the delicate conscience of the Saint, he went so far as to quote the example of Our Lord, Who feigned to the disciples of Emmaus that He would go farther. The effect of this diplomacy was to falsify the history of the Rule. Thus, when, after having obtained the approbation of the Rule by the Holy See in 1750, the Sisters asked from the Bishop the approbation of their Constitutions, they stated in their request: "These Constitutions have been drawn up for the most part by Mgr. Falcoia, Bishop of Castellamare, of the Congregation of 'Pii Operarii'." We cannot even see a feeble attempt at reparation towards Mary Celeste in an obscure allusion to the rule God had reserved for her, in these words taken from their Chapter book: "The new Rule, as well as the

Constitutions, were dictated by Mgr. Falcoia, who had received Supernatural light regarding them."

Finally, this is how these good Nuns some years later wrote the history of the origin of their Order: "After the foundation of this Monastery, the Nuns lived for some time under the Rule of St. Francis de Sales. Under the direction of Thomas Falcoia, priest of the Congregation of 'Pii Operarii' and later Bishop of Castellamare, they made much progress in virtue. It came to their knowledge, however, that St. Francis de Sales insists on each monastery being founded by a Visitandine Nun, and on its being united to the other convents of the Order. Now they had not taken this into account when founding their monastery, and this double omission might create difficulties for the future. The Sisters then became very much disturbed and anxious. They felt they were not true religious, since their foundation was lacking in two necessary elements prescribed by the founder of the Order. They began therefore to desire to be under some Rule, so that their position might be regularized, yet they had no preference for any special Rule. They spoke of this many times to their director, Monsignor Falcoia, who not only would not hear of it, but humiliated them on this account, even depriving them of Holy Communion. The more he opposed it, however, the greater grew their desire, and the more insistent their requests; until finally Monsignor Falcoia, seeing the unanimity and constancy of the Sisters, and knowing also their desire to imitate Jesus Christ, composed for them from the Gospels some Rules on the imitation of the Savior. He did this after much opposition both on the part of Mgr. Guemere, Bishop of Scala, and of numerous priests and laymen of that town. All the opposing parties, however, changed their opinion later, and expressed their regret even to the point of coming to the Monastery to ask the Nuns' pardon. Finally, with Mgr. Guerriere's permission, on Whit-Monday, 1731, Monsignor Falcoia imposed his Rule on the Nuns, who at once conformed to it."

We can only hope that the Nun who wrote these lines knew nothing of past events, being herself deceived by the mis-statements of her predecessors. Yes, in truth all the Sisters who entered the Monastery of Scala later must have ignored even the very existence of St. Alphonsus, and of Mary Celeste. They were therefore obliged to believe the false legend which made Falcoia their founder.

Needless to say, this legend could only be confined within the walls of Scala. The companions and first sons of St. Alphonsus were too well aware of the facts concerning the origin of the Order to allow such an error to enter their thoughts. St. Clement Hofbauer, the apostle of Warsaw and Vienna, who was raised up by God to transplant the Congregation of the Most Holy Redeemer beyond the Alps, had been instructed and formed by them. Therefore, when his disciple and successor, the Venerable Father Passerat, Vicar-General of the trans-Alpine Congregation of Redemptorists, sent his spiritual daughter, Eugenie Dijon, accompanied by the Countess of Welsersheimb, to drink in the spirit of the Order at the Monastery of St. Agatha, he did not dream of directing them to Castellamare to the tomb of Falcoia, but told them to go to Nocera to the tomb of St. Alphonsus. They arrived there on November 11th, 1830. The lines written then by that great Frenchwoman, who is justly considered as the foundress of the Redemptoristines outside Italy, are decisive on this subject. "... We remained all morning in the Church," she says, "at the foot of the altar, where are preserved the relics of Blessed Alphonsus. We received Communion there and heard several Masses. Afterwards we recited out loud the Litanies of Blessed Alphonsus, imploring him with tears to deign to receive us among the number of his children, and to intercede with God to obtain the authorization for the Order of his spiritual daughters to be established in Austria. And what happened? Our beloved Father deigned to give us a proof of his paternal affection by obtaining from God that the decree of authorization should be signed that very same day by the Emperor."

Justly proud to be the true daughters of that great Doctor of prayer and of Divine love, the Redemptoristines beyond the Alps have held in grateful veneration and affection the two great souls whom God united for the foundation of their Order, Mary Celeste and St. Alphonsus.

To return to the Sisters of Scala, living under such an unfortunate delusion, it was only in 1855 that they remembered her to whom they owed their holy Rule and their very existence as Nuns of the Most Holy Redeemer. That year brought round the centenary of Mary Celeste's death. The immense crowd of people who went to Foggia to venerate the body of the Venerable Sister and the wonders wrought at her tomb made a great sensation in the surrounding country. The echoes of all this reached the Sisters' ears. They were much impressed by it. The Superior of Scala, who was then Mother Mary Alphonsus of the Will of God, wrote to the Superior of Foggia, Mother Mary Teresa of Jesus, a letter which is no longer in our possession, but whose import is clearly indicated by the following reply:

"To the Very Reverend Mother Mary Alphonsus of the Will of God, Superior of the Monastery of the Most Holy Redeemer at Scala.

"MY MOST HONORED SUPERIOR AND SISTER IN JESUS CHRIST,

"You cannot imagine what joy your letter gave me. You express a desire most dear to my heart, that is to know a few details concerning the life and death of our Sister Mary Celeste Crostarosa, foundress of this monastery where her body lies buried. A true odor of sanctity emanates from these holy remains, parts of which, in particular the hands, have been preserved intact. This wonder makes manifest the mercies with which God deigned to overwhelm her during her hard life.

"On the 14th of September this year a century had gone by since the glorious death of her whom all named 'the holy Prioress of the Most Holy Redeemer of Foggia.' On my request, with the episcopal sanction, an anniversary office was celebrated; but not a Requiem, for this holy soul who must now certainly be in possession of her heavenly crown. However, the Church has not yet authorized the homage which we one day hope to render her. An immense crowd gathered for this anniversary. We were all the more astonished, as we had not sent out word of it to the faithful. They came by all roads and from all parts, saying to one another: 'Let us go to venerate the holy Prioress' body, for to-day the centenary of her death is being celebrated.' At the unveiling of the reliquary placed in the wall of our Church on the Gospel side, in which since 1809, by order of Cardinal Firrao, her precious remains have been preserved, the fervent devotion, the cries and tears of the crowd, knew no bounds. Added to this was the noise made by people who wished to enter and could not do so on account of the crowd, so that the Chaplain of the Monastery, fearing difficulties with the police or, worse still, damage to the holy body, was obliged to close the Church. The crowd grew so excited that an attempt was then made to open the doors and let them enter once more. The effect was worse than ever, so that the Chaplain ended by locking the doors and carrying off the keys. A crowd is easily pacified. They were promised permission to come every day if they would come quietly. Since then, the procession of people of all classes is incessant. Lately the Capitulary Vicar of Troia, accompanied by several priests, asked to see our saint. He thought her wonderful. We have obtained permission to print her picture. This picture is venerated in all the houses of Foggia, and her protection is invoked in all circumstances. Not a day passes without some favor being received through her intercession. In this holy cloister we keep the manuscript of her life written by her own hand. At present it is in the episcopal palace, the Capitulary Vicar having expressed a desire to read it. This Life is quite voluminous and could not be copied without much fatigue. Our Mother relates therein all that she suffered for the reform of this monastery, and all that she prophesied to St. Alphonsus, as you know. I have the advantage of knowing one of our old Sisters, Mother Mary Gertrude of the Heart of Jesus, an exemplary religious who knew not only the holy Foundress, but also St. Alphonsus, Brother Gerard, and other saintly members of the Congregation. Though I was very young at the time, my greatest pleasure was to listen to her stories. Their memory lives with me. In order to help you I will wait until the book in question is returned to me, and will then copy shortly for you the essential facts. Rest assured that it will give me pleasure to do this for you.

"Would you satisfy my curiosity by telling me how you came to think of asking for the life of this Nun, your Sister and our Mother? What has happened? A century has gone by since her death (not counting the eighteen years which preceded it, when she was a member of your community) and we have never been questioned about her. What had brought you to do so now? It fills me with hope since nothing occurs without God's Will. Who knows what designs God may wish to realize through you!

"I beg of you to remember me in your prayers. I ask the same of your daughters, my Sisters in Jesus Christ. I need prayers. Obliged to direct a large Community of sixty-six people, I need the fervent spirit of my holy Foundress. Alas! I am far from that. Therefore, I recommend myself to souls pleasing to God, such as you and your daughters. And I, unworthy as I am, shall not fail to pray for you, since Our Lord hears us all. My good Sisters here will pray with me. They send their affectionate homage to you and to your Community. I join myself to them, embracing you in the Hearts of Jesus and Mary, and I sign myself your very humble and devoted servant and sister. SISTER MARY TERESA OF JESUS, Superior of the Monastery of the Most Holy 10th *November*, 1855. Redeemer of Foggia."

The hopes of the Superior of Foggia were not realized. God's designs were only to be accomplished later; nevertheless the Superior of Scala inserted in the archives of the Monastery the following account: "Warning and Notice" Herein registered is the copy of the memoirs relating to our former Sister Mary Celeste Crostarosa, one of the foundresses of this monastery, authentic memoirs which have come straight to us from the Superior of the Monastery of the Most Holy Redeemer at Foggia, Sister Mary Teresa of Jesus. These memoirs were sent to me on my request by the kindness of the aforesaid Superior on August 9th, 1857. A picture and piece of clothing belonging to Sister Mary Celeste were sent with them. All this was sent free of charge.

"The portrait is kept in our Choir, for in our Community we had completely forgotten the memory of this Sister. Indeed, after receiving the revelation which she communicated in the confessional to St. Alphonsus de Liguori, of the Most Holy Redeemer, as is stated in her Life, she left this monastery and went to undertake the reform of a community at Cava, then of another, that of Carmillo, at Nocera; and from there she went to Foggia, where she founded the monastery still in existence, that of the Most Holy Redeemer, which numbers actually sixty-five Nuns, including choir-Sisters, lay-Sisters and postulants. There, after having written the Rules, her Life and other mystical and ascetical works, she died as Superior in the odor of sanctity. Her venerated remains are preserved in the Church of the aforesaid monastery in a special sepulcher, and her soul, with all its virtues, enjoys the eternal beatitude of Heaven.

"May this great Servant of God deign to look down mercifully from above on her daughters who form this abandoned Community. May she keep them united in bonds of charity and in humble and perfect observance of the Rules. May she also pray for her who has done all in her power to procure this precious book of information. *Fiat, Fiat!*"

All honor to this worthy Redemptoristine! Her prayers have been heard. To-day the flourishing Community of Scala, living now in the full light of Justice and Truth, are second to none in their devotion to the Venerable Mother. The memory of Mary Celeste lives in the Monastery. Wherever some particular scene of her life occurred a tablet is placed recording the incident taken from the Autobiography of the Servant of God.

CHAPTER IX
THE PRIORESS OF FOGGIA AND THE REDEMPTORISTS

HE Congregation of the Most Holy Redeemer was to afford more consolation to Mary Celeste's heart than the Sisters of Scala had done. The Brothers' dispositions at the time of the process of beatification bear witness to the fact that in their Congregation the Venerable Mother had always been looked upon as a holy soul favored with great supernatural gifts. Therefore, whenever their ministry called them to Capitanate or to Pouille, they did not fail to visit the holy Prioress. St. Alphonsus set them an example in this, and their meeting, which took place in 1745, is worthy of record.

That year fifteen Redemptorists, under the direction of their Blessed Father, went to preach a mission in the four parishes of Foggia. The Saint preached in the Cathedral where, from her shrine, the Madonna of the Seven Veils presided over the exercises. The miracle with which the Holy Virgin rewarded her Servant's zeal is well known. One evening whilst the Saint was preaching on Our Lady with his usual fervor of soul, suddenly within the silver oval which framed the Madonna's face the features of the Virgin appeared, fresh and rose-tinted, standing out in relief like those of a living person. A shining ray of light came forth from Mary's face and illuminated the features of the holy preacher. Falling immediately into ecstasy under the eyes of the immense crowd, Alphonsus was raised a few inches above the floor of the pulpit, with his arms extended towards Mary as though he were about to fly towards his beloved Queen.

"During this mission," says Father Berthe, "Alphonsus went to visit Mary Celeste and to condole with her over past sorrows. Whilst admiring the fervor of the Monastery and the virtues of the foundress, whom the whole town venerated as a Saint, he adored the decrees of God, Who leads His elect to Heaven by paths known to Himself alone." Moreover, St. Alphonsus had always kept his holy friend in mind, and followed her in spirit through all her vicissitudes. He had been very much preoccupied by the financial difficulties she had had to face at the beginning of the foundation. Yet how could he help her, having no resources himself? Whilst urging Mary Celeste to put her whole trust in Providence, he sent one of his Fathers to beg alms for the venerable foundress from the wealthy families of Foggia. "Armed with the Saint's authority," says the Rev. Father Berutti, from whom we learn this detail, "the ambassador succeeded wonderfully in his mission, which greatly rejoiced the heart of Alphonsus."

A little incident gathered from one of the Saint's letters to a Nun of the Monastery of the Annunciation at Foggia shows us the intimacy which never ceased to exist between Alphonsus and Mary Celeste.

In the above-mentioned monastery an Apostolic Visitor had suppressed all music known as "figured chant," as it had a worldly character and generally necessitated the cooperation of seculars. Now the Superior of this Convent intended to write to the Sacred Congregation of Bishops and Regulars to have this prohibition withdrawn. A fervent member of this Community wrote to St. Alphonsus asking how such a scandal could be prevented. The Saint replied on January 30th, 1747, that the Nun in question should write herself to the Sacred Congregation, setting forth the objections to this secular music and begging that it might not be again introduced into the Convent, The Saint even took the trouble to explain to this Nun how she should begin and end her letter. The difficulty, however, arose as to the forwarding of the letter, for, should it pass through the Superior's hands, she would at once suppress it. St. Alphonsus finds a way out of the difficulty. He told his correspondent to give the letter privately to Sister Mary Celeste of the Convent of the Most Holy Redeemer, telling her that it came from him and that, for the glory of God, she would pay for it and send it to its destination. This detail is very suggestive, for it is only from an intimate friend that one could ask such a service.

Also at Foggia God granted to Mary Celeste the friendship of a holy Redemptorist who, after St. Alphonsus, was the greatest glory of the new Institute. We speak of St. Gerard Majella, the humble lay Brother whose sanctity was the admiration of all, and whose miracles roused the enthusiasm of the whole population. The meeting of the holy Brother with the venerable Mother came about in the following manner: writing to one of his spiritual daughters who was a Nun in the Monastery of the Most Holy Redeemer, Gerard said to her among other things: "I desire to love God, to keep myself constantly united to Him. I desire to do everything for the love of God." Mary Celeste read this letter and was delighted with these dispositions, which accorded so well with her own feelings. Soon after this the fervent Brother was introduced into the Monastery by the Redemptorist Fathers, and the venerable Mother realized immediately that the lines just quoted exactly portrayed the soul of him who had written them. From that time onwards she honored him as a great Servant of God.

On his part Gerard was not long in discovering the treasures of holiness with which the Divine Master had enriched Mary Celeste, A holy friendship founded on mutual esteem sprang up between two souls who were so well able to understand one another, and this spiritual friendship ended only with death. "As for Gerard," says one of his biographers, "to know Mary Celeste was for him to be in intimate union of soul with her. Therefore, on each of his numerous journeys to Foggia he looked upon it as a privilege to visit the Monastery of the Most Holy Redeemer, and there, as in the parlor of Avila, the celestial colloquies of a St. Teresa with St. John of the Cross were renewed."

"Mother Mary Celeste," writes Father Tannia, "was happy to confer with the humble Redemptorist Brother, and he on his part enjoyed the spiritual conversation of the holy Prioress. I know not whether Gerard or the Nun enkindled the other to fervor; but both mutually exhorted each other to the greatest perfection."

Moreover, the Bishop of Troia, Monsignor Fraccoli, and later on his successor. Monsignor Di Simone, knowing of Gerard's influence on souls consecrated to God, had many times begged the worthy son of St. Alphonsus to help Mary Celeste in the work of sanctification she had begun so well. It is easy to guess how great must have been the spiritual profit enjoyed by the Nuns of the Most Holy Redeemer from the interchange of lights and graces between these two great souls. They were accustomed to say that Gerard's words enkindled within them ardent desires for eternal good. When he opened his mouth to speak of wisdom, holiness, the power of God, the merciful goodness of Jesus and Mary, his heart, like a burning fire, gave out flames which enkindled their love. He no longer seemed to be a man, but a seraph with face aflame, looking towards the infinite.

How great must have been the consolation of the Mother and Sisters when once, on the eve of the Feast of the Most Holy Trinity, they were allowed to be present at one of the most marvelous of the holy Brother's ecstasies. Here is the account, taken from the process of beatification:

"Gerard was in Choir during the first Vespers of the Feast. Hardly had the words of the holy liturgy in praise of the One God in Three Persons sounded in his ears than he entered into ecstasy. Transported by a mysterious power, he crossed the Choir, repeating aloud the words of St. Paul: 'Oh riches, oh Wisdom, oh unfathomable depths of Divinity I How unsearchable are Thy Judgments, O Lord!' (Romans 10:33.) In the meantime the chanting of the psalms ended, but the ecstasy continued. On leaving the Choir, Mary Celeste and her Sisters were struck with wonder at the sight of the Saint absorbed in God. They saw him stiffen as though defending himself against an invisible power, but he was gloriously vanquished and cried out: 'Love God, my Sisters, let us love God!' He ceased and remained still, his eyes looking towards Heaven, then, miraculously raised from the ground, he remained for several seconds suspended in the air, after which the ecstasy ended."

The devotion which this holy Brother showed to Mary Celeste's religious family was proved by many miracles. A lay Sister being on the point of death, Gerard made the sign of the Cross over her and restored her to life. Another time a postulant, given up by the doctors, was restored to health in the same manner. Again, one of Mary Celeste's daughters was dangerously ill and the holy Brother begged prayers for her, writing to one of his spiritual daughters in the following burning words: "I do not wish her to die, no, I do not wish it; tell Our Divine Master that I wish her to become more perfect. Ask God only to call her to Himself in her old age, so that she may spend long years in His service. In the name of God I implore you not to let this excellent Sister die. This very day I am beginning a novena to the All-powerful God." Heaven heard his ardent supplications—the sick Nun recovered and lived to an advanced age.

Gerard held Mary Celeste's direction in such esteem that he made it his business to procure subjects for her monastery. He entrusted his own niece to the "Venerable Mother," as he called her, and himself took the young girl to Foggia. An amusing incident is recorded of this journey. As they drew near to the Monastery, Gerard constantly exhorted his niece to become a saint. The young girl listened in silence and recollection of heart. Suddenly they came to a river, and Gerard, turning to her, exclaimed in the passionate Neapolitan manner: "Once for all, do you intend to become a saint? If not, I shall throw you into the river!" We cannot doubt that the young girl, overwhelmed by such ardent exhortations, resolved to work hard at her sanctification.

One more example.

The two daughters of Don Capucci, in obedience to Gerard's counsels, resolved to enter the Monastery of the Most Holy Redeemer with twelve companions to whom they were related. Capucci wished to accompany his children and place them in the hands of Mary Celeste. Gerard also, like a faithful guardian angel, joined the little company to bring them safely to port. As was to be expected, on the way he exhorted them to charity and to generous love of God. In this manner they reached Cervaro at a point where stepping stones crossed the river. But recent rain had caused the waters to rise, and the little group stood on the bank gazing helplessly at the angry waters. What was to be done? It was then that a miracle took place which has since been sworn to by eye-witnesses. Gerard held his hand over the waters and commanded them to part. Instantly the waters stood still and rose like a wall, leaving a dry passage over which the little group passed in safety. When they had reached the other side the waters, with a tumultuous noise, regained their natural course.

At this period a child called Gertrude of Cecilia was being educated in the Convent of the Most Holy Redeemer. Gerard was very fond of the little girl, and through his prayers she obtained the grace of a religious vocation. Yet at first she felt no attraction for the cloister, and longed for the time when she should be free to leave school and return home. One day the holy Brother warned her, saying in serious tones: "Know that if you leave this house you will be sorry for it. You will be enslaved for a time by worldly vanities, but the grace of God will bring you back here."

Deeply impressed by these words, Gertrude renounced the world and became a Nun in that monastery. Shortly after her profession, however, a serious illness obliged her to return to her native country, San Severo. The Saint's prophecy was then fulfilled. The spirit of the world, against which she was not as yet sufficiently strengthened, took hold of her and led her to lead a worldly life. Fortunately, however, the remembrance of Gerard's warning brought her to a spirit of repentance. She returned to the Convent and led an exemplary life until her death in 1830. This was Sister Mary Gertrude, of whom in 1855 Mother Mary Teresa will speak to the Superior of Scala. As for Gerard, the hour of his supreme trial was at hand. He had a presentiment of this. Holy Week was drawing near and he felt an irresistible desire to spend it in the Monastery of the Most Holy Redeemer. God drew him towards this sanctuary that he might find light and strength near Mary Celeste, who had passed through her own great trial. Gerard says of this time: "I spent these days in great consolation." It was peace before the storm.

A few weeks later the storm broke and the holy Brother was enveloped by the dark cloud of calumny. His Superiors forbade him to go out and he was relegated to the solitude of his call. People knew vaguely that he was in disgrace, and Mary Celeste was deeply grieved by it. Ignoring the true cause, she imagined that he had been giving away too much in charity, and she wrote him the following little note: "We are sorry to learn that you are suffering through your own over-generosity. This time the devil has succeeded in preventing you from coming to edify us. May God's Will be done! We are praying constantly for you, and trust that the powers of evil will not gain the victory. Wherever we may be, let us seek only God. Let us go to Him by doing His adorable Will. And then let us love Jesus Christ, Who has so loved us!" This letter must indeed have brought consolation to poor Gerard's broken heart.

As his end drew near the holy Brother seemed to seek out every possible opportunity of being of help to Mary Celeste. Through the influence of a Jesuit Father he had obtained precious indulgences for his beloved monastery. In writing to inform Mary Celeste of this the faithful friend penned the following lines, which were probably the last he addressed to her:

"Jesus, Mary!

"Dear and Most Venerable Mother,

"May the Divine grace and the consolation of the Holy Spirit be in your soul and in that of your daughters. You will find enclosed the brief of the Indulgences accorded to your community. Keep this document carefully, so that the Nuns who come after you may also profit by it. They will then understand that I have a little right to their gratitude, and after my death their charity will inspire them to gain some of these rich indulgences for the profit of my soul. I also beg from the future Superiors of the Monastery the alms of some of their Communions. Particularly, I beg of the Prioress who will be in office at the time of my death [this Superior was Mother Mary Illuminata, who succeeded her sister, Mary Celeste, and governed the Monastery until her death, which occurred in November, 1773] to apply to me for eight days the Sisters' Communions, and whatever indulgences they may gain. On my part, I will pray God to make them Saints."

This letter, full of a gentle and melancholy and anxious preoccupation for the eternal years, prophesied the approaching death of its writer, and the still closer approach of Mary Celeste's own death. The future will show that this impression was justified.

On Friday, September 14th, 1755, Gerard, on the point of death himself, saw Mary Celeste entering the realms of the Blessed. "Brother," he said to Etienne Sperduto, his Infirmarian, "to-day Mother Mary Celeste has gone to Heaven to receive the reward of her great love for Jesus and Mary." Events confirmed the truth of these words. Shortly afterwards they learnt that the holy Prioress had expired on the day and at the hour mentioned by Gerard. On that day he seemed to be happier than usual, yet at the same time could not hide a certain sadness. His joy was caused by Mary Celeste's triumph; his sadness by a longing for Heaven. These two souls, so united in divine charity, were not to be separated long. On the following October 16th Gerard in his turn took his flight to the heavenly country to share with his holy companion the ineffable happiness promised by God to those who love Him. Mary Celeste, who was born a month after St. Alphonsus, and who died a month before St. Gerard, seems to be guarded by these two great saints, who are her protectors in the Order of the Most Holy Redeemer.

CHAPTER X
THE HOLY PRIORESS

HE holy Prioress! Such was the name given to Mary Celeste by the inhabitants of Foggia; a name by which she is still known in that town at the present day. As at Nocera, the holy Mother was held in great veneration. To her came all who needed counsel in doubts and difficulties, while those in sorrow went to her for consolation and asked the help of her prayers. Numbers of young girls, attracted by her reputation, sought admittance to the Monastery of the Most Holy Redeemer.

Let us pause awhile and contemplate the venerated portrait of the servant of God, both from the physical and moral point of view. An authentic portrait of Mary Celeste is preserved at the Monastery of Foggia. From this portrait hundreds of reproductions have been made. It is from this picture that our frontispiece has been taken.

At first sight, the portrait gives us the impression of an open mind allied to a dominant personality. Yet this impression, caused by the rigid pose of the head and body, disappears after a more attentive examination. The sloping shoulders indicate calmness of mind; the attitude of the arms and hands denote gentleness, the eyes are rather watchful than piercing; the mouth discreet rather than disdainful. In fact, if this portrait gave us at first the impression of a proud and dominating spirit, we soon change our minds. It is so easy to mistake strength for boldness, and to see ambition where there is only greatness. In reality, the picture represents the portrait of a valiant soul, one who scorns difficulties and is full of high ideals. Such a character, if unsupported by faith, could easily turn to pride.

Upheld by faith and guided by virtue, it rapidly attains to heroism. Such examples abound in the Gospels. Peter is ready to give his head when it is a question of confessing Christ. Asked to make restitution of ill-gotten goods, Zacheus is ready to return all four-fold. Is a neighbor in distress, what does the Good Samaritan do? Then again, look at the conversion of Magdalen. In all these we see the gift of self, given without counting the cost, the gift of great souls, generously given. It is this very magnanimity which is expressed in the features of the Venerable Mother. Yet her look, full of majesty and grace, is tempered by modesty and sweetness. See the expression of the mouth, ready to smile; therein we trace a tenderness of heart in proportion to the strength of character, and which completes her portrait from a moral point of view.

The history of her life confirms this impression. At once noble and simple, pure and gentle, while possessing an ardent soul untiring in the pursuit of perfection, Mary Celeste belongs to the family of great souls. Her clear, pure mind had no difficulty in reaching the heights. Though quite unlettered, she composed works full of thoughts and beautiful metaphors. No one could resist her words.

Above all, she had a heart of gold. The Divine Master, jealous of this heart, warned her that He would allow her friends to be a cause of grief to her, in case she should become too attached to them, because of her inborn inclination to gratitude. Naturally straightforward and proud, she had a horror of all dissimulation and untruth. "God is Truth" she goes on to say. One day a postulant pretended that she had seen the eyes of the statue of the Infant Jesus open. Mary Celeste saw by the girl's face that this was not true. She corrected her in public and imposed a severe penance on her. On this rich foundation of nature, God sowed seeds of the highest virtues. The Venerable Mother's whole life has been an uninterrupted exercise of faith. Therefore it is only natural that she should extol this virtue in all her writings.

Speaking of prayer, which she likens to the degrees of Jacob's ladder, she says: "Oh, my sweet Lord and God, grant that my tongue may express what my heart feels about this holy faith. Although this theological virtue is placed on the first rung of this mystical ladder, yet it is the only path by which we can reach the last rung. The soul in this ascension must travel by a royal and princely road, and faith is the sure guide which leads it to union with God. This is the mysterious ladder seen by Jacob, reaching from earth to Heaven. The earth is the Holy Catholic Church where the holy Faith is planted, and every Christian soul rests on this firm foundation whose cornerstone is Christ. The Angels, seen by the holy patriarch ascending and descending this ladder, are the symbol of the knowledge and the light communicated by God to the soul, by means of these celestial spirits concerning the mysteries of faith, and also the light given to the holy Fathers and interpreters, to explain the Catholic Truths revealed by the Holy Ghost.

"In very truth, I can affirm that the ascension of all the degrees of this mystical ladder, up to the top where the holy patriarch saw God seated, is the work of Faith!" And Mary Celeste cries: "Oh, holy Faith, how great is thy work, since through thee the soul receives all treasures Thou art the sole door through which I can enter into God, and through which He can give entrance to me. How I grieve for the misfortunes of this miserable world, which appreciates Thee so little. Contemplatives are rare, and the number of truly faithful and Christian souls is restricted, because Faith is almost dead. The knowledge of the Divine mysteries in all their truth is the way of prayer, and how few are those who Practice this knowledge. Their number could be easily counted. Oh God, the number of Thy saints is small, because few are really faithful, for if all were truly faithful, all would be Saints."

Her hope rested on the immovable foundation of Faith. Our Lord Himself bore witness to this: "What fills Me with love for you," He deigned to say, "is that you have not placed your hope in any worldly thing, neither in your own strength, nor in any creature, but in Me alone!" St. Paul has said: "Love is the fulfilling of the law." If we were to attempt to portray here how great was the Divine love in Mary Celeste's soul, it would mean repeating all that we have already said in the course of this history. Moreover, we shall speak of it later, in the chapter concerning her spiritual doctrine. It must suffice, therefore, for the present to say that the love of Jesus was the sole passion of her life. Her heart burned with such ardent love that she was obliged, even on winter nights, to remain for some time at the open window of her cell, in order to cool the fire which consumed her whole being. The Nuns of her monastery affirm that she was so much upheld by Divine love that, when walking, her feet scarcely touched the ground. They were wont to say to one another that her heart must be entirely consumed and destroyed by the fire of love which devoured it. This great love, however, was allied to the most simple and tender piety. At Foggia the Nuns still preserve ai statue to the Infant Jesus, lying in a cradle and carrying a dove in His hand. It is called "The holy Prioress' Infant Jesus." At Christmas time she loved to fondle it, and sing hymns to it, which she had herself composed. During Lent she organized processions, in which she and her Nuns carried the instruments of the Passion. Her piety always took its inspiration in the liturgy, and Our Lord did not fail to reward her for this. Indeed, every Feast-day she received some special grace, often an extraordinary one, but always corresponding to the spirit of the mystery which the Church was then celebrating. Her principal devotion seems to have been the Blessed Sacrament. Her most beautiful hymns are inspired by devotion to this mystery. She instituted in her monastery perpetual adoration every Thursday, and herself often spent the night at the foot of the Tabernacle.

And what can we say of her love for the Most holy Virgin, whom Jesus had given her as Mother, and who had accepted her as daughter for ever? She assures us that Mary had delivered her from countless dangers of body and soul. In addition to canticles in her honor and many beautiful meditations on her mysteries, in particular on each verse of the *Magnificat*, she wrote the following prayer which she recited each morning:

"Most Holy Virgin, Mother of God and my Mother, thou art all my hope, after Jesus. Thou art my love, my consolation, I have recourse to thee. My dearly beloved Sovereign, I wish to love and to die in thy tender arms. Therefore I renew my homage to thee, kissing the ground three times; and I ask of thee to be my help, my defense and my comfort during this holy day, and to place me as thy devoted daughter under the folds of thy virginal cloak. I kiss thy holy hands, and implore thee to bless me, and to obtain for me that of the most holy Trinity. *Nos cum prole pia benedicat Virgo Maria.*"

A remarkable occurrence shows how greatly pleased was the holy Virgin by her privileged daughter's devotion. One day, whilst Mary Celeste was in prayer, the divine Mother appeared to her, and presented her with a picture of herself. This picture was later on sent to Rome, where it was in great demand by the sick, to whom it sometimes brought healing, and always consolation. The holy Prioress was not content with words, she joined severe mortification to her prayer. Like many saints, she had engraved on her breast, with a red-hot iron, the adorable name of Jesus. She often took the discipline to blood, and wore on her body spiked iron chains and a hair-shirt. On her breast she often wore a wooden cross with iron points. Her director was obliged to moderate this vigor of her penances, at least during her more severe illnesses. The instruments of her penance, found after her death, were divided between her Nuns, who kept them as relics. And all noticed that a sweet odor emanated from them. When she interrupted her prayer at night to take a little rest, it was to lie on the ground with a brick for her pillow. She usually took her meals kneeling, or sitting on the ground, and her food was mixed with bitter herbs and cinders.

The Venerable Mother was as gentle to others as she was hard towards herself. She learnt this grace from Him Who said: "Learn of Me because I am meek and humble of Heart." He had said to her: "My daughter, receive the spirit of meekness and gentleness. ...You will look on your neighbor with that love which I bore towards My apostles and disciples. With this love you will look on the companions with whom you live. With My compassion you will pity their weakness. With My charity you will console their sorrows. With My gentleness you will speak to them of the Kingdom of God. With My patience you will bear with their human failings, and will never speak in anger to them, so that in you shall be accomplished what is written of Me: 'Milk and honey are hidden in his tongue.' May your words be all gentleness and love."

We must not imagine, however, that this evangelical gentleness hindered the Prioress from correcting her daughters when charity necessitated it. Her gentleness was not of the kind which would hurt nobody because she feared all. Our Lord had also said to her: "You must never hide the truth out of human respect, when it is a question of My glory. If, out of zeal and love for Me, you give counsel to your neighbor, which the latter takes badly, do not worry. The gift which he has repulsed will return to your own soul, and I will give you all the graces which he would have had if he had profited by your words. Therefore, in future, do not be afraid to tell the truth to your neighbor, even when he does not accept it, and thinks badly of you because of it. To stop on that account would be self-love, and no longer zeal for My glory."

To enable her to obey the Divine Master's direction, Mary Celeste had at her disposal a miraculous power. The following instance is an example of it: One day, being surrounded by her Nuns, she called for a basket of apples. There were as many apples as Sisters, and each apple was in excellent condition. "These apples represent you," said the Prioress to her daughters. Having said this, she placed the basket at the foot of the altar, and prayed over it, She then took the apples and showed them again to the Sisters. But what a change had taken place! Not one single fruit was without blemish, and one of them was completely rotten. Through this miracle the holy Prioress had wished to make her daughters understand in as forcible and delicate a manner as possible that each one had some fault to overcome, and that one of them was, alas I in a desperate condition. This latter Sister did in fact leave the Monastery and abandon her vocation, after the death of the foundress.

But the best lesson given by Mary Celeste was that of her own example. She was the most faithful observer of all the Rules, her daughters tell us. We know, indeed, how much she loved this Rule given to her by Our Lord, and which tends wholly to transform the soul into Christ, by the imitation of His examples and virtues. She esteemed most highly her religious vocation, a life of continual sacrifice, but of sacrifice inspired by love, a life lived in union with Jesus and in continuation of His work of redemption. She had so well understood and retained this lesson of the Divine Master: "My daughter, you ask Me what can please Me most and procure Me the greatest glory in this world? I will tell you, not only for your own good, but for the good of others. It is to observe this Rule given by Me, and which is nothing less than the imitation of My holy life. May your Sisters Practice it in My spirit, and then I shall be united to them. My daughter, receive the spirit of your Institute, to engrave it on every soul who desires to receive it, and by its means to become united to Me. Enter lovingly into the remembrance of My life at all the hours prescribed in this Rule which is both Mine and yours. Thus you will live in My spirit and in My life. At each hour of the day, at the time prescribed by the Rule, you will call to mind the remembrance of one or other of My actions, and in this exercise you will receive a great abundance of grace, of gifts, of virtues, and of union which will lead you to a high degree of perfect contemplation. The remembrance and imitation of My life, that is the spirit of your Order. Your life consists in following the example of Magdalen in holy contemplation. Happy are those who shall Practice with loving vigilance the intentions assigned to each hour, recalling the works of My life. My holy Humanity will be their dwelling-place, they shall be My beloved doves who make their nests in the hollow of the corner-stone, where the wicked serpent cannot devour them."

Mary Celeste's solicitude for the perfection of souls was not confined to her religious family only. Like St. Paul, she gave herself to all, and first of all to her dear sinners, as she called them. Reparation occupied a great place in her spiritual life. She says to Our Lord: "What affliction do I not feel, piercing my soul like the point of a sword, at the sight of so many creatures indifferent and cold towards Thee, even among those to whom Thou dost grant Thy choicest graces. The sight of this pierces my soul, my sweet Savior."

The Divine Master, in a symbolical vision, asks her as He did Margaret Mary, for reparation for the insults He receives, especially in the Sacrament of the altar. The following is Mary Celeste's account of this vision:—

"After Communion, I heard these words: *Ecce Agnus Dei, Qui tollit peccata mundi.* I seemed to see a mountain, on the summit of which was a little lamb surrounded by raging dogs who sought to tear it to pieces. There were also numbers of cruel men who struck at it with lances and other weapons, striving to hurt it was much as they could, with great cruelty and barbarity. But this little lamb remained on the ground at their feet without moving, wounded and as though dead. From its mouth came forth a liquid like a sweet-smelling balm. During this time, I heard the voice of Purity speaking to me thus from the Tabernacle: 'See how sinners wound Me on the Calvary of the holy Altar! By their sacrileges they would kill Me in a worse manner than did the Jews. This balm which comes from My mouth is the commiseration with which I pardon them when they repent with their whole heart, and these dogs which I have shown you are the devils of hell, trembling with hate towards Me and striving to make sinners insult Me and to make them die in their sins.' Then I said," continues Mary Celeste, "and what can I do to repair so much evil? And Thou didst reply: 'My daughter, weep for them before My Father, and pray incessantly for these ungrateful sinners.' Oh, my Sovereign Good, Thou hast indeed grieved my heart, in showing me the cruelty of ungrateful men. Alas! I am the most ungrateful of all Thy creatures, in spite of Thine innumerable benefits and Thine infinite love. To think that whilst Thou dost sacrifice Thyself on our altars, to satisfy for our sins, Thou dost receive only insults and injuries! Tell me, what can I do to console Thee, to make reparation for these sins and to prevent them?" To reparation she added prayer. The Venerable Mother explains the nature of the apostleship of prayer, which as a true contemplative she never ceased to exercise. She calls it a "charity infused by God in the soul for the needs of the Church, or of the public, or of some sinner, or of the souls in Purgatory, or for the utility and perfection of just souls." And she adds: "God gives to the soul an interior assurance which springs from confidence in Him, and which makes the soul pray for whole days at a time, with its mind fixed on God. The soul tells Our Lord what it desires of Him, speaking with filial abandonment, confident in its God. It is God Himself Who moves the soul to act thus, because He wishes to pour forth His mercy on all creatures. Therefore the sold feels as great a sense of security as if it had already obtained what it asked. Yet there are certain things which the soul desires to ask, yet it finds it impossible to do so, experiencing an interior repulsion and feeling itself obliged to ask other graces from God, rather than those it had intended. This is a sign that God does not wish to grant its prayer, for the greater good of souls and for His own greater glory."

This apostleship of the servant of God was especially exercised in favor of her dear town of Foggia, which she had adopted. Mary Celeste's prayers preserved the town from a fresh earthquake, and made the shock to cease throughout that region. On this subject, we read in one of her talks with Our Lord:

"I remember a favor which Thou didst grant me two months ago, and which I cannot pass over in silence now that my desires have been granted.

"It was at the time when Thou were afflicting the world with the scourge of earthquakes. My soul was troubled and frightened to see Thee angered against Thy poor and miserable creatures. Because of their sins. Thou hast destroyed whole towns. I thought of this town of Foggia. I was bold enough then to ask Thee why Thou wert so angry with the creatures that Thou hast made. Answering my prayer, Thou didst deign to tell me that it was because of die grave offences committed by men through their cupidity and avarice. They were full of greed and attached to the things of this world. Therefore by this earthquake. Thou didst bury their bodies, together with the worldly goods they loved; and thereby Thou didst show to all men how passing are the things of this world, and the riches for which men care.

"I implored Thee then with the greatest ardor to make this scourge cease, since it was my birthday, which falls on the Vigil of All Saints. At this humble request, Thy love towards me made Thine anger to cease. Thou didst promise me that because of Thy love for me. Thou wouldst at once make the earthquake to cease, which Thou didst indeed do through Thy goodness. Moreover, Thou didst promise me to forgive their sins, and to save many sinners. From that day, indeed, the earthquakes have entirely ceased." Happy are the towns who possess as mediator between man and God's Justice a community of contemplative Nuns, urged on to prayer and reparation by the example of a holy Prioress!

CHAPTER XI

MARY CELESTE'S SPIRITUAL DOCTRINE

THE quotations given throughout this book will have given the reader some idea of the Venerable Mother's teaching. Now, however, that we are considering her at the very height of her life as Foundress, it is time to make ourselves acquainted with the ensemble of her spiritual doctrine, which is contained in her writings—where, by order of her directors, she has left us an account of her communications with God. Her doctrine has therefore been lived. In speaking of it now we are not interrupting, but continuing, the story of her life.

The theme of these writings: "Meditations on the Gospel," "The Soul's Converse with her Spouse Jesus," "Novena for Christmas," teaches us that Mary Celeste has based her spirituality on the mystery of the Incarnate Word, that Mystery of Love which has been made manifest in the Flesh, justified by the Spirit, revealed to Angels, preached to nations, believed in the world, and finally raised to glory. Moreover, her vocation itself was to show forth and teach many souls the meaning of the words of St. Paul: "For me to live is Christ."

"May Jesus be my life," is the tide she has given to her Autobiography. Out Lord has asked her to be the apostle of this mystery. "Beloved of My Heart," He says, "write of Me! What I have told you in secret, proclaim publicly. For My Will is that you should make known the truths which you have learnt of Me concerning My Incarnation and the value of the works I accomplished by taking on Me the nature of man. Oh, how many secrets regarding My life and death are hidden from Me! I command you, therefore, to write of Me, so that My Name may be glorified on earth, and that all creatures may know that My Father has placed in Me His treasures and His eternal riches." The devotion Mary Celeste professed for the Incarnate Word sprang from her inward conception of the greatness of God, Who had Himself imbued her soul with this idea. "This day Thou hast made me see my nothingness," she says, "and Thou hast surrounded me with the immensity of Thy Divine Being. In the little world of my soul I hear with the ears of purity a trumpet resounding with overwhelming force. It announces that existence is found only in Thee, and that all creatures must humble themselves to the depths of their nothingness. The most perfect men are but as phantoms before Thee, and as though they did not exist. I see Thy Divine Majesty containing and governing all things. Thou dost show me that I do not exist save in Thee. My poor and miserable spirit bows down in humble respect and in deep adoration, I am plunged in the abyss of my nothingness, I am without thought, without movement, and my solitude is so intense that I could not explain where my senses are."

Our Lord never wearied of instructing His docile pupil on this fundamental point of spiritual life. "All is in God and lives by Him. In every reasonable soul this Divine Spirit is the principle and the source of life. He is its support and its providence at every moment. It is He Who puts into each soul a continuous aspiration towards immortality, towards a center which is Himself. As such He is the great torment of the lost souls in Hell, for they also have their being in God, which makes their suffering so terrible that it is beyond our comprehension." Therefore Mary Celeste in her works often returns to this great thought of the Divine Being: "Outside of Him, in Heaven as on earth, in reasonable creatures as in unreasoning creatures, there is only nothingness. In Heaven the Angels feel this, although their humility and annihilation cannot be as ours, who are creatures composed of soul and body, and weighed down by sin. The annihilation of these spiritual beings comes from their very beatitude, in contemplating God and in considering that they have received all from Him. The greatest of their joys is to see the Supreme and Infinite Being existing alone, and to know that outside of Him all is nothing, since He is the source of their life and their beatitude. Oh God, how can I explain a thing so high, so hidden, and yet of such great truth? In what does the greatness of the Saints in Heaven consist, if not in their annihilation? They alone are truly humble, and not we, poor creatures traveling on this earth. The reason of this is that they, being in light and in truth, contemplate God without a veil; they see that He is the Principle and the End of all their being."

And she exclaims: "Oh, light of truth in my soul, shining brightness. Thou dost force me to bow my head in respect and fear, even lower than the feet of Lucifer s when I see Who Thou art and Who I am in my misery."

Jesus said: "No one can come to Me unless My Father draw him." Mary Celeste knew this, but she also knew that drawn by Jesus, we go through Him to the Father; and she prays: "Eternal Father, my God, Truth itself. Infinite Sanctity, show me Thy Son, Eternal Wisdom, in Whom Thou dost place Thy happiness and eternal joy, so that through Him I may possess Thee. Most holy Father, may I love Thee with His love, may He show Thee to me, that I may know Thee in truth and love Thee as Thou dost desire to be loved, and as Thou dost command me to love Thee. Oh, inaccessible Light in which I see all knowledge reflected; light which darkness cannot approach, and which enlightens my ignorance! Holy Father, give me this Son, Thy Word, He Who has ransomed me. In Him I place all my hope, my soul burns for love of Him and I cry to Him day and night, consumed with regret, anguish, and ardent desire for Him. Give me Him Whom I love, in Whom I hope, for Whom I live. Give me my help, the possession of this supreme Good which is my All; give me my Salvation, my Peace, my true and eternal pledge of safety."

Such vehement desires could not but be heard. Listen to what Mary Celeste has to say: "Oh, Heavenly Father, Thou hast given me Thy Divine Son, so that He may live within me, and that I may live in His Divine Heart, where infinite treasures are revealed to me."

And speaking to the Divine Son Himself, she says: "Oh, my Beloved, help me to give to Thy Divine Father infinite praise and thanksgiving, which should only end with my life. By my death, they will begin to bring forth fruit and to be more perfect."

The Venerable Mother has also made known to us the great favor by which the Heavenly Father revealed to her the beauty of His Son Who was both God and Man: "Thou didst make the harmonious voice of purity to sound in the depths of my soul, saying, 'Enter into the Choir of the Cherubim,' and I entered that Angelic abode ... there I saw the two natures, the Divine and the Human, united by an act of Thine almighty power, and Thou didst show to me the Cause of eternal happiness. Oh, Eternal Word, Thou didst explain this mystery to me without words. I saw how Thou art the happiness and the wisdom of the Father, Infinite Light, Almighty Power, Glory, Beauty, Mercy, Truth, Justice, Holiness; a pure Mirror in which is reflected all Perfection, receiving all beauty and happiness from the Father. Thou art the Principle of all good, of all the works and marvels of creation, of the redemption and conservation of all creatures, by a single and eternal act. Thou art the light and glory of the Angels ... Oh, my Jesus, Word of the Father, Thou art the happiness of the just, the throne and the fulness of the Divinity. This act has no beginning and no ending, and is for ever renewed. In this instantaneous and eternal act is to be found the true eternal happiness of the Divine Being, O Eternal Word; and Heaven itself is contained in this happiness, through Thee, O my beloved Jesus, So much for Thy Divinity! And what of Thy Humanity? What an Infinite Treasure Thou art! As Man Thou alone art well-pleasing to the Father. God loves all men in Thee. Sanctifying grace is given to Thee for all men. In the name of all men Thou doest despise the honors and riches of the world. Thou dost plead and implore for us all. Thou dost love God for us all. Thou art the Dispenser of all supernatural graces and gifts. Thou dost enlighten our mind to understand the mysteries of faith. Thou dost even communicate to men a portion of Thy Divine power, by allowing the just to work miracles. The Gifts of the Holy Ghost are communicated to the elect, and to the Church by Thee. Thou art the true Light which enlightens our sojourn on this earth, and awakens within us the remembrance of eternal gifts. Thou hast enobled our nature by allowing it, through Thee, to be united to the Word made Flesh. Oh, when shall I see Thee face to face? Thou art incomparable in goodness, power, mercy and all good. Compared with Thee, everything in the world is distasteful to me."

Mary Celeste felt the need of singing of her love, of repeating again and again the wealth of riches she discovers in Jesus, and of affirming that the contemplation of Christ's Humanity leads to a knowledge of the Divinity: "Let me sing of Thee in all freedom, Oh love of my heart!" she cries, "for Thou art my love, my life and my soul. Tell me, my Beloved, why dost Thou consume my heart with love of Thee? On hearing Thy Name, I am on fire and as it were saturated with happiness. All my desires are towards Thee. ... I could never express what Thou art to me. Many loving hearts have died for Thee, in particular Thy divine Mother, who knew Thee more intimately than anyone. Her love was like a flame of light, which being attracted towards Thee, was separated from its earthly life. Oh my King and Sovereign Good, let me tell Thee for my consolation something of what Thou art. I look upon Thee as the eternal Sun, clothed by Thy Father, the supreme and infinitely wise Artist, Who, desiring to lighten the world in its darkness, made of Thy Divinity a robe crystal clear and transparent, which was Thy holy Humanity, in which Thy Divine splendor appeared also, all the riches and infinite treasures which are enclosed in Thee Who art His Word. The Father placed this Sun, thus robed, in the world, so that He might become the light of all men. ... As for me, Thou art my Jesus, deign to be so in very truth ...

"... How could I see the Divine Sun if I did not first contemplate the brightness of the crystal globe in which this Sun is enclosed? In this crystal orb are to be found all the works of Thy wonderful life, perfectly and artistically wrought as in fine gold. There are to be found even the smallest actions of Thy holy life, and thus Thy Holy Humanity is adorned and embellished. My heart is on fire with love. It cannot but love this Sun in this crystal orb, and this orb which encloses the Sun. Oh, my Jesus, what should I do in this world without Thee? With Thee all suffering is changed into joy; and I would dare to say that even were I in hell and could think of Thee, the frightful torment which one must suffer there would be changed into joy and peace for me. No one can separate me from Thee, my Beloved."

Our Lord invited Mary Celeste to dwell within this globe which she has just described; therein to contract an intimate union with the Holy Trinity by contemplation of the faith. "Enter into me, your God, and you shall possess Me. I am the pure Mirror, look at Me and you shall have life in My Father Who is pleased to look on Me in His eternal joy. As an object can be seen in pure crystal, so you shall see the Father in Me, and in the Father you shall see His Word. ... There united in eternal bonds by the Spirit of love, you will be consumed by that fire which burns with infinite sweetness, and which will destroy all earthly blemish in thy heart. Contemplate Me always, Who am the Mirror of My Father, and you shall be purified by love from all stain, and shall merit to possess My Father, and shall be rewarded with the fruits of eternal life."

Jesus told His faithful spouse that this blessed globe was more especially His Heart: "My Divine Heart is your center. See what a wealth there is for you in this dwelling. Do not leave this cell prepared for you. On the Cross I opened the door to give you entrance to it. There you will find all satisfaction both in time and in eternity. In life's sorrows you will there find peace; in temptation and persecution, refuge; in affliction and desolation, comfort. You will there find your friends and all those who love Me. Every time that you wish to seek consolation with My Saints, you can enjoy their company without speaking, in gentle communications and a peace which the world cannot give. There infinite good is to be found, which is beyond all human understanding."

And Mary Celeste, once inside this globe, sees only Jesus in all things and sings of the effects of her union with Him. "Pure Mirror of Divine Beauty, Word, Man- God, Power itself, I contemplate Thee with Thy Divine eyes, and see Thee in all creatures. I embrace Thee with sweetness and joy, since I have forgotten all for love of Thee and desire to possess Thee only. I see Thy splendor in the sun, in the moon, the stars, the sky, the earth, the sea, in all plants, trees, fruits, birds and beasts, in the elements of the air, in the whole world; I see only Thee. For Thou alone hast given existence to all things. ... Thou alone, Oh Christ, art the one hope of my soul, in Whom alone I trust. ... My union with Thy Will unites me to my Heavenly Father, because He looks on me in His love, which is naught but Thee, Eternal Word. There I lose sight of my miseries and the remembrance of my sorrows."

Mary Celeste thus shows that she has remembered the lesson which God gave to her on the mystical Body of Christ, when He spoke to her in these words: "When I address you as My beloved spouse, with so many titles and so much love; when I clothe you with an incomparable beauty, I do all these things to My Christ within your soul. When I call you friend, spouse, I say all this to you, but above all I say it to Him Who is the Life of your being, and through Whom your soul is My spouse. It is by union with Him that every soul becomes My beloved spouse. Be not surprised, then, at the sublime acts with which I honor the souls I have created, for in loving My Incarnate Word I love you, in espousing Him I espouse you. All souls are one in Him, and He is one in all. They are marked with the same seal, with the same impression; making one nature, one spouse and one love." Thanks to this union, Jesus turns all the vicissitudes of life to the good of the soul.

Again addressing Our Lord, Mary Celeste says: "Beloved Spouse of my heart, great as are my infirmities and my miseries, still greater is Thy bounty. It is thus I see all in the pure light of Thy truth, my Divine Lord, and all becomes clear to me. Thou art my whole good, for when Thou dost deign to visit me, I lose all taste for human consolation. Thou dost imbue me with the purity of Thy love, removing from me all else. If I fall in my weakness. Thou dost stretch forth Thy Hand to save me. Thou dost look on me with love, giving me confidence, and all turns to my good. If Thou dost permit grief, persecution and suffering to hurt me through man and through those near to me. Thou, dost strengthen me interiorly, encouraging me to suffer by recalling to me Thy life of suffering on earth in order to accomplish Thy Father's Will, and thus Thou dost make me understand the price and worth of the Divine Will. The happiness of Paradise is hidden in this Will, and through this I enter into eternal glory. Should the devil attack my soul and body by temptation and disturbance of soul, Thou dost teach me, O God, to make a pure act of faith—light in darkness. Then united to Thy Divine Will I suffer with patience all the attacks of the enemy. Thus I could endure my suffering for a thousand years, without desiring anything else, since I know that Thou art there, and without being able to hear Thee, I feel that I possess Thee and that Thou art within me by Thine Essence and by Thy power. I find Thee in my sufferings, my afflictions, my joys, but neither suffering nor joy can enchain me, for I abandon myself to my beloved and only God. Thou alone dost possess my heart. In spite of what may happen, I breathe in the Man-God, crucified and loving. There I find all wealth and happiness, and all sufferings are as pearls of eternal life shining with the love of my God."

Again Mary Celeste cries in the transports of her love: "My Jesus, how can I find words to express what Thou art to me? . . , Thou dost govern me and subject me to Thy rule. As a Master Thou dost command me, as a Father Thou dost provide for my needs, as a Mother Thou dost nourish me, as a Spouse, Thou art inseparably united to me in pureness of love. What shall I say of Thee, since Thou hast communicated to my understanding a fulness of knowledge which submerged me in silence and in an ocean of joy?"

But the spouse of Jesus takes care not to forget that union with Him will make of her a co-redemptorist. "O Father, Thou hast taught me that every soul who, with humility and ardent desire, unites her will, her mind and all her powers to Thy Divine Son, shall participate in the perfect sacrifice of the Divine Word; sacrificing herself with Him Who is the Life of all men. Not only will this soul be purified from all stain, but, united to the Immaculate Lamb, she will be able to satisfy for the sins of men, for the souls in Purgatory ... United to Jesus, the soul will have the will to be sacrificed in Him to the Divine Father, and to satisfy for the sins of all its brothers, and to co-operate with Jesus in the Redemption."

Our Lord had encouraged Mary Celeste in the practice of all virtues, by showing them to her as an exercise of love. "My beloved child," said Our Lord, "you warm Me by bearing cold; you clothe Me by mortification; you feed Me when you fast; you rest Me when you keep silence, speaking only when necessity obliges it; you sing canticles of love to Me, when you unite yourself to Me by continual aspirations; you press Me to your heart when, in order to serve Me, you overcome your weakness, indispositions, and bodily pains; you embrace Me at every act of love done to your neighbor for My sake; you give Me exquisite pleasure each time that you make an exterior or interior act of gentleness and humility. Your trust, dependence and diligence ate so many keys with which you lock Me in your heart."

The Divine Master, moreover, teaches His faithful disciple to find in this union with Him three virtues, three treasures, which are all manifestations of perfect love.

The first of these is Zeal for Souls. Our Lord asks it of her in Holy Communion: "This morning," says the Divine Master, "I desired you in My Heart in a special manner. I awaited you most anxiously, so that in espousing Me you could espouse every soul, not only those who already belong to My Church, but also those who are still without the fold. I wish you to love them with the same burning love as I do. Just as I thought more of them than of Myself when I was on earth, so must you forget yourself and think of these souls whom I love so dearly."

The Divine Master explains also to her the reason of His great love for souls, saying:

"Enter into My Heart and consider the beauty of these souls which I have created in My Image. You will then no longer be astonished that I came from Heaven and died on the Cross for them. All this is the effect of that love which, as God, I bear towards Myself, because in these souls My goodness, wisdom and power, spiritual substance and all united good is made manifest. All this is found in My Divine Heart. At present I am He Whom you espoused in love, henceforth I wish you to espouse also the objects of My love, that is to say, souls."

Again Our Lord had said to her:

"With My right hand I press you to My Heart, so that you may embrace within this Heart all creatures . . Receive My Heart in your heart, to love it as your own, and to bind within it all souls with the cords of charity. Love especially the souls of this Community in which you live. Love them, take to heart their spiritual good. I give them to you. My beloved, they are My spouses and yours; henceforth you must love in Me and Me in them."

Let us listen to the inspired words of Mary Celeste, after she had received the Heart of Jesus in the place of her own:

"I felt that Thou didst place Thy Heart within me, so that mine melted into Thine like wax. There I could hear Thy Heart beating. No words could describe it. I heard also the beating of the hearts of those who love Thee, and all the souls which Thou hast created and redeemed were enclosed within Thy Heart. My heart was with them in Thy Heart. ... Now, when I speak of Thee as my Spouse, I include them all in Thee, through Thee and by Thee."

The second treasure contained in the union with Jesus, through love, is that of Abandonment. Our Lord uses a striking metaphor in order to teach Mary Celeste the necessity of entering into this pure and perfect path of abandonment. He says: "Know that I am pure Justice. All men separated from Me, perish. Live in My sight, in this knowledge. Contemplate what you are in truth. You are like a little child who, at its Mother's breast, does nothing without its Mother, and is nourished by the nourishment she takes."

After having thus shown her the necessity of union with Him, the Divine Master develops this teaching on the practice of abandonment which is so necessary and has such consoling results. "I wish you to be like a child at its Mother's breast. Desire nothing except what comes from this breast which nourishes you, and where you are in safe keeping. You will then be sheltered from all dangers. You will do this by abandoning yourself to My good pleasure. Have no other desire than to rest within this stronghold where nothing can harm you. Seek rest there in all difficulties, in pain, in doubt, in temptation, in fear, in persecution, in humiliation. Sorrow cannot penetrate this enclosure. Live a life of love. Do not judge My plans from a human point of view, nor strive to understand more than I show you. Do not mix yourself up in other people's business, nor be anxious about your own affairs. Do not trouble about earthly things, but rest in the arms of My Divine

Providence. You are as powerless as a wisp of straw exposed to a violent wind, so also are all creatures. Why, therefore, fear their judgment and their actions? Live as a child at My Breast."

Finally, the third treasure to be found in union is Love of the Cross. This is the supreme test of love. It gives us a perfect resemblance to the Divine Spouse; by it, souls are redeemed. To encourage her in this, Our Lord invites Mary Celeste to contemplate Him as continuing and completing His Passion in her.

"Listen to Me from the pulpit of the Cross, which I have planted in your heart," says her Divine Master. "In this transitory world you will contemplate only Me crucified in yourself; crucified by your extreme misery, crucified in your body, by its weakness and infirmities, crucified in your soul by its aridities and loneliness, its sadness and loss of all human consolation. In order to make you resemble Me as I was during My life on earth, I shall send you nothing but crosses and sufferings. You will suffer persecution, calumny, scorn, blame, misunderstandings, confusion and temptations of all kinds. You will be misjudged by the world and laughed at, moreover, you will suffer from the weight of your bodily infirmities. But this will not take from you the glory of the love of My Divine Heart, where you will always be united to My Will, one with Me in My Father. You will deserve to understand that you are pleasing to My Father, when you are united to Me on the Cross. You will then be rewarded in a single moment for all your trouble, and you will enjoy a repose that no words can express nor mind understand." The Divine Master wished her to aspire to the last supreme degree of suffering, that which He endured on the Cross. But a mere creature could never attain to this last degree unaided; and Jesus tells her: "Seek to make Me live in your heart. Desire Me night and day. Let Me be your only nourishment. Then you will find true happiness and eternal joy. Whatever be your crosses, they will always come from God for your good. Yet you will never reach the supreme degree of suffering to which you aspire in order to be entirely like Me. You will think your suffering nothing in comparison with your Beloved. Live, therefore, united in spirit to the last sufferings of My life, when I was consumed in sacrifice on the tree of the Cross, offering to My Father My pure and perfect love for Him and for souls."

Docile to the voice of her Divine Master, Mary Celeste dwelt on Calvary.

"How great is the beauty which I see on this Mount of Calvary," she says, "I seemed to see a river of blood which watered and gave life to tender grass and fresh flowers. Thou didst tell me that these flowers were the holy martyrs and all souls who are suffering a martyrdom of love and who desire the Cross and bear the yoke of mortification and suffering. Thou didst show me also how much to be prized in eternity are the fruits of patience, because they flow from the beautiful fountain of pure love. Oh, my Beloved, grant me a place among these flowers, for in my past life I was far from Calvary. O send me suffering! Grant me also, O my God, a patient and pure love, that I be no longer unfaithful; and may the rest of my days be spent on that mount of love where Thou art, O my Spouse."

Finally, if we would know how her great love of Jesus Crucified was rewarded, Mary Celeste tells us in the following words:

"It is always a subject of astonishment and of admiration to me when Thou dost enlighten my mind to understand the wonderful things Thou art accomplishing in the depths of my soul. When I see ail Thy love and Thy mercy, and how Thou dost remove all earthly thoughts from my heart! Thou dost work within me and lead me without any effort on my part. Thou dost lead me above, away from creatures and the things of this miserable world. There I enjoy Thy beauty and Thy sweetness. There no noise and tumult can trouble the peace which springs from this happy center, and my soul cannot Relate all it learns there. If here on earth my weakness can already comprehend so much of Thy goodness, what is there not reserved in Heaven for those who love Thee?"

We cannot end this chapter better than by quoting a prayer addressed by Mary Celeste to Our Lord:

"O may Thy Word, like a fiery arrow, pierce my soul to wound it for ever with Thy- Divine Love. Thou dost tell me to be like a flaming torch, always burning before Thee to lighten souls. But how can I be so, since of myself I am only darkness? I will be a torch, a sun even, if Thou wilt always remain united to me. I beg of Thee, by Thine infinite mercy, that it may be so."

CHAPTER XII
MARY CELESTE'S SPIRITUAL DOCTRINE
(continued)

 UR Lord had given Mary Celeste St. Catherine of Sienna to be her spiritual Mistress, and the whole doctrine of the Venerable Mother is contained, one might say, in the beautiful prayer of the Saint: "Oh, my God, make us live as though dead, in the true and perfect light!"

This death which we must undergo in order to live in the true and perfect light is none other than that "annihilation" spoken of by St. John of the Cross, and called by Mary Celeste "purity." This is the central point of her spiritual doctrine. In order to make our outline of the Venerable Mother's teaching more complete it will be necessary to devote a few pages to this doctrine.

This purity is the *"abneget semetipsum "*of the Gospel, the renunciation of self, that is to say of self-love, which is antagonistic to the love of God. Let us hear what Our Lord said to Mary Celeste on this subject: "My daughter, you can never realize sufficiently to what extent creatures are subject to self-love, to pride and to the thirst for happiness. These are like heavy chains binding the soul to earth. However, in My goodness and providence, I come to their help in order to break these chains bit by bit. I send them trials which thwart their natural inclinations, which are harmful to their spiritual advancement. Yes, My daughter, this self-love is the great obstacle to man's perfection. That is why so few are perfect, though many try to walk in the way of perfection. A great many stop half-way without understanding the nature of the obstacle. I will explain it to you, so that you may enlighten others who may desire to profit by it." And the Divine Master explains to His pupil die subtle manifestations of self-love in weak and cowardly souls, in more advanced and courageous souls, and even in souls who are truly loving and perfect. In conclusion He says:

"My daughter, watch over your heart so as to purify it interiorly and exteriorly. Let all your acts spring from love of Me. Let all your desires be for My Divine pleasure, and your thoughts and words only for My glory. Let all you do, either for yourself or for your neighbor, be free from human respect and fear. Thus all your actions will be done as coming from Me, and will have great value in My sight."

In order to combat self-love it is necessary to hate the sin which springs from it as from its root. Our Lord imbues Mary Celeste with this hatred by saying: "There are two extremes—a Supreme Good, which is My Divine Being, and a supreme Evil, which is sin. On these two extremes depend the two eternities. I am the Being of Beauty, Virtue, Perfection and Eternal unmeasured Bliss; whilst sin is the extremity of ugliness, misery, misfortune and evil of all kinds. You can never comprehend so great an evil. Being incapable of penetrating the greatness of My Divine Being, you are incapable of sounding the depths of evil, which is sin. Just as I contemplate in myself the goodness of which I am the Source, so I condemn and punish even the smallest sin. See, My daughter, how much you should hate sin. Think that whatever wrong you do, however slight, is not small in My eyes, for I hate even the shadow of sin.

. . . Think that in committing a single venial sin you deserve the hatred of all creatures. Therefore I, the only Good, in order to remedy this, took on Myself your likeness, so as to destroy what you love—that is, your self-love, which takes the place of the love you owe to Me."

Our Lord shows her also how His life on earth was the

condemnation of self-love, by the poverty, suffering and shame with which it was filled. This is the mystery of the Cross, which the Divine Master proposes to Mary Celeste for her meditation. "Meditate day and night on the mystery of the Cross," He says, "and have an ardent desire to see yourself on the Cross with Me, so that your self-love and the desire of honors and pleasure be crucified in you. Keep yourself firmly bound to the Cross, and embrace it with love, hating your self-love and all attachment to evil, and uniting yourself to Me, the supreme Good."

Having denounced the evil and indicated the remedy. Our Lord explains the act of purity by which the soul attains to union: "You must act in such a manner that by loving aspiration your soul takes its flight towards Me, and that all your aspirations be reduced to one act, one pure intention in Me your only End. Your slightest thoughts, words and actions should be animated by this same principle."

In this manner the precept of the Gospel is fulfilled: "Be . . ye therefore perfect, as your Heavenly Father is perfect." The two following beautiful virtues are less the fruit of purity, as Mary Celeste understands it, than the exercise of purity itself. Hear what Our Lord says to His servant on this subject of the first of these virtues, which is simplicity: "Charity is to be found in simplicity. My dwelling is in pure and simple souls. I rest in them as one would rest in the midst of a journey, communicating to them the true spirit of peace. My daughter, do all your actions in this beautiful spirit of purity. I wish you to be simple like a pure dove. That is the path I mark out for you. When you no longer feel that familiar love so dear to you, it is because you have neglected simplicity of soul and thought. It is I Who, through the love I bear to your soul, make you experience aridity in prayer when you neglect this simplicity in your dealings with your neighbor. I do this in order to make you abstain from all judgment, as far as it is possible in this world, among men. In this way you will be freed from self-love.

This latter resembles a venomous serpent which turns its tail towards him who would crush its head. Often I seek to deliver souls ensnared by this love of self, by sending them humiliations or allowing them to be humbled by their neighbor. Alas! instead of profiting by them, they change the remedy into poison and, like the serpent, turn the tail of their self-love against Me or against the neighbor who has humbled them. Instead of being resigned to My Will, they take everything badly, committing many imperfections and conceiving aversion for their neighbor. Their love becomes cold, and still greater evils ensue. My daughter, beware of this serpent and warn your neighbor when you see him likely to be caught in its toils, so that he may not allow it to take possession of his soul."

The second great virtue is humility. Our Lord explains this to Mary Celeste in the following manner: "All the degrees of humility are a Practice of truth, which is purity. Look at the first degree of humility, which is the knowledge of your own nothingness. It is to be found in this purity, for it considers Me and not self in all its works, and thus recognizes its nothingness.

"The second degree of humility consists in the knowledge of your own miseries and baseness, the conviction that you are a sinner, worse than nothing. This same purity of intention, which looks towards Me as the supreme Being, gives birth to this feeling of your own lowliness. Those who look towards Me alone as the supreme Beauty and supreme Good are penetrated with deep respect for My majesty and truth; and in the light of this greatness they condemn themselves as being but falsity and ugliness.

"The third degree of humility is not to desire honor and the esteem of men, and even to hold them in contempt. Purity of intention has this effect also. It hates and despises all that is not truly good, all that has not Me alone for Object.

"The fourth degree of humility is to love scorn and contempt and to rejoice in abasement. This disposition is also to be found in purity of intention, for it tends to unite itself to the life I led on earth in My Humanity, and it considers only My Divine pleasure.

"The last and most perfect degree of humility is to give Me all honor and glory, and to attribute all grace to Me. This is the special aim and desire of that purity of intention: to give all honor and glory to Me, in the perfect annihilation of self. Purity of intention is therefore a guide to that perfect truth which is called Humility. If the soul does 'not find this virtue by the path I have marked out, she Will never find it elsewhere."

Our Lord ardently desires to unite Himself to the soul of His faithful servant; and He explains to her that the condition of this union is silence, which also springs from the exercise of purity. He says: "Do not allow yourself any act, any word, any thought which is not the outcome of purity. In order to facilitate this work, keep a perpetual silence, having as sole aim pure love of Me. Be silent at all times. Be silent in mind, in heart and in tongue. Be silent when you are spoken of, be it in praise, blame, scorn or exaggeration. Be silent, whether the opinion of men be favorable or unfavorable to you. Be silent when you receive gifts, graces and lights. Be silent in the changes and vicissitudes of this life; do not seek to speak either in time of consolation or of sorrow. Let all be lost in purity. Do not seek enlightenment, either from your Superiors or your equals. May your life be henceforth pure Love, Who is your Spouse, the Word. Be exact as regards silence, and if you are obliged to say a few words because of living in common with others, do it always in gentleness and in the pure peace of the Word. Before speaking, recollect yourself, seeking wisdom from on high, and then speak only briefly. In the same way, do not be anxious to speak either good or evil of yourself. Consecrate yourself to the silence of pure love."

Mary Celeste understood this Divine Lesson and repeats it: "Thou dost make me understand," she says, "that I must apply myself to resembling Thy purity in all my actions as far as my weakness is capable of. The lesson that Thou dost give me is to keep my eyes fixed on the Divine Being, never ceasing to look towards Him. This pure act of Divine Love must be uninterrupted, whether in conversing with my neighbor or in silence or solitude, whether eating or drinking. Thus Thou dost make me see what the life of my soul should be in Thee; ... My Beloved, Thou dost teach me to behave towards Thee like a child with its Mother ... I must ignore all created things and all human judgment ... With total abandonment, I must rest happily in Thine arms, as a child on the breast of a beloved Mother."

Mary Celeste warns us that it is necessary to keep the Presence of Jesus within us by the light of Faith, so as not to lose this treasure of purity. "It is certain," she says, "that if my soul wanders away even for a quarter of an hour from that look of Faith, if it is not attentive to keep Thee in sight, it sins in thus not looking towards Thee, O supreme and infinite Being. I do not mean to say that any action done without this intention is a sin, but nevertheless, far from Thee, one can easily sin. My experience teaches me that to do anything without special reference to Thee easily brings a stain upon the soul. That is why it is not astonishing that worldlings so often fall into sin. Our nature is so weak and corrupted that we fall the moment we lose sight of Thee. ... The soul who desires to attain perfection must not imagine that it can be achieved without this constant looking with love towards its God. ... O God, grant in Thy goodness that my soul may never lose sight of Thee, otherwise I might be drawn into evil."

Our Lord tells Mary Celeste that this act of purity can raise the soul to Heaven, where it finds its repose in God. "The higher the flight of the bird, the purer is the air it breathes, and the greater its security from hunters. Thus the Christian soul is safer from the attacks of the enemy the more it penetrates into the heaven of My Divinity. Mount, therefore, as high as possible into the pure and calm air of My Divine Being. ... From there you will see the earth like a round cage, in which all creatures are imprisoned and are flying hither and thither in perpetual agitation and suffering. Those just souls who mount upwards to My Divinity enjoy, on the contrary, great liberty, uninterrupted happiness and interior peace. The most happy are those who have the greatest strength in their wings, strengthening them by being convinced of the nothingness of all things, and of their own nothingness, and so they mount higher towards the Infinite Being Who is All."

The Angels are models of this angelic purity, and Mary Celeste in the spiritual exercises (third day) says "Thou dost show me that the Angelic Choirs are steadfast in the pure act of their being and that they contemplate Thee without ceasing. Thou dost wish me, like unto them, to keep the eye of my mind fixed on Thee. Like these pure spirits, I should look upon earthly things as so many atoms seen in the rays of the sun. I should live in the company of the Angels, animated by their spirit."

What is the source of this purity? Jesus invites Mary Celeste to draw it from His Wounds.

"My five Wounds are so many arrows that wound just souls with the love of the Cross. ... Henceforth I wish My Wounds to send forth arrows to transfix your soul, so that you may not remain one hour without being wounded by them. You will thus continue attached to the Cross. Wish rather to die than to be unfaithful."

It is especially in Holy Communion, however, that Jesus communicates this virtue of purity: "This interior purification is brought about in an especial manner by sacramental Communion," He says. "When I was living on earth, the mere touch of My garments healed the sick, a single look from Me was sufficient to remit sins and the punishment of sin. How then can I enter into the heart of souls dear to Me, souls who long for My coming with love and humility, without purifying them still more by the fire of My charity. This Divine fire bums away those involuntary stains which have been contracted through human frailty. That is why, when you receive Me sacramentally, you should have the desire of wearing again your baptismal robe, washed in the Blood of My Heart."

In another place Mary Celeste warns us that the increase of grace through Holy Communion grows in proportion to the care with which the soul has kept that which she has previously received. She adds: "Thou hast opened the eyes of my soul and made them understand how important it is to use care and fidelity in keeping the graces already received, and augmenting them by the practice of holy virtues. Thou dost show me, O my Beloved, that grace flows like a river for fervent souls; for weak souls it is only a stream; for cold and tepid souls it flows but in drops; if they are not careful to gather up at least these few drops, they will become dried up and without life. The sanctification of each soul depends on the measure of grace, and the loss of so precious a gift results in the damnation of a great number."

It belongs to the Holy Ghost, by virtue of His gifts, to lead the soul to that degree of purity which assures its perfect union with God as far as it is possible on earth. In the Dialogues we read:

"This morning in Holy Communion Thou didst call on me to make a profound act of humility, abasing myself in my nothingness. Through this. Thou didst unite me to Thy Divine Being. In the brightness of Thy light, Thou didst give me the seven gifts of Thy Spirit, teaching me and communicating to me by them seven kinds of self- abasement or annihilation."

The wonderful little treatise on the seven Gifts of the Holy Ghost left us by the Venerable Mother describes the seven states of annihilation which constitute perfect purity; it is a luminous commentary on the doctrine of St. John of the Cross on the same subject. The soul raised to this degree of Purity has no other desire than the pleasure and Will of God. It is an aspiration such as this which drew from Mary Celeste's heart the following inspired words:

"O sweet and precious Will of God! How can I, a miserable creature, express what Thou art? It suffices to say that Thou art the substantial Cause of the work of Creation and of Redemption. The Will of my God is the very Being of my God. And because Jesus loves God above all creatures, He alone loves God's good pleasure more than any other creature. That is why in the Gospel He calls it His food. That is why, if He had been called upon to be born, to suffer and to die for one single man. He would have considered this painful and shameful death as naught, because by it the Divine pleasure would have been satisfied."

Evidently she is describing her own soul when she adds: "The soul to whom it is granted to understand something of the meaning of the Divine pleasure in the life of union with Jesus, that union which is the canal through which flows this water of Paradise; such a soul becomes, in my opinion, as firm as a rock, which neither crosses nor tribulations nor sorrows can move. Such a soul would allow herself to be cut in pieces by creatures rather than do a single act contrary to the Divine pleasure. She suffers, therefore, in peace all that God sends. Not only does she suffer with patience but with great joy even her combats with the evil one, and the revolt of her own corrupt nature, in those things which are the most contrary to her wishes and desires. She is solely attentive to destroy in herself everything contrary to God's Will. She never allows herself an uncharitable word or thought. ... She lives only in seeking the Divine pleasure. Should God send her dryness and aridity, she is equally pleased, because she rejoices only in her Beloved. If the devil torments her interiorly, she suffers certainly, but it is not a cross for her, since it can only happen by the Divine permission. In short, she never complains to God of what He arranges for her. But in whatever regards the honor of God, seeing that His creatures care so little for His glory, she sighs and weeps over it; not for herself, but for her Beloved."

We need not hesitate to say that the Venerable Mother did not reach at one bound this sublime degree of purity, and in consequence of union. Our Lord kept on asking it of her, especially in Holy Communion. "Look at Me, O My beloved," He said, "with the eye of purity I desire you to be entirely pure ... I wish your heart to bum with love, so that I can pour My graces into it."

And Mary Celeste replies: "O my God, I contemplate Thy sacred and glorified Body I It is a thousand times more beautiful than a sun of purest crystal. How can I ever resemble such purity? Do this for Me, Thou Who canst, for of myself I could never attain to it." She knows well her human powerlessness, and cries to Our Lord: "The greatest remedy for my misery is in a total mistrust of self, for I am incapable of responding faithfully to Thine advances, and of being immaculate as Thou dost wish me to be. Thou alone, O God, canst grant me this. Thou knowest that I can do nothing of myself. ... I implore Thee not to leave me ... I shall never tire of speaking of Thine infinite mercy."

During the first years of her religious life Mary Celeste had not yet attained to that perfection of purity demanded by Our Lord, as His words to her bear witness: "Continue to hear Me, O daughter of My Heart. You have not yet let Me take possession of you wholly and entirely. Not through reserve and want of good-will on your part, but through weakness and instability."

She accuses herself humbly of her own imperfections. "My God," she says, "Thou hast .enlightened my heart with the light of truth, which shows me that in the past I have often neglected occasions of exercising virtue, by which I could have gained great merit and grace. Alas 1 I allowed myself to be dazzled by self-love and ambition. Several times when my neighbors have misinterpreted my actions I have sought to justify myself before all, so that nobody should think badly of me, and I have grieved over it as though it were an injustice and something unbearable."

Do not let us be misled, however, by Mary Celeste's humility. A favor she received from God speaks for itself and shows us the dispositions of her heart:

"After Holy Communion this morning," she says, "whilst I excited my heart to a fervent act of love, it seemed to me that Thou didst receive all my thoughts and works that were pure, and didst place them within Thy Heart, taking great pleasure therein, but all the imperfection that through frailty I had committed in my works Thou didst take and throw into a deep pit which yawned at Thy Feet.

Thus Thou didst show me that my faults were to be buried and forgotten by Thee, through Thy mercy, symbolized by this pit. Thou didst place my little acts of love in Thy - Heart, to signify that by Thine infinite love, my love had become worthy in Thy sight."

By another symbolical vision the Divine Master showed her the pleasure He took in pure souls:

"Whilst I was praying in particular for certain souls, Thy spouses, who had asked my prayers," she says, "I seemed to see a rock, on which was placed a large stone covered with short grass. From this stone a stream of clear and limpid water flowed, in which, O my Jesus, Thou didst quench Thy thirst with great pleasure. I then heard the voice of Thy purity saying to me: "This represents those pure souls in whom I satisfy My hunger and quench My thirst.'" And Mary Celeste cries: "O Purity, how precious and beautiful Thou art! ... Thou art the Beloved of God. In Thee He dwells and is nourished. It is of Thee that the sacred Spouse of the Canticles says, 'My love feeds among the lilies.'"

And she addresses the following prayer to Jesus:

"O beloved Spouse, I earnestly desire to clothe myself in a new robe of purity, so as to please Thee, for purity is beautiful in Thine eyes. Unfortunately I am full of sins and imperfections, of ingratitude and self-love, which Thou dost detest. I come therefore to Thee, my sure Refuge, so that by Thy power Thou mayest give me this perfect purity. How should I obtain it without Thee, miserable creature that I am, incapable of accomplishing one good action without imperfection? ... Even my good actions are imperfect in Thy sight. O immaculate King of Purity, have pity on my misery and purify me Thyself. I await this grace with hill confidence."

Mary Celeste's prayer was heard, and Our Lord answered:

"I will grant you all that you ask Me, for in you I find but one desire, that of pleasing Me. This pure act draws Me so gently to your heart that I cannot prevent Myself from inclining towards you, O My pure dove. Strive to augment this purity which is so dear to My Heart." He then calls her by this name: "Beloved, purity of My Heart!" Oh, how sweet is this name to Mary Celeste! "O God of my heart," she says, "what joy I felt on hearing Thee pronounce this beautiful name of purity. For not only dost Thou give me this name, but also the effects of this name. What a difference between Thy language and the language of creatures. They teach, but can effect nothing. How different with Thee! Thou art All-Powerful. ... My mind effaces itself before Thine all-power. Thine infinite mercy and the splendor of Thy majesty, which overwhelms my mind when it contemplates Thee."

Let us close this exposition of Mary Celeste's doctrine of purity, which is the condition of Divine union, by the following lines which the Venerable Mother addresses to Our Lord:

"I hereby abandon my whole being irrevocably to Thee. Keep me, O my Love! I am resolved to suffer a thousand deaths rather than displease or sadden Thee by the slightest shadow of fault; but all this I promise through Thy grace and by Thy help. O my Beloved, Thy spirit of love gives me the spirit of peace, of praise, of thanksgiving, of offering. I see the absolute necessity of breaking with creatures and with the world, by a complete separation even from things good in themselves, and from holy friendships. It is the only way of preserving purity of heart, for Thou, O God, art far from the commerce of men. O how true it is that Thou dwellest in purity, and that worldly and earthly things have no resemblance to Thine infinite purity! O how necessary it is for me to live as though I were alone on this earth!

"Hear me, O souls who desire to possess your God for ever. He warns me to dwell here below in spirit little or not at all; and He says this not only to me, but to all souls who love Him and who desire to find Him and to live for ever united to Him."

CHAPTER XIII

MARY CELESTE'S SPIRITUAL GIFTS

 ET us end the study of Mary Celeste's beautiful soul by consecrating a few pages to the extraordinary supernatural favors of which she was the object. We mean those gifts which do not of themselves sanctify, but which sometimes accompany mystical prayer, though they are independent of it, gifts which God grants less for the personal advantage of the recipient than for the help of the faithful.

These favors are not signs of the measure of God's love for souls; still less are they the measure of the love of souls for God. The Divine Master took care to warn Mary Celeste of this: "Know, My daughter," He said, "that in the world there are many faithful souls who are dear to Me, and on whom I have never conferred these favors and supernatural gifts. I prefer one ounce of pure love in a soul to all the extraordinary graces with which she may be endowed. These favors are dear to Me, certainly, as enriching the souls who possess them, and in whom I have placed them; and I expect these souls to keep them with perfect fidelity. But I receive as much glory from those who love Me and who have not been enriched by these favors, for they glorify Me in great purity of love by their humility. I hide Myself within them with great joy. Thus in Heaven souls will be glorified according to the measure of their love, not of their gifts. In the Heavenly country strange things, unguessed by the world, will be revealed, for the world esteems souls enriched by extraordinary graces. In My Kingdom many souls who have followed the ordinary way will have a higher place than those favored by supernatural gifts, because a great number of the former surpass in love those more highly favored; and on earth they have received neither honor nor esteem."

Yet Mary Celeste is herself of the number of these privileged souls, and without presumption we may endeavor to indicate the reason. These supernatural gifts and favors were necessary among the faithful of the Primitive Church. They were necessary to establish the Faith. Since then, however, the Holy Ghost has not left the Church. In the course of centuries He has communicated these same gifts to the principal members of the mystical Body of Christ, to those whom He has chosen to be the instruments of His works, to accomplish a difficult mission, or fill a prominent role in the Christian community. He has favored, in particular, founders of Orders, those patriarchs of religious life who were destined to have a great posterity.

The Venerable Mary Celeste has been chosen to be a powerful instrument in the hands of the Redeemer. It is therefore not surprising to discover in her those gifts mentioned by St. Paul. The gift of Wisdom, or the gift of interpreting the most profound mysteries, is brought out in her commentaries and in her Dialogues. The following lines bear witness to this:

"After Holy Communion, Thou didst open the eyes of my soul, O my beloved," she says to Our Lord, "and I saw how Thou didst enter into me and didst change me into Thyself. There I rejoiced in Thy Divinity, which is the source of all virtues. ... I heard in the depths of my soul these words, 'substance of the Father.' This was said with love in the very center of my soul. Then I was admitted to see all the virtue and justice of my God, that is to say, the essence of His holiness in each of His works. I saw Him shine in His creatures. O my God, Thou hast shown me the whole of Thy holy life whilst Thou wert on earth, also the value of Thy Divine works, and the union in Thy Person of the human nature with the Divine; also the union of all men to the Divinity through Thee, and the worth of the Catholic Church enriched by Thee with inexplicable treasures, whereby I understood perfectly and in an instant all the mystery of the ceremonies of Holy Church. I saw the price of Thy Precious Blood, but all this I saw in Thee."

The gift of Knowledge, or the gift of explaining elementary truths, is allied to the gift of wisdom in the meditations which the Venerable Mother composed for her Nuns; beautiful commentaries on the Gospel, especially on the Holy Childhood, and the Passion of the Redeemer. This gift shines forth particularly in Mary Celeste's teaching on the spirit of purity so necessary to Divine union. In a passage of the Seventh Dialogue she speaks of the five senses, showing how each one should be dedicated to God alone. "These five senses," she concludes, "should make me enter into my own nothingness, so that by true self-annihilation Thou dost live in me and not I myself; that I may be wholly and entirely Thine, renouncing all knowledge for love of Thee."

We cannot linger over the gifts of prophecy and discernment of spirits, as this would mean rewriting the history of the Venerable's relations with St. Alphonsus, with Mother Mary Joseph, and with the young Sister Mary Columba. But we will cite two instances of her faith. The first of these is the gift of healing, the second the power of working miracles.

"One day the head workman of the monastery returned home late for his dinner. His wife scolded him for letting the dinner get cold and asked the cause. The good man then explained that he had been detained at the Convent, as the holy Prioress had met with an accident. Whilst standing at an open window a heavy shower of water from a leaking pipe had fallen on her. The woman then began to complain of the holy Prioress, who had been the innocent cause of her husband's late arrival. The poor man listened in sorrowful silence, when the housewife, having advanced into the porch, received on her head and shoulders a cascade of water from the same pipe and was instantly seized with the same illness and fever as the holy Prioress. The unfortunate woman now changed her tone and humbly prayed and implored Mary Celeste's intercession. When the man returned to the Monastery the Prioress knew of what had happened before being told, and said to him: "Do not be anxious, your wife will be cured at the same time as myself!' This prediction proved true."

Another time there was no more oil in the Monastery. The Sister Bursar and the lay Sisters, having assured themselves that the jars were empty, came to tell the Prioress. The latter, having prayed a moment, said to them, "Go and look again." They obeyed and found the largest jar full of oil. In utter astonishment they ran to tell the Venerable Mother of the miracle. Mary Celeste merely replied that probably they had not looked properly the first time; but in saying this she colored and hastened to the Choir to thank Our Lord present in the Blessed Sacrament.

There are certain graces which, by their extraordinary nature, can hardly be allied to the preceding gifts, though they are wonderfully sanctifying f6r the soul who receives them. Mary Celeste's life was full of such graces. We can only mention a few within the limits of this book. For our instruction the Divine Master often revealed to Mary Celeste the operations of His grace in fervent souls, especially through Sacramental Communion. Here is an example:

"God of my soul," writes the Venerable Mother, "Thou dost declare to me that through the Eucharistic Sacrament Thou dost inundate my soul with graces. Again this morning Thou didst act thus. In Thy goodness Thou didst take from Thy side a globe of light, from whence Thou didst draw two garments. The first was white; it was the robe of innocence. Having dressed me in it. Thou didst clothe me also with the other garment, which was red, the robe of charity. Thou didst tell me that these two garments were bought for me with Thy Precious Blood. I saw all this clearly, though not materially, and I felt myself enriched with Thine eternal wealth. O Divine Heart of my Beloved, I rejoice in seeing an evil creature like myself changed into an angel of light through Thy most Precious Blood."

And on another occasion she writes:

"To-day being the Epiphany, my spirit was rejoicing in Thee, O my true God. My heart seemed to be united to the Eastern Kings, and to adore Thee with them, not so much in the stable as in the Blessed Sacrament of the Altar. There I offered my three gifts with the holy Kings; the gold of pure love, the incense of all my actions, even the slightest, done solely for Thy glory, and the myrrh of mortification of the senses, by renouncing all satisfactions which have not Thy Divine pleasure solely in view. As usual, Thou didst wish to reward me for this little gift, and didst admit my soul to a secret and intimate embrace, uniting me to Thyself and manifesting to me how Thou wast united to the Church Thy spouse, and to all souls who are Thy faithful spouses.

"In this union of purity. Thou didst raise me far above the things of sense, and I heard Thy Voice pronouncing the following words: 'My pure daughter, I wish to pay you for these three gifts. For the gold, I give you My love; for the incense, I give you the works of My life and My merits; for the myrrh, I give you the suffering of the Cross.' It seemed to me that Thou didst then lock my heart with a key of gold, and place this key in Thy Divine Heart. At the same time Thou didst explain this action to me. I understood that henceforth no creature and no earthly affection must have entrance into my heart, and the golden key signified the pure love which I must bear for Thee until death. O Eternal Purity, what joy Thou givest me. Human language could never describe, nor brain understand, the wonderful effects Thou dost produce in souls."

Here is another example, showing that it is indeed in Holy Communion that our souls grow like to their Divine Model: "After Holy Communion," writes Mary Celeste, "Thou didst deign to unite Thyself to my soul in that purity of which I have spoken; Thou didst show Thyself to me with the eyes of my mind. Then, taking my right hand in Thy left Hand, in which Thy glorious wound shone like the sun. Thou didst place therein a rich and precious stone. Then Thou didst the same to my left hand; after which, bringing Thy Heart near to mine, Thou didst place a third precious stone in my heart. Thou didst then explain to me that the first precious stone signified the love of scorn, the second signified the love of the Cross, whilst the third signified pure love. I saw that Thou hadst placed these stones within me as a pledge of Thy love, and didst promise me that I should keep them for ever. O goodness of my God, how can I thank Thee for so much love towards Thy miserable creature?"

The following is a still more remarkable favor:

"Seeing me suffering, O my God," she writes, "Thou hadst compassion on me, and in Thy goodness Thou didst fortify my soul as with a precious ointment, giving me new strength and new life. Then, impressing on my heart Thy sweet Name, Thou didst say: 'I am your Jesus, Who, enclosed in the little cell of your heart, wishes to dwell there eternally, for I am your Life.' At this moment, O my Beloved, Thou didst print Thy beautiful Name on my heart, and I felt within my soul a consolation which strengthened and renewed my-whole being."

Another time she related an even more marvellous grace: "The world seemed to me a dreadful prison, and I myself like an earthworm," she said. "Thou, O my God, dost know my sorrows, and this morning in Holy Communion, to ease my suffering, Thou didst hold me for a few instants in Thine arms, saying with Thine accustomed love: 'Always on the Cross, always loving, you will suffer much, but all for love.' During this time, although I seemed to see Thee crucified in my heart, I felt myself glorified in beholding myself in Thy Divine arms, and my soul was full of peace and joy."

Sometimes the Most Blessed Trinity appeared to Mary

Celeste to enrich her with precious graces. Thus she writes on September 10th, 1751:

"Being in prayer before God concerning a matter which had been recommended to me, the Divine Father showed Himself to me in a shining light and said: 'I am your Father; leave to Me, your Father, the care of all things and of yourself, and I will grant whatever you desire.' Then the Three Divine Persons showed themselves to me; the Father, receiving me as His daughter for ever, gave to me a rich robe which signified His Divine Will. He wished me to be clothed in it always, as His true daughter. Then the Word named me His spouse for all eternity, and with great love presented me with a magnificent ring and little cross of gold, covered with diamonds and precious stones. The ring also was set with precious stones; it signified that I must be faithful in all my actions until death. The Holy Ghost likewise adorned me with celestial jewels. This beautiful Cross, with its five precious stones, represented the five degrees of humiliation endured by the Word of God, my Spouse. His annihilations. His insults. His scorn, His 'hidden life, and His abandonment. The gold was the love He bore for the Cross. The rubies represented the value of His merits and graces, with which He adorns the souls who are dear to Him. Then, taking in His Hands His Divine Heart, shining like crystal, and wherein the drops of Blood appeared to be shining rubies. He said to my soul: "Receive this Heart, in order to love Me eternally with My own love.' Then my soul rested in God in the purest joy and loved God with the love of the Word, its loving Spouse."

Mystical authors tell us of words which can he heard by those wrapt in contemplation. Having described to us the admirable ways in which God usually spoke to her, Mary Celeste adds:

"He has also another way of speaking; this is through the medium of heavenly messengers, or through my Guardian Angel, who is very faithful to this office with which he has been charged from my childhood. My Angel fulfils this either by inspirations and spiritual impulses, or by formal words, according to whatever God ordains for my good. And I have experienced this, not only from my guardian Angel, but also from other celestial spirits, whose action I was able to perceive in the light God gave to my intelligence in the before-mentioned union. O Father of mercy, I thank Thee for the great goodness Thou dost show towards a creature so vile and unworthy as I."

As a true daughter of the Most Holy Redeemer, Mary Celeste had a great devotion to the holy Apostles, whose protection she could not fail to enjoy. "I experienced within me," she wrote, "a bright light, and in this light I saw a company of celestial spirits. ... Next I saw Thy dear Apostles, Peter and Paul, and in a moment I understood the glory which they now enjoy. They promised me their protection and showed me the place which Thou hast prepared for me near to them in Eternity. I also saw the place of the other Apostles, of St. James in particular, whose Feast the Church is celebrating to-day."

Among her favorite saints Mary Celeste numbered St. Thomas a Becket, for which she gives us the following reasons, saying:

"In order to cure me of my weakness, O my God, Thou didst send to me the holy Archbishop of Canterbury, St. Thomas the martyr. Dipping his finger in his blood, with great charity he made the sign of the Cross on my eyes, and thus delivered me from my suffering. My soul then experienced a sweet repose in Thee, O my eternal Rest.

"Several times at differing intervals during my life this great Saint has been pleased to come and assist me by his presence during my prayer, and, uniting my spirit to his, led me to Thy Bosom, there to contemplate his love for Thee, and Thy love for him. My soul then enjoyed heavenly contemplation of union with God such as he himself possesses. I thank Thee, O my

Spouse and King, for the mercy Thou hast showered on me by means of Thy servant. My soul received great increase of virtue from this heavenly society."

But our quotations are becoming too long and must cease. We know that these extraordinary supernatural gifts should always be accepted and not sought after, welcomed with reserve and submitted to obedience and tried by contradiction; we know also that they should produce in the soul a more profound humility, greater generosity and a more perfect application to duty. This was the effect produced in the soul of Mary Celeste by the marvellous graces with which her life is filled. She herself has never sought these .extraordinary manifestations, desiring only to be led by the light of Faith. It was with the greatest repugnance that she wrote down her experiences in obedience to the orders of her directors. We could fill pages with the touching expressions of her humility. For example:

"What have I done to deserve so many favors, O my God? I only deserve to be buried in oblivion, scorned, and treated as unworthy and ungrateful. Why dost Thou overwhelm me with so many graces, since I am so unfaithful to Thee, my only Good?"

We cannot close this chapter without one more quotation which reveals to us the depth of the Venerable Sister's humility and the purity of her love, while at the same time it speaks of a favor which must have brought the greatest consolation to her heart:

"I was deeply troubled," she says, "thinking that during the course of my life I might possibly have attributed to myself the glory that is due to Thee in Thy gifts and graces. O my God, even the thought of this horrifies me. I pray Thee to deliver me from such a misery. Let me remain in the nothingness to which I belong. I return to Thee, O God, all the gifts which Thou has placed in me.' Having made this prayer, I experienced peace of mind and Thou didst allow me to rest in Thee. And Thou didst awaken me with these words: 'I love thee from all eternity. My beloved one.' My heart being inflamed with love, I implored Thee to show me Thy love by confirming the Rules Thou hadst dictated to me. Thereupon the Three Divine Persons gave me the wished-for confirmation by the approbation of Thy Vicar on earth, at the same time asking me two things: death to myself by a continual mortification, and deep humility. But Thou must accomplish this Thyself in my soul, O generous Giver! I hope all from Thee, knowing my own weakness."

Monsignor Gay has said: "There is nothing more touching on earth than to see the singular love of God for certain creatures. It is a revelation of His Heart, surpassing the discoveries of even the most eminent theologians. ... God is an ocean. It is He Who makes the rivers into which He pours Himself."

Mary Celeste has surely been one of these rivers, with deep and limpid waters. Should the question arise to what other saint we might compare her, she seems to us to be the sister of St. Gertrude, who had made of her heart a sweet dwelling-place for Jesus.

CHAPTER XIV
THE CONSUMMATION

E are now coming to the term of this life of labor for God; a life in which the supernatural workings of Providence are shown at each step.

The hour is drawing near when Mary Celeste will contemplate in Heaven Him Whom she has so loved on earth.

"How greatly she had desired this hour! In the following passage of her Dialogues, we seem to hear the echo of the words of the great St. Teresa:

"O my Beloved God and Spouse, I feel that I cannot live one moment, no, not one single hour without Thee, and my soul can only rejoice at the thought that every day and every hour brings me nearer to the eternal joy of seeing Thy Divine Face. My heart grieves when it is moved by self-love, and although that does not happen often, yet it makes me suffer intensely. This life on earth becomes bitter at the thought that I have ever offended Thee. My neighbors' conversation gives me no pleasure and no consolation and I feel myself, displeasing to everybody, and words fail me. I take no interest in anything except to speak of Thee; that alone fills me with joy and delights my heart, or else when I, or others, sing canticles of love to Thee. Then am I full of peace and joy." And she cries with St. Paul: "O how much I desire to leave this prison of flesh, my poor body, that I may never lose sight of Thee, my only Treasure!" God was soon to hear the ardent desires of His servant, and to grant her a last favor. As Mary Celeste's special vocation had been the imitation of the Redeemer, so her death will bear a touching resemblance with that of Jesus. All

CHAPTER XV: THE CONSUMMATION

witnesses are unanimous in saying that this death was not preceded by any illness or particular infirmity, nor even by pain which might have indicated that the end of this precious life was near.

It was on Friday, September 14th, of the year 1755, the Venerable Mother had received Holy Communion as usual that morning. In the evening, full of ardent love, she asked for the Holy Viaticum and the Sacraments of the Church. Knowing that she would soon see her Savior face to face, with what fervor must she not have received Him for the last time under the Sacramental Veils. Her thanksgiving ended, she asked her confessor, Don Nicholas Lombardi, who was present, to read to her the Passion of Jesus Christ in St. John's Gospel. When the priest came to the words, 'Consummatum est,' she bowed her head like her Divine Master, and breathed her last. At the same moment an earthquake shook the house, and a noise of chains was heard, as if to show the despairing flight of the devil who had never once been able to overcome the Saint who was now beyond his reach for ever.

At this same moment, as we have already related, St. Gerard Majella, lying ill at the convent of Capolele, far from Foggia, said to Brother Stephan, his Infirmarian: "I have just seen the soul of Mother Mary Celeste wing its flight to Heaven like a dove, to receive there the reward she has merited through her great love for Jesus and Mary." The vision of the holy Redemptorist Brother was but the fulfilment of a promise made by Our Lord to the Venerable Mother. The Divine Master had said to her at the very beginning of her trials: "My daughter, know that in this world you will always be united to My Passion, and that you will receive afflictions and infirmities in abundance, for one cannot love without suffering, and all that I arrange and do for you is the outcome of love. You must be very patient and I promise you faithfully that as soon as your soul leaves your body, I Myself will bear it to Heaven, so that it can enjoy Me for all Eternity."

The mortal remains of the great servant of God preserved all their freshness and gave out a sweet perfume. Her countenance expressed sweetness and holiness. Her daughters the Nuns, shedding many tears, carried her to the choir in their Church. They could not doubt, however, that their holy Mother was already in possession of eternal happiness. God Himself was to bear witness to this. When the body of the Venerable Mother was exposed in the Church, Don Benedict Salerni, the Superior of the Monastery, commanded it to make the sign of the Cross. To the astonishment and consolation of all present, the corpse obeyed, and after having made the sign of the Cross, fell back into its former position.

The whole town was roused to enthusiasm. "The Saint is dead, the Saint is dead!" was the cry heard on all sides. And the whole populace ran to the Church of the Most Holy Redeemer. Each one demanded a piece of her garments or an object belonging to her; each one wished to look for the last time on the features of the holy Prioress. The funeral obsequies were solemnly celebrated that same day.

Among the crowd in the church was a woman who had been blind from birth. Hearing the cries of admiration and joy from those who had seen the venerable Nun, she was grieved at not being able to enjoy the same happiness. In the midst of her tears, she implored the holy Prioress - to grant her the gift of sight. Her prayer was instantly heard. This miracle caused great enthusiasm among the populace, who repeated unceasingly that a great Saint had just died at Foggia.

The body of Mary Celeste was placed in the ordinary sepulcher of the religious, in the place reserved for Prioresses. It is to be noticed that since the beginning of the monastery the bodies of defunct Sisters had not been buried in the ground nor enclosed and walled up in niches, but simply placed on wooden pedestals, the funereal room being only closed by a door. On the coffins enclosing the mortal remains were inscribed the family names and the names in religion, also the date of death.

CHAPTER XV: THE CONSUMMATION

However, in the case of the Venerable Mother, her daughters had placed a tombstone in the wall in front of the pedestal on which her coffin rested. It bore these words: "Mary Celeste of the Most Holy Redeemer, in the world Julia Crostarosa, Foundress, Mistress, and perpetual Superior of the College of Virgins." This form of burial, although truly extraordinary, was providential. God had arranged it in this way for the glorification of His servant. For, every time the Nuns had occasion to enter the vault on the death of any of the Sisters, they did not fail to visit the body of their Foundress, and to change her garments, which soon became rotten with the dampness of the place.

In 1785, thirty years after the Venerable Mother's death, they had occasion to fulfil this pious duty. Their emotion was great when, in attempting to unfasten the inside tunic which had wound itself round the right leg, they saw blood spring from it in abundance! Three years later, another death in the Community caused the Sisters to re-enter the vault. On this occasion they washed to change the handkerchief which covered the holy Prioress' face. They found it covered with blood. The Superior of the Monastery at that time was Don Saggese, who had a report concerning this marvellous occurrence drawn up by three lawyers. Being eventually named Bishop of Montepoloso, he went to Rome to receive his episcopal consecration, and presented the miraculous handkerchief to Pope Pius VI.

The same marvel was renewed a third time in 1809, under still more remarkable circumstances. We cannot do better than quote the account of it made by Canon Riccardi, Superior of the Monastery, and Vicar-General to Cardinal Firrao, Bishop of Foggia, together with the latter's reply.

BLESSED MARY CELESTE: PART III

REPORT DRAWN UP BY CANON RICCIARDI, VICAR OF THE
MONASTERY OF THE MOST HOLY REDEEMER AT FOGGIA, TO HIS
EMINENCE THE CARDINAL FIRRAO,
ON THE 10TH DAY OF JANUARY, 1809.

Your Eminence,

The spirit of prophecy, lights from God, celestial
communications and miracles have never been wanting to holy
souls in the church of Jesus Christ. Sister Mary Celeste
Crostarosa, after her revelations and prophecies which she had
made known to Monsignor de Liguori, to whom also she gave
the Rules for the Congregation of Missionary Priests he was to
found: Sister Mary Celeste, I repeat, went from Scala to reform
another convent of Nuns at Nocera Di Pagani; from there, being
called to Foggia, she built this monastery of the Most Holy
Redeemer, of which she is the Foundress and of which your
Eminence is at present the honored Superior. This Servant of
God passed to a better life on September 14th, 1755, that is fifty-
four years ago. The heroicity of her virtue is proclaimed by
public opinion. After her death, her body remained in a state of
perfect preservation, so much so that the Nuns, each time they
were obliged to enter the vault, on the death of any of the
Sisters, took advantage of the circumstances to change the
garments of their Mother and Foundress. On January 1st, 1785,
that is thirty years after her death, the Nuns went in this
manner to change her clothes. They found the tunic adhering
to the right leg, and in seeking to detach it, blood began to flow
in abundance, so that the Nuns' hands were covered by it. In
the same way on September 19th, 1788, they went to perform
a like office, and found that the linen cloth which had been
placed over the face three years ago was now covered with
blood, especially near the mouth. On this same occasion, blood
was seen to flow from the nostrils. An account of this was
drawn up before three lawyers, by Monsignor Saggese, Bishop
of Montepoloso, then a Canon of that Church and Vicar of the

aforesaid Monastery of the Most Holy Redeemer. Several ecclesiastics and laymen were present. Monsignor Saggese, at the time of his elevation to the Bishopric, took this linen cloth to Rome and presented it to Pope Pius VI. Just lately, an old lay-Sister died. It became therefore necessary to re-open the vault, a thing which had not taken place for many years, as the Community have been free from illness and epidemic. The Nuns were greatly excited. Above all, they desired to look once more on their Foundress, Sister Mary Celeste Crostarosa. All remembered what had occurred in 1785 and in 1788. I could not therefore do otherwise than undertake to examine the vault. As your Eminence knows, I had procured all the necessary permissions beforehand. I went down into the vault, therefore, armed with all the necessary guarantees. My first act was to note the state of the opening which gave into the cave. It was well made and absolutely dry, it was evident that no one had entered the place since the last burial twenty-one years ago. Mary Celeste's coffin was unnailed, in my presence and in the presence of all the confessors of convents in the episcopal diocese (I had desired the presence of these priests as witnesses); numerous seculars were also present. We found the veil and wimple covered with bright blood. The upper part of the tunic was also covered with a blood so liquid that it stuck to our fingers. The blood was more abundant on the right side of the chest, where two ribs were to be seen, also covered with blood. Blood was also visible near the back of the head. Two doctors and two surgeons who were present examined this extraordinary phenomena with great attention. Convinced of the existence and the nature of the blood, they wished also to analyze it; they compared this congealed blood with blood which for the purposes of comparison they drew from themselves. Both specimens were tested by the same process and produced the same results. ... I then drew up a complete, authentic and solemn account of these wonders. The Nuns now removed the blood-stained linen and replaced it with fresh garments.

The vault which serves as a burial-place for all the Nuns is situated in a damp place, and this might injure the holy Foundress' body as it has already destroyed the face. Moreover, it seems to me hardly respectful to leave the remains of this Servant of God and Foundress in the common sepulcher. I think, therefore, and the Nuns desire it also, that the body of Mary Celeste Crostorosa should be enclosed in a well-sealed coffin, which could then be placed, either in the Church or in the sacristy of the monastery. Thus, should God deign eventually to glorify His faithful servant by means of miracles, it would be easier to obtain precise information. I send to your Eminence part of the veil and habit covered with blood. Meanwhile, I await respectfully whatever orders your Eminence may deign to give, and remain your respectful and obedient servant.

CANON RICCIARDI,
Vicar of the Monastery of the Most Holy Redeemer at Foggia.

January 10th, 1809.

THE CARDINAL'S REPLY TO THE PRECEDING REPORT.
NAPLES,
January 18th, 1809.

The Cardinal Firrao, Almoner in chief to His Majesty, to M. the Canon Ricciardi, his Vicar for the Monastery of the Most Holy Redeemer at Foggia.

The wonderful phenomena of which your Lordship has sent me an account concerning the remains of the Servant of God Mary Celeste Crostarosa, from which, fifty-five years after her death, flows bright red blood, deserves our highest consideration.

Since, together with this wonderful phenomena, witnessed

by you with every precaution and all the necessary prudence, is joined a life of great holiness led by the above-mentioned religious in her quality of Foundress of this monastery, I willingly approve the legitimate desire expressed by your Lordship, by the Nuns and the population of Foggia, that the body of Sister Mary Celeste Crostarosa should be transferred to a place apart, and placed in a new tomb with a suitable epitaph. I entrust this pious duty to your wisdom, so that, acting as my Vicar, you may arrange all in such a manner that it be done in good order and with the requisite devotion. Let all be done quietly. It must not be noised abroad. I hope that the Almighty will deign to manifest His glory by means of new miracles accomplished through the intercession of His Servant. I am pleased to hear that the good Nuns on this occasion arc further strengthened in the practice of virtue and of those duties which they already fulfil so well under your watchful direction, and I urge them to keep always before their eyes the example of their Foundress' life.

May God bless your Lordship's zeal and the Nuns' obedience.

CARDINAL FIRRAO.

The Cardinal's orders were executed. The saintly body was transferred to the Monastery church. Placed in a reliquary open in front but sealed below, it stood near the door on the Gospel side, slightly raised from the ground. The reliquary was closed by two keys, one of which bore the four seals of the episcopal tribunal. They were kept by the Ecclesiastical Superiors.

Further miracles occurred when the holy remains were transferred. Don Anthony Mary Guadagno, Canon of the Cathedral of Foggia, and for twenty-four years Chaplain of the Church of the Most Holy Redeemer, swore on oath at the Introductory Process of Mary Celeste's cause, that he had been told by his father, who was an eyewitness at the time of the transference of the body, the following facts: "The body on its removal had all the appearance of life; the limbs were perfectly flexible, therefore they had no difficulty in clothing it with fresh garments. The Canon, Superior of the Monastery, ordered the corpse to make the sign of the Cross, and to the astonishment of all, the body obeyed. Still greater was the universal admiration when the holy remains obeyed a second order from the Canon. He commanded the dead Nun to allow herself to be bled. Thereupon a surgeon who was present opened a vein, and all the eyewitnesses saw bright blood flow from the wound, until it was closed."

Another witness at the Process made an identical deposition. These phenomena were, however, only the prelude to the miracles by which God was about to glorify His faithful Servant.

CHAPTER XV
THE GLORIOUS SEPULCHER

ROM the day when the mortal remains of Mary Celeste were laid to rest in the Monastery church an incessant procession of pilgrims demanded to gaze on the Saint's features, and to solicit her intercession. From the very beginning the visitors were not only the inhabitants of Foggia, but people from the whole province. Pilgrimages began to be organized, but these were immediately forbidden, in case a public worship begun too soon might later prove an obstacle to the beatification of the Servant of God.

Sister Mary Henrietta de Fazio was able to make the following deposition at the Introductory Process of the Cause. "In my opinion," she states, "devotion towards the holy Foundress is augmenting rather than decreasing. It is kept up by people of either sex and of all conditions. Moreover, this crowd of people has not been in any way invited. They are inspired by Faith, and their numbers grow daily on account of the singular graces with which they are rewarded."

On three occasions, in particular, the crowd at Mary Celeste's tomb was immense. The first of these occasions was on the centenary of her death, September 14th, 1855. The crowd then demanded insistently the beatification of the holy Prioress. The next assemblage took place when the people were informed that the Bishop of Foggia, Monsignor Bernadino Frascolla, was sending a petition to Rome to obtain the Introduction of the Cause. And again, in 1878, the crowds gathered when the Bishop, Monsignor Cosenza, reiterated his predecessors' petition.

Since Mary Celeste's death, numerous are the requests for relics of her garments. Her picture is honored in countless family circles; often a lamp is kept burning before it, and if any stranger asks, "Whose portrait is that?" the invariable reply is: "It is a portrait of the holy Prioress!"

As Sister Mary Henrietta stated, the people's devotion was increased by many miracles due to the intercession of Mary Celeste. More than fifty of these miracles were related in full at the Introductory Process of the Cause.

On this subject we must remark: first, that most of the miracles were accompanied by the apparition of the Venerable Mother, Mary Celeste, appearing to the sick, saying: "Have confidence, God will cure you!"

The following is an account of a particularly interesting cure. The fortunate beneficiary was a doctor, Vincent Nigri, who makes this deposition himself: "In February, 1864, I was attending soldiers attacked with purple typhus, at a time when the epidemic was violent. Two doctors had already succumbed as a result of their devotion to duty; and I myself, after twenty days of untiring work among more than six hundred sick men, was attacked by the terrible disease in its most virulent form. By the third - day I had become unconscious; on the eleventh day I was at death's door. At this crisis my wife, seeing that all remedies were in vain, made me swallow in a little water a tiny particle of the holy Prioress' habit, at the same time placing one of her pictures under my pillow. I was told that towards midnight I awakened as from a deep sleep and, calling my family, said to them: 'A Nun has been to visit me; she has taken away all my pain, and now I am cured.' It was indeed so. The next morning I had recovered the use of all my senses and was completely cured without experiencing any of the after effects of the dreadful disease. To my mind this was a wonderful miracle. Only God could do it, through the hand of His saint." Secondly, we must remark on the wonderful variety of the miracles related in the Process.

CHAPTER XV: THE GLORIOUS SEPULCHER

If it has been stated that Mary Celeste, like St. Gerard, is particularly kind to mothers in assisting them at the birth of their children, we must also recognize that no type of miracle seems to be beyond her power, and all classes of people are included.

Some had already received the Last Sacraments, and their life despaired of, when they were completely and instantaneously cured by Mary Celeste. Such was the case of Raphael de Mita, an old man of eighty-five. Also Sominic Vinciguerra, who was dying of congestion of the lungs. The doctor had declared death to be inevitable, and had even stated the probable hour of it. Preparations for the funeral were even begun. But Dominic had a daughter who was most devout to Mary Celeste. The Saint appeared to her and announced her father's cure. He did indeed recover perfect health at the very hour at which the doctor had prophesied his death.

Then there were those afflicted by incurable diseases. The holy Prioress appeared to some amongst them and cured them by the touch of her hand. A young man named Elvirus Vitali was attacked by a nervous illness which caused periodical attacks of insanity; he was cured by touching the Venerable Mother's picture.

Concilia Urbana was cured of a painful disease of the eyes by a vision of the holy Prioress. There are also numerous accounts of cripples who have recovered the use of their limbs. A young man named Lorenzo had one leg much shorter than the other and could only walk with crutches. On the day indicated by Mary Celeste in an apparition to his mother, Lorenzo threw aside his crutches. His leg had suddenly become longer and he was able to walk like other people. ...

Augustin Tancredi, a child who was never able to stand as his legs were too weak to support him, was carried to the holy Prioress' tomb by his mother, full of faith and hope; a few days later the latter saw the child gaze fixedly at Mary Celeste's picture, then leave his chair with a bound, stand straight and firm on his feet and run to his mother's arms.

Sister Mary Celeste loved the poor and was always ready to help them. A poor workman had fallen seriously ill, but he had a devotion to the holy Prioress; she therefore gave proof of a motherly care towards him. It was known by all that in the reliquary of the Venerable Mother her head was resting on two pillows. The case was always closed by a double lock and sealed with the episcopal seal. One day it was noticed that one of the pillows was missing. Consternation was great. Where could it be? This was soon learnt. Mary Celeste had appeared to her servant, the sick workman, and had given it to him. Scarcely had the sick man leant his head on this pillow than he was completely cured. Naturally they did not deprive him of the Venerable Mother's gift. The fortunate man kept it as a precious relic in his best cupboard, and there it was often seen by Canon Dominic Potignonne, the worthy man's confessor, who has given testimony to this fact on oath.

Mary Celeste has also performed miracles of a different kind, but no less admirable. People divided by a deadly hatred became suddenly reconciled; families threatened with misery and unmerited disgrace testify to having had a vision of the holy Prioress assuring them of unexpected deliverance. A person grieved at not being able to procure for her brother the treatment which would save him prayed to Mary Celeste, and on opening her drawer found there the necessary sum.

A young girl, Marie-Vincente Palazzo, had never thought of entering the religious life. The Venerable Mother appeared to her and spoke to her, when the young girl decided forthwith to consecrate her life to God.

Another time a postulant, Marie-Assumpta, had scarcely entered the Convent when she was seized with a profound distaste for religious life, and with bitter regret at having left her family. She resolved therefore to return home the next day. Mary Celeste appeared to her in a dream and so changed her heart that, on awakening, Marie-Assumpta felt as much joy in the practices of religious life as she had before felt distaste, and was never again tempted to abandon her vocation.

The holy Mother also concerned herself with less important matters. Don Vincent Ricotta, rector of the Church of St. Augustine at Foggia, was to preach; worn out with worry and anxiety and incapable of thinking clearly, he was yet obliged to go into the pulpit without having had time to prepare his sermon. He invoked the help of the holy Prioress and astonished all, for never in his life had he spoken with so much ease and eloquence.

It was, however, especially in favor of her own dear monastery that she used her credit with God. After her death she appeared several times to her daughters, sometimes to console them in times of sadness, at others to encourage them to fervor.

Mother Marie-Therese was Mistress of Novices. One day at Holy Mass she raised her eyes towards the picture of the Foundress placed in the Choir. She noticed that the eyes of the picture seemed to cast sad and indignant glances in the direction of two novices. Mother Mary-Therese, however, could not distinguish which of the two attracted the holy Prioress' attention. Time soon made this clear. After the revolution of 1860 one of these two young girls left the Monastery, and led henceforth an unsettled and scandalous life.

On another occasion the Venerable Mother appeared to Sister Mary Celeste del Comte and informed her that Mother Mary Teresa of Jesus was going to be elected Superior. This seemed to be impossible; all the Sisters and the Bishop himself were opposed to this election; besides, the Nun in question was seriously ill and obliged to follow a treatment outside the Monastery. Shortly after, however, the Bishop died, and Mother Mary Teresa was unanimously elected Superior.

The Nuns of the Most Holy Redeemer have borne witness to four miraculous cures performed in the Monastery through the intercession of Mary Celeste. Moreover, ten among them have given testimony to having been themselves miraculously cured through the holy Prioress. We will quote the following marvellous occurrence which was subjected to a searching examination on the part of the Ecclesiastical judges, and which ended in being declared an undeniable miracle. We quote Sister Candida Cittadini's own words:

"For some months I had been charged with the office of baker. It happened that for some reason or other the miller did not send the usual provision of flour to the Monastery; and at the end of four days the Community, consisting of fifty Nuns, was without bread. I told the Superior of it. She told me to look again. I replied that it was useless to do so, as the provision had been exhausted four days ago. The Superior then raised her eyes to Heaven and called on our holy Foundress to help us, saying: 'O holy Mother Prioress, it is for you to provide!'

"For my part, out of pure obedience, holding in my hand the key of the flour-bin, which never left me, I went to look again. A lay Sister accompanied me. We opened the bin, on which I had pasted a picture of Mother Mary Celeste, and saw that it was quite empty; only a few specks of flour adhered to the four corners. I told the Sister to gather up these remains and to take them to the Superior, in order to show her that there was really nothing to be done. But as the Sister gathered these crumbs they multiplied, soon forming an enormous quantity, far greater than the amount we usually had. Full of joy and admiration at the miracle, we ran to tell our Mother and Sisters. We all returned thanks to Divine Providence and to our holy Protectress, who had come to our assistance in such a motherly way. The Community enjoyed the bread made from this flour and called it the miraculous bread."

On July 5th, 1877, a fire broke out in the houses next to the Monastery. The flames were so fierce that they reached the Convent itself and burnt away the doors. The Nuns saw before them the necessity of leaving their holy enclosure to avoid being burnt alive. They called on Mary Celeste to help them, and in an instant the fire was extinguished.

Mary Celeste also protected her monastery against a still greater peril. On July 25th, 1859, Father Moscato, a Jesuit, came to Foggia with six companions in order to venerate the holy Prioress' body. During their pious contemplation the seven pilgrims saw the Venerable Mother's body raise itself slightly, lift one hand, and utter deep sighs. They were overcome with astonishment. Hearing their cries of alarm, the people rushed into the church. All who were witnesses of this miraculous occurrence hastened to inform the Bishop, who himself came at once to the Monastery to hear their testimony and drew up an account of it. This miracle was a warning of the terrible persecution soon to be let loose against religious communities. It foreshadowed the protection with which Mary Celeste would surround the Monastery of the Most Holy Redeemer. In the following year, in fact, the revolution which was to overthrow the kingdom of Naples broke out. All convents were declared the property of the State. The Nuns were either expulsed or condemned to die of hunger through the confiscation of their goods. It was then that Mary Celeste's miraculous protection overshadowed her monastery. All the convents in Foggia were closed and their Nuns expulsed. The Convent of the Most Holy Redeemer was destined to undergo the same fate. Several times an order to this effect was given, and each time Providence suspended the execution of it. One day the revolutionary agents came right into the house, intending to expel the Sisters. Suddenly they changed their mind, asked the Sisters to stay, and declared themselves their defenders.

Several Nuns from other convents, relying on the protection of the holy Foundress, came to seek refuge in the Monastery of the Most Holy Redeemer and asked to join the Community. Mary Celeste's prophecy was indeed fulfilled. She had said to her daughters: "You will never be turned out of this monastery."

During those sad days of persecution the Nuns feared for

the safety of their holy Mother's relics. They therefore asked permission from the Bishop, Monsignor Bernadino Frascolla, to place the body in a safer place. Permission was granted, but Mary Celeste evidently wished to remain with her daughters in the sanctuary where she had received so many prayers and worked so many miracles. She remained there, in fact, until the last Nun of that monastery had died, and was only removed in triumph when the Monastery was obliged to be pulled down for purposes of public necessity, when the glorious remains were confided to the care of the children of St. Alphonsus.

CHAPTER XVI
MARY CELESTE'S CAUSE FOR
BEATIFICATION

O great a reputation for sanctity, and so great a number of miracles, was bound to inspire the desire of all to see Mary Celeste raised by the Church to the honor of the Altar. This was indeed the wish of the Bishops, and of the faithful of Foggia, as well as that of the Nuns of the Most Holy Redeemer.

In 1788, Monsignor Sagesses himself took a petition to Rome and laid it before Pope Pius VI, together with documents for the Introduction of the Cause. Cardinal Firrao had given precise instructions to the Sisters on the subject. Monsignor Frascolla began the diocesan process, but he was turned out of his episcopal See by the Revolution. Monsignor Cosenza, who continued the work of his predecessor, addressed petitions to Pope Pius IX. Mother Mary Teresa of Jesus had placed the affair in the hands of Don Anthony Rubiao, a distinguished priest in Rome, but the political troubles, and also, it must be owned, the poverty of the monastery, always seemed to prevent the Cause from going any further.

In 1891 Monsignor Peter Crostarosa, a grandnephew of Mary Celeste, and Canon of St. Mary Major, became Postulator of the Cause, at the request of the Nuns of the Most Holy Redeemer at Foggia. The Cause, which was taken up with great zeal, proved most successful. The examination of the Venerable Mother's manuscripts by the Sacred Congregation of Rites, ended in the following declaration: "There is nothing in the works of the Servant of God which could prove an obstacle to the Introduction of her Cause." This decree of the Sacred

Congregation was confirmed by Pope Leo XIII on December 2nd, 1895.

Finally, in 1901, Mary Celeste received the title of "Venerable" by a decree of the Sacred Congregation of Rites, confirmed by the Sovereign Pontiff, a decree which we will now quote in its entirety as being the *resume* and justification of this book.

DECREE

In this decree several petitions are mentioned as having been addressed to the Holy See for the Introduction of Mary Celeste's Cause. Among these the reader will have remarked that of the Superior-General of the Redemptorists, at that time the Reverend Father Mauron. It is particularly noticeable because it confirms the close link which binds Mary Celeste to the new Congregation of the Most Holy Redeemer, and also the intimate conviction which not only St. Alphonsus, but all the Redemptorists of his time had, of Mary Celeste's holiness and supernatural gifts. It is also interesting to note among these eloquent petitioners, the names of Cardinal Sanfelica, Archbishop of Naples, Cardinal Capecelatro, Archbishop of Capone, and author of a very beautiful life of St. Alphonsus; also the Bishop of Nocera, and the Archbishops and Bishops of the neighbouring provinces of Foggia; and finally, the Redemptoristine Nuns of the Monastery of Malines, in Belgium. Mary Celeste was proclaimed "Venerable." It seemed therefore that the Cause of Beatification would follow its normal course, and that the Church would not delay in raising the holy Nun to the honors of the Altar.

God's designs, however, which often upset our human calculations, are always admirable and worthy of adoration. Mgr. Crostarosa, who had consecrated all his energies and all his fortune to the Cause of his glorious relative, died soon after the promulgation of the Decree just quoted. His death seemed to be the death of the Cause also. The Nuns of the Most Holy Redeemer were not able to continue it. Persecution had decreased their numbers, besides which extreme poverty left them no other resources than prayer and sacrifice.

Foggia, however, did not relax its devotion to the holy Prioress. A distinguished member of the Cathedral Chapter, Canon Bucci, was placed in charge of the Church of St. Savior, where the Venerable Mother's body had been placed. In 1920, encouraged by his Bishop, Mgr. Farina he founded a periodical under the title of *The Hidden Pearl: or the Venerable Mary Celeste Crostarosa*, a monthly magazine designed to promulgate the beatification and canonization of the holy Prioress. It was a splendid effort, worthy of all praise, yet it proved insufficient to stimulate the Cause, and to bring it to a happy conclusion. And now in 1930, on March 22nd, the Feast of Our Lady of the Seven Veils, Patron Saint of Foggia, the Very Reverend Father Murray, Superior-General of the Congregation of the Most Holy Redeemer, addressed the following letter to the Reverend Father d'Orazio, postulator of the Causes of his Congregation.

PATRICK MURRAY
Superior General and Rector Major
Of the Congregation of the Most Holy Redeemer,
to the Reverend Father
and beloved Brother in Jesus Christ, BENEDICT D'ORAZIO,
Greetings in the Lord.

You must know how much the remembrance of the Venerable Mary Celeste is kept alive in our Congregation, because of her holy friendship with our Father St. Alphonsus, and how close are the bonds which unite her to the origin of our Institute.

As many desire to see the Servant of God raised to the dignity of the Altar, the Nuns of the Most Holy Redeemer founded by her in the town of Foggia, and the Very Reverend

Peter Crostarosa, a relative of Mary Celeste, began together the Introduction of her Cause of Beatification, and brought it to a successful issue as far as the Decree for the Introduction of the Cause, promulgated by the Sovereign Pontiff Leo XIII, August 11th, 1901.

But the Very Reverend Peter Crostarosa being dead, and the former Monastery of the Most Holy Redeemer no longer existing, this Cause which had begun so well has fallen into oblivion. Nevertheless, the desire to see the Servant of God inscribed in the catalogue of the Saints has always been very near to our heart, and to the hearts of the Nuns of the Most Holy Redeemer, also to those of the clergy and people of Foggia, who glory in possessing the Venerable Mother's body.

Therefore the worthy prelate, Monsignor Fortune Farina, Bishop of Foggia, and the honored members of his clergy, have earnestly begged our Congregation to do all in our power to further the Cause of the Venerable Mary Celeste Crostarosa.

Having fully considered the matter in conjunction with my Counselors, I have decided to grant this request with great pleasure. For this reason, I entrust to you by this letter, in your quality of general Postulator of our Congregation, the charge of re-opening the Cause of Beatification and Canonization of the Venerable Servant of God, Mary Celeste Crostarosa, and I give you all necessary powers, even to establish, if necessary, Vice-postulators, so that with the help of God you may follow up this Cause with all zeal and bring it to a happy conclusion..

Rome, from our house of the Most Holy Redeemer and of
St. Alphonsus, March 22nd, 1930,
on the Feast of Our Lady of Foggia,
The Madonna of the Seven Veils.

This letter seems to us of the utmost importance. It is in his quality of Postulator of the Causes of the Institute of the Most Holy Redeemer, that Reverend Father d'Orazio has been charged with promulgating the Cause of the Venerable Mary Celeste. This act on the part of the Superior General of the Congregation of the Most Holy Redeemer marks the official and glorious re-entrance of the Venerable Mother, into the Institute from which she was expulsed two hundred years ago.

A more recent and still more solemn act, however, has corroborated this, and gladdened the hearts of all those who have a devotion to the Venerable Prioress. Since September, 1930, her precious remains are no longer in the Monastery of her Church. Prior to the above- mentioned date, a decree was issued by the civil authorities for the destruction of the sanctuary and of the Convent; the latter being uninhabited since 1923, on the death of the last Nun. This decree was not a hostile measure by any means, but the site of the Convent was required on which to build the Governor's palace. It became necessary therefore, to transfer Mary Celeste's body. Authorized by the Sacred Congregation of Rites, this transference took place with a splendor worthy of the fervent love the people of Foggia had always borne for their "holy Prioress." Permission was not given to open the reliquary. The solemn ceremony took place on September 11th, presided over by his Excellence Monsignor Farina, Bishop of Foggia, assisted by the Venerable Chapter of the Cathedral and by the secular and regular clergy. The Very Reverend Father Murray, Superior of the Redemptorists, accompanied by the Very Reverend Father Di Coste, Consultor-General, and by the Very Reverend Father d'Orazio, Postulator of the Cause of Mary Celeste, was present, as if to take official possession of the holy remains.

The reliquary was placed on a pedestal decorated with fresh flowers. It was carried by eight Nuns, representing all the religious communities of the town. The procession started amidst general enthusiasm. In addition to the religious authorities already mentioned, there were representatives of the civil and military authorities and of all pious organizations of men and women bearing their insignia and banners. An immense crowd lined the route which lay through the principal streets of the town, and another crowd followed in the wake of the procession.

Thus they reached the Church of St. Dominic where the reliquary was deposited in a place of honor. On the following days, the 12th, 13th and 14th of September, a solemn Triduum was organized in honor of the Most Holy Trinity to obtain the hastening of the day of Beatification so long desired.

In 1931, the Bishop of Foggia wished the Nuns of the Monastery of the Most Holy Redeemer at Scala to come to Foggia, and re-establish the Convent founded by the Venerable Mother. After overcoming many difficulties, a valiant little band of Sisters set out, headed by Mother Mary Philomena, the Superior of Scala, and were enthusiastically received by the people of Foggia, who rejoiced as only Italians can do to see the red and blue habit once more in their midst. The travelers arrived at Foggia at midnight, accompanied by Mgr. Cesarano, Bishop of Aversa, himself a Redemptorist. Notwithstanding the hour, they went to the episcopal palace, where Mgr. Farina was waiting for them. As it was past midnight, Mgr. Cesarano said Mass immediately and gave Communion to the Nuns, who then went to take a little rest after their long journey.

Next day, after a grand High Mass and Sermon, the Nuns were conducted processionally to their temporary abode in the Convent of the Marcellines. Later on they moved into their own house, which had curiously enough been built by Mgr. Cavalieri, uncle of St. Alphonsus and Bishop of Foggia.

The first care of the Sisters was to build their Church, so as to be able to receive the holy body of their Mother. Thus was fulfilled the prophecy of the Venerable Mary Celeste, who told her daughters that after her death their Convent would flourish for many years and do untold good; but that later on it would be destroyed and another raised in its place would give great glory to God. The Redemptoristines are settled in Foggia, where they will carry on the work of their holy Foundress, and pray unceasingly for the happy day when she who so generously followed the Way of the Cross in the footsteps of the Most Holy Redeemer will, by the Voice of the Church, be granted her well-merited place in the court of her risen Lord.

Epilogue
by Ryan Grant

Fr. Favre was right to long for Sr. Maria Celeste to find her place among those in whom God's glory was particularly shown forth. Sadly, it would not happen during his lifetime.

Nearly eighty years after the original publication of this book, the process began to move again. On 13 June 2013, the Congregation for the Causes of the Saints issued a decree on the exercise of heroic virtue by Mary Celeste (AAS 2014 909). Then, on 14 December 2015 a miracle attributed to her intercession was examined and approved (AAS 2017 1156). This miracle was the healing of a deaf nun at Foggia in 1955, which had been examined by the diocese in 1988, and finally, since the Ecclesiastical machinery can operate with all the speed and agility of a lumbering elephant, in 2013 it was approved by the Congregation of the Causes of the Saints, resulting in the decree of 2015.

Consequently, on 18th June, 2016, Mary Celeste was beatified at Foggia, and her feast day placed on 11 September in the calendar (AAS 2017 1257).

The following is taken from the decree of Beatification:

"After consulting the pleas of our brother Vincent Pelvi, Metropolitan Archbishop of Foggia-Bovino, as well as of a great many other brothers in the episcopate on behalf of many of Christ's faithful, and the Congregation of the Causes of the

Saints, by our Apostolic authority we exercise the faculty that the Venerable Servant of God, Maria Celeste Crostarosa, a nun and Founder of the Order of the Most Holy Redeemer, a humble imitator of Christ and faithful witness of His salvific love, henceforth be given the name of Blessed, and her feast can be celebrated every year on the eleventh day of September in every manner and place in which it has been lawfully established. In the name of the Father, and of the Son, and of the Holy Spirit."

BLESSED BE GOD IN HIS ANGELS AND IN HIS SAINTS

The Revealer of the Globe

Christopher Columbus & His Future Beatification

Part One:
*Exposé and Historical Background
of the Cause*

LÉON BLOY

Translated by Richard Robinson
Preface by Jules Barbey d'Aurevilly

Sunny Lou Publishing Company
Portland, Oregon, USA
http://www.sunnyloupublishing.com

2nd Edition: March 1, 2024
Original Publication Date: June 2, 2021

ISBN: 978-1-955392-60-0

* * *

This translation from French is based on the A. Sauton
Libraire-Editeur, Paris, 1884, edition of
Le Revelateur du globe.